Contents

Acknowledgements

The authors and publishers are grateful to those who have given permission to reproduce material.

Every effort has been made to contact copyright holders of material reproduced in this book. Any omissions or errors will be rectified in subsequent printings if notice is given to the publishers.

The publisher would like to thank David Floyd for acting as a consultant for this publication.

Text acknowledgements

Amazon, amazon.co.uk – page 123
Assael, H., *Marketing Principles and Strategy*, London: The Dryden Press, 1993 – page 132
Broadcasters' Audience Research Board (BARB) – page 157
CACI Ltd – page 148
Cannon, Tom, *Basic Marketing: Principles and Practice*, London: Cassel, 1997 – page 145
Dibb, Sally et al., *Marketing Concepts and Strategies*, Boston: Houghton Mifflin, 2001 – pages 150, 172
Friends of the Earth (England, Wales & Northern Ireland) – page 50
Kotler, Philip, *Principles of Marketing*, Englewood Cliffs: Prentice Hall, 1996 – page 143
Manchester United – p. 49
Microsoft product screen shots reprinted with permission from Microsoft Corporation – pages 116, 118, 119
National Readership Survey – page 149
Nielsen Media Research – pages 159, 182
Office of National Statistics – page 148
PIMS Study – page 136
Research Machines – page 175
Schumpeter, Joseph, *Capitalism, Socialism and Democracy*, New York: Harper and Row, 1974 – page 127
Shipley, D., *Pricing Objectives in British Manufacturing Industry*, Journal of Industrial Economics, vol. 29, no. 4 – page 169
Stewart, Rosemary, *Managers and Their Jobs*, Nuffield Foundation, 1965 – pages 70–71
TREE AID – page 4
World Advertising Research Center/DIMS – page 183

Crown copyright material is reproduced under Class Licence No. C02W0005419 with the permission of the Controller of HMSO and the Queen's Printer for Scotland.

Photo and logo acknowledgements

Alamy – pages 8, 57(a), 60(b), 69, 76, 125
BBC – page 14
The Body Shop – pages 2, 13
Corbis – pages 38(a)
Dyson – page 60(a)
Empics – pages 38(e),(h), 70(a)
Friends of the Earth – page 50
Getty – pages 1, 38(b),(c),(g), 59(a)
Investors in People – page 40
Livewire – page 63
Nestlé – pages 2, 40
Oxfam – page 3
P&O – page 85
Rex Features – pages 5, 10, 38(d),(f), 43, 59(b), 70(b)
Rosabeth Moss Kanter – page 47
Shell – page 2
Tesco – pages 2, 13
Virgin Atlantic – pages 2, 57(b)

Introduction

Welcome to your Edexcel GCE Applied Business course. The term 'Applied Business' is used to describe your course because it is focused not just upon learning about business organisations but also upon finding out and investigating how people within such organisations behave and make decisions. The Edexcel qualification is designed to 'provide you with a broad introduction to a vocational area and help you to apply knowledge in a variety of work-related situations' by 'exploring the world of business in a highly practical way'.

Edexcel places considerable emphasis upon getting you to learn within realistic business contexts. Your course will involve using theory as part of your learning and finding out how that theory relates to all of the decisions and activities that are undertaken by people within organisations at a variety of different levels. You will also undertake a range of investigative coursework activities which provide you with a first-hand opportunity to learn within and outside a classroom about many of the important activities and functions of business by undertaking many of these functions yourself. In this way your course is closely 'work related' and is designed to give you a much deeper and meaningful understanding of the sort of activities that people in business are involved with, so that you gain both knowledge and experience.

The Edexcel Applied Business qualification is flexible because it provides you with a real choice about which parts of the qualification you want to undertake. Just like the more traditional A levels, the Applied GCE adopts the AS and A2 structure of GCEs.

The Edexcel *AS Single Award* comprises three units which must be taken. These are:

Unit 1: Investigating People at Work (Externally Assessed)
Unit 2: Investigating Business (Internally Assessed)
Unit 3: Investigating Marketing (Internally Assessed).

In this course you will complete both external and internal assessments. The external assessment will relate to a business scenario to provide an appropriate context for the vocational element of your studies. For the internally-based assessments you will be asked to undertake realistic activities that relate to a vocational scenario, each of which you will be able to undertake in tandem with your learning within each unit. You will be assessed within 3 bands, the lowest of which is Mark Band 1 and the highest Mark Band 3. Your assessment criteria for each activity will identify all that you have to do to achieve the outcomes within each banded activity.

Throughout this book key words or concepts are highlighted in bold or italic. Many of those in bold are explained further in the glossary at the back of the book.

Enjoy your Applied Business course. By succeeding with your course you are opening up avenues so that you can either go into the workplace or go into higher education following your course.

Rob Dransfield
Dave Needham

UNIT 1

Investigating people at work

This unit contains four parts:

1.1   Business aims, objectives and organisation

1.2   How businesses obtain employees

1.3   How businesses motivate employees

1.4   How people are influenced at work

Introduction

Businesses need to have a sense of direction. Therefore they need to define their aims, i.e. the ends that they seek to achieve. Having created a general aim for the organisation it is then possible to set out more specific objectives which provide guidance for the people who work for the organisation. Businesses also need to be structured in such a way that they are well organised to achieve their aims and objectives.

To provide goods and services, businesses rely on the people who work for them. It is therefore important to have an understanding of how and why people work in business, and what influences them at work.

What you will learn in this unit

* Why businesses have aims and objectives
* Typical aims of business organisations such as survival, growth and making a profit
* Different types of business organisations and how this affects the way they operate

FIGURE 1.1 *Motivated employees enjoy their work and help businesses to achieve their objectives*

* The functions and structures of business organisations
* How businesses obtain employees
* Effective ways of recruiting, selecting, and training employees
* How businesses motivate their employees
* How businesses can use theories of motivation in the workplace
* How external issues, such as environmental issues, influence people at work.

1.1 Business aims, objectives and organisation

Businesses are decision-making units that have been designed to make goods and provide services. A **good** is anything that a customer is prepared to buy because they believe that it will make them (or the person they buy the good for) better off. For example, you will probably have bought a mobile phone, computer game, or CD because you believed that it would give you more enjoyment.

A distinction is often made between a physical good, such as a sandwich, motor car or lawn mower, and **services**, which are benefits provided for consumers to enjoy but they do not have anything to take home with them (except for the benefit they have enjoyed). Examples of services include window cleaning, hairdressing or a visit to the cinema.

The term **product** refers to something offering a benefit that we can touch and see, for example a tube of Smarties or a compact disc. Production refers to the process of making these products, for example on a production line. However, the term product is also often used today for things such

PHYSICAL GOODS	SERVICES
Tangible goods (you can feel and see them)	Intangible services
A razor 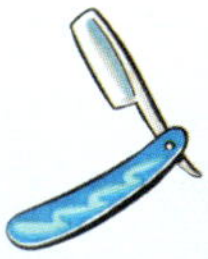	Being given a shave by a barber 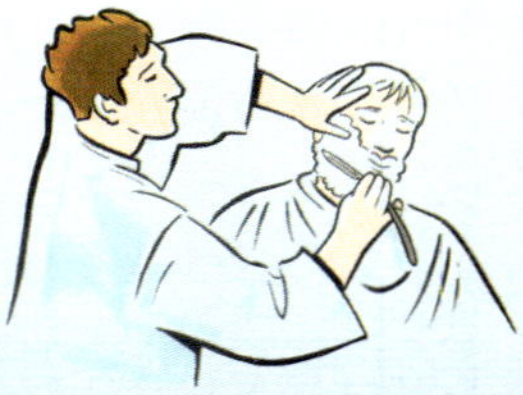
A packet of sandwiches 	Being served in a restaurant 
A piano 	Listening to a musical concert 

FIGURE 1.2 *Goods and services*

Divide the following up into physical goods and services. Explain why you have put each in the category that you have chosen:

A taxi ride, a theatre visit, a bottle of milk, a pen, a textbook, a business studies class, the work of a tree surgeon, a foot massage, treatment from a dentist, a toothbrush, an eye test, a driving test, a motor bike, a tube of glue.

What types of goods and services are produced by businesses where you do work experience or have a part-time job?

Find the logos of six businesses that you have not come across before by examining the business pages of a national newspaper: What do the companies make, or what service do they provide? Does the company where you have part-time work or where you are carrying out work experience have a logo? Perhaps you could make a display in your school or college of the logos of the companies that your group works for.

as insurance policies and other types of service outputs – the product is the complete article which a company sells to you as a discrete item.

There are many different types of business with their own particular purposes. An important distinction can be made between businesses that seek to make a profit and 'not for profit' businesses.

For profit businesses are ones that are owned by:

* individuals, such as **sole trader** (one owner) businesses

* a group of **partners** working together

* **shareholders**. A shareholder owned business is called a company.

Private companies are owned by private shareholders, and shares in them can only be bought privately with the permission of the **Board of Directors**. Anyone can buy shares in a **public company** (PLC). Shares in PLCs are traded on the **Stock Exchange**.

For profit businesses set out to make a profit. The profit can be used in the following ways:

1 For further expansion of the business

2 To be distributed among the owners. In the case of a company the owners are the shareholders and their share of the profit is given to them in the form of a dividend. For example, if they have 100 £1 shares in the company, and the company pays a dividend of 5p a share, then the shareholder will receive £5 worth of dividends.

Look at the following company logos. Can you identify the name of the company, and the type of business they are in?

FIGURE 1.3 *A logo is an important part of a company's image*

Not-for-profit organisations come in two forms:

* Charities
* Voluntary organisations.

A **charity** is set up for a specific charitable purpose, e.g. Oxfam is a charity that is best-known for providing famine relief. Other charities have aims related to education, or providing sports and leisure activities to the community. Charities do not make profits. Instead they can make a surplus which is where the costs of running the charity are less than the proceeds in a given year.

FIGURE 1.4 *Oxfam – a charity providing famine relief*

Another form of not-for-profit organisation is a **voluntary organisation**. A voluntary organisation like the Women's Royal Voluntary Service (WRVS) is staffed by unpaid volunteers, whereas people who work for a charity are often paid.

Carry out research in your local town to find out the name of six for profit organisations and six not-for-profit organisations. Share out the task in your group of finding out the stated objectives of the six not-for-profit organisations.

The aims businesses have

Aims and **objectives** are the ends that you seek to achieve when you carry out a particular task.

The aim can be seen as the general end that you are working towards while objectives are sub-components of that aim. Often objectives can be **quantified**, i.e. numbers can be attached to them.

Many businesses today create what is termed a **mission statement** setting out the general aim or purpose of their organisation. Typically, missions are short statements such as Oxfam's mission 'Oxfam works with others to overcome

CHARITY LIKE OXFAM	COMPANY LIKE SHELL
When the revenues of Oxfam are greater than the costs of running the business a surplus is made which goes back into running the charity the next year	When the revenues of Shell are greater than the costs of running the business a profit is made which can be ploughed back into the business or distributed in dividends to shareholders

FIGURE 1.5 *Distinction between a for profit and a not-for-profit organisation*

CASE STUDY

Charities need to be business-like

Today charities have to operate in a business-like way if they are to be efficient.

Miranda Spitteler, the chief executive of the small development charity TREE AID, says:

'…passion for the cause is vital but it's not enough. People need to offer professional skills and experience. They'll be expected to work as hard and to meet as many targets and deadlines as in any commercial company. We're under more scrutiny than ever before, so we have to perform in order to survive.'

Rob Farace, the head of recruitment at Cancer Research UK, says that if anything charities have to be meaner and keener than commercial companies as they have to be accountable both to their donors and to the people they are helping. 'We have to be even slicker as we know how hard people have worked to collect our money.'

Identify three charities and state their key objectives. Research your answer by entering the name of the charity as an internet search.

Learning activity

Typically mission statements set out:

* Why a company exists
* What the company believes in
* What makes the company special
* How the company behaves

Carry out an internet search using the key words mission and the name of a company you are interested in.

1 To what extent is their mission clear?

2 To what extent does the mission communicate the four points listed above?

FIGURE 1.6 *Ryanair is a low-cost airline*

poverty and suffering'. You can see that this gives a sense of mission or purpose to everyone that works for the organisation and tells everyone outside the organisation what it stands for. The mission of leading supermarket chains typically involve statements such as 'To provide unbeatable value for our customers, while providing first class careers for our employees'. Often mission statements also mention the importance of creating growth for shareholders and building an excellent reputation in the community.

The mission of well-known organisations can typically be broken down into discrete objectives.

For example, the aim of Ryanair is to be 'Europe's leading low cost airline'.

To achieve this aim, there are a number of supporting objectives, such as:

* To undercut the fares of rivals
* To take over other airlines
* To increase sales each year.

Ryanair will want to quantify some of these objectives, e.g. to increase sales by x% in 2005, to sell tickets at y% less than rivals this year, etc.

In order to achieve aims and objectives an organisation will need to create plans which help it to achieve the desired ends.

The table illustrates the relationship between plans and aims and objectives for a company.

AIM	BUSINESS PLANS
To be Europe's Number 1 low-cost airline	Plans to raise finance e.g. by selling shares and borrowing.
Objectives (examples)	Plan to recruit and train high quality friendly staff
To operate efficiently at low cost, achieving sales and profit figures of x per cent in a given time period.	Marketing and operating plans
To fly to new destinations	Promotional plans
(aims and objectives are the ends to be worked towards)	(business plans are the means to achieve the ends)

A business plan will include details such as how the business will raise the finance it needs, who are the customers that make up its market, the type of people that it will need to employ, and so on.

SMART objectives

In business we often say that a good set of objectives is a **SMART** set of objectives. The term SMART stands for:

* **S**pecific
* **M**easurable
* **A**chievable
* **R**ealistic
* **T**ime-related.

For example, Manchester United Football Club set itself the target for the 2004–2005 season to win the European Champions League, and one major trophy in this country.

This was SMART because:

* This objective is clearly specific, it is easy to understand and everyone will know whether they have been successful in achieving the objective.

* The objective is also measurable – if they won the Champions League and a major trophy in this country they would have achieved the required measure.

* The objective is also achievable. Manchester United started the season in a position where they could easily qualify for the Champions League, and they were already well placed in the Premier League in this country.

* The objective was realistic. Manchester United had been this country's most successful football team over the previous decade and had the players and manager to achieve success.

* The objective was also time related – it related to the 2004–2005 season.

FIGURE 1.7 *Objectives should be SMART*

Why objectives apply to certain businesses

One of Ryanair's main aims in recent years has been that of growth – to expand into new routes and to attract more customers. However, growth is not the only aim of a business.

The main aims are:

1 Survival
2 Meeting stakeholder needs
3 Maximising sales revenue (income)
4 Maximising profit (surplus)
5 Growth.

1 Survival

Walk down any High Street and you will find a selection of businesses that have been there a long time – they have survived. Some of the survivors like Marks & Spencer or WH Smith may have seen better days. At one time it would have been unthinkable that Marks & Spencer would have to struggle to survive. Up until the 1990s Marks & Spencer went from strength to strength and represented the very best of British quality. It was said that you could walk into any room where people were gathered together and know with certainty that the majority of women would be wearing Marks & Spencer underwear.

However, by the 1990s many other new stores were springing up and there was a rapid change in consumers' tastes and the desire to become more fashionable. M&S were left behind and their profits started to suffer. Fortunately M&S woke up to the problem and in recent years they have completely revamped many of their stores and employed state of the art designers to make their clothing desirable. However, today M&S is engaged in a real battle for survival in an intensely competitive market place. For example, in recent times ASDA have started selling cut-price school uniforms to threaten M&S's hold in this area. At the same time companies like WH Smith have had to fight hard to survive faced by competition from internet-based booksellers (e.g. by setting up their own online bookstore).

We can therefore say that the prime objective of any business in the modern world is that of survival.

2 Meeting stakeholder needs

A business does not just serve the needs of its owners such as shareholders. Rather it must serve the needs of a range of **stakeholders** who are individuals and groups with an interest in how that business runs. Of course the shareholders are a very important interest group and so they have a lot of influence over decision making.

3 Maximising sales revenue (income)

The term **sales revenue** refers to the income that a business receives from selling goods or services. In accounts it is also referred to as turnover.

Many businesses will seek to steadily increase their turnover in order to win a larger share of the total market. In business there is a saying that if you win the lion's share of the market then the profits will follow. This makes sense. For example, if a business has 51% of the market its nearest rival can only gain 49%. The firm that sells in bulk is able to reduce its costs through a process known as **economies of scale**. Economies of scale are the advantages of producing on a grand scale which enable a firm to reduce the cost of producing and selling each unit of output.

The way in which firms seek to maximise sales revenue is illustrated by the mobile phone market where there are a number of competitors such as Nokia, Orange, and O_2. In the industry today the battle is well and truly on to grab and keep those

CASE STUDY
A multiplex cinema

FIGURE 1.8 *A multiplex cinema*

The case of a multiplex cinema provides a good example of an organisation with a variety of stakeholders as illustrated by the table below:

STAKEHOLDER	INTEREST AND INFLUENCE
Shareholders	The major owners of the multiplex. Some of them will be individuals while others will be **institutional investors** (i.e. large organisations that invest in shares, e.g. pension funds). The shareholders want the business to make a profit so that their dividends are high and the share price increases.
Employees	Managers and staff at the multiplex want to see it being successful because their job security and pay depends on it.
Customers	Customers want the multiplex to show interesting and enjoyable films at value for money prices.
The government	The government benefits from the taxes paid by the cinema. The government also regulates the types of films that can be shown, and makes sure that the premises meet regulations such as health and safety requirements.
The local community	People in the local community benefit from having entertainment on their doorstep. However, they may not be happy about the noise and congestion caused by the cinema complex.
Other businesses	Other businesses may be able to make a profit from setting up around the multiplex, e.g. cafés and restaurants.
Competitors	Competitors have an interest in how the business is run. They will complain if they feel that the multiplex is gaining an edge over them, for example if the local council allows the multiplex to stay open longer or to engage in new activities.

Organisations will seek to meet the needs of their various stakeholder groupings and failure to attend to the needs of any of these groupings may have enormous consequences for the business. For example, failure to keep the local community happy may lead to protest and adverse publicity. **For an organisation of your choice, outline five key stakeholders and their interests.**

FIGURE 1.9 *Arsenal Football Club is sponsored by O_2*

	1999	2000	2001	2002	2003
Sales revenue of O_2 (£000)	2,618	3,200	4,276	4,874	5,324

customers who will pay to download games, send photos, pictures and e-mail.

O_2, the sponsors of Arsenal football club, have been particularly effective in the mobile telephone market with about one-third of the text messaging market.

4 Maximising profit/surplus

A lot of people believe that the main objective of businesses is to maximise the profits they make. Although businesses probably seek to achieve high profits in the longer term they may have different short-term objectives. For example, in order to gain market leadership a firm may have to invest heavily in the short period so that short-term profits fall. By sacrificing short-term profit maximising a firm can secure its long-term survival or long-term profitability.

5 Growth

Earlier we stated that growth is an important business objective, and that Ryanair is a good example of this process. Ryanair has come a long way since it started in 1985. Its first route was

CASE STUDY

Corus

Corus was formed by the joining together of British Steel and the major Dutch steel manufacturing company Hoogovens in 2000. Steel manufacturing is intensely competitive and there were too many steel plants in Europe. Corus therefore made the tough decision to sack nearly 10,000 workers and to cut back some of its loss-making plant.

Fortunately for the company the world price of steel soared in 2004 as a result of surging demand from China which continued throughout 2004. The combination of falling costs and rising prices (and hence revenues) has helped to turn round the losses made by the company into profits, as shown below:

CORUS (OPERATING PROFITS £)	
2000	-133m
2001	-389m
2002	-400m
2003	-66m
2004	+340m

Corus is a good example of a company that has cut costs in order to increase its long-term ability to make profits. In a similar way, as we saw earlier, Marks & Spencer have invested heavily in updating the look of their stores, in retraining staff, and in creating new and attractive stock, as well as supporting these changes through exciting advertising campaigns. Manchester United is a business that pays careful attention to controlling costs. One of its cost objectives is to keep costs at under 50% of turnover (the value of sales). For example:

TARGET TO KEEP COSTS AT UNDER 50% OF TURNOVER		
Year	Costs as % of turnover	Profit change since previous year
2003	46	Up
2004	45	Up

Why do Corus and Manchester United seek to control costs?

Learning activity

Using examples from your own experience and newspaper and internet research identify an industry in which:

✴ some businesses are growing

✴ others are cutting back.

1 What are the advantages of having a growth strategy in that industry?

2 What are the potential drawbacks of the growth strategy?

from Waterford in Ireland to London, but it grew quickly, adding routes from Dublin to a number of European cities.

It made heavy losses until, under Michael O'Leary, who became chief executive in 1994, it embraced the low-cost model typified by America's Southwest Airlines.

The company has not looked back. It quickly grew to dominate Anglo-Irish services, and went public in 1997. It operates almost 100 aircraft, but if it continued to grow at its current rate, it would have 1,000 aircraft in 20 years – more than double the number operated by British Airways.

6 Non-profit objectives

Not-for-profit organisations may have different objectives from for profit ones. We have already seen that charity organisations have a range of objectives and purposes.

For example, an important objective of a number of organisations in this sector is to care for the environment, e.g. Friends of the Earth, Greenpeace, The Woodland Trust, etc.

Today the objectives of a charity which are recognised as being lawful include:

✴ the prevention and relief of poverty

FIGURE 1.10 *Band Aid is a not-for-profit organisation*

Learning activity

Carry out an internet search using the terms environmental protection and either charity or voluntary organisation. What are the key objectives of the organisations that your search reveals? Why do you think that these organisations have these not-for-profit objectives?

✴ the advancement of education

✴ the advancement of health

✴ the advancement of culture, arts and heritage

✴ the advancement of amateur sport

✴ the advancement of environmental protection and improvement.

How the way a business operates is influenced by ownership, control and financing

The owners of a business are the people the business belongs to. For example, Fred's corner store may be owned by Fred on his own. In contrast Makepeace, Patel and Amin the solicitors is a partnership.

Sole trader and partnership businesses are not only owned by the owners, they are also controlled by them. Control refers to decision making. Fred makes his own decisions about what he sells, who he employs and when he opens and shuts his shop.

In companies, however, there is a distinction between the ownership and the control of the business. Companies are owned by shareholders, but it is often managers who make decisions and hence control the business.

Different types of business are also financed in different ways. Typically large public companies have access to a much wider range of finance than small sole trader businesses.

A **sole trader** business is owned and controlled by one person. It is the most common form of business and is found in a wide range of activities (e.g. window cleaning, plumbing, electrical work, busking). No complicated work is required to set up a sole trader business. Decisions can be made quickly and close contact can be kept with customers and employees. All profits go to the sole trader, who also has the satisfaction of building up his or her own business.

But there are disadvantages. As a sole trader you have to make all the decisions yourself, and you may have to work long hours (what do you do if you are ill or want a holiday?). Another disadvantage is that you don't have the legal protection of **limited liability**. What this means is that should the business run up debts these debts become the responsibility of the business owner. The debts are unlimited and the owner may be forced to sell their house and other personal possessions to pay off their business debts.

The sole trader typically provides much of their own finance, although they may also borrow from a bank, or friends. As a sole trader you need to be a jack-of-all-trades, and just because you are a good hairdresser does not necessarily mean that you have a head for business!

A **partnership** is usually formed by signing a **Deed of Partnership** with the paperwork being supervised by a solicitor. Partnerships are typically found in professional work, e.g. a medical or dental practice, a group of accountants or solicitors. People in business partnerships can share skills and the workload, and it may be easier to raise the capital needed.

FIGURE 1.11 *A sole trader business is owned and controlled by one person*

FIGURE 1.12 *Partners can share the workload and decision-making*

For example, a group of vets is able to pool knowledge about different diseases and groups of animals, and two or three vets working together may be able to operate a 24-hour service. When one of the vets is ill or goes on holiday, the business can cope.

The **Deed of Partnership** sets out how profits will be shared and the different responsibilities and payments to partners.

The main disadvantages of partnerships are that people can fall out (she doesn't work as hard as me!), ordinary partnerships don't have limited liability, and partnerships can rarely borrow or raise large amounts of capital. Business decisions may be more difficult to make (and slower) because of the need to consult all the partners. There may be disagreements about how things should be done. A further disadvantage is that profits will be shared.

A **company** has to be registered before it can start to operate, but once all the paperwork is completed and approved the company becomes recognised as a legal body. The owners of

the company are its shareholders. They elect **directors** to represent their interests. A managing director is the senior director on the Board. The Board consists of executive directors who make the major ongoing policy decisions about the business. The Board will also have some non-executive directors in its membership. Non-executives are there to provide specialist advice and because of their links with other businesses.

Shareholders are able to have a say about the way the company is run when they attend an Annual General Meeting each year. At the Annual General Meeting highlights of the company's report will be presented to shareholders as well as the annual accounts. At this time the shareholders

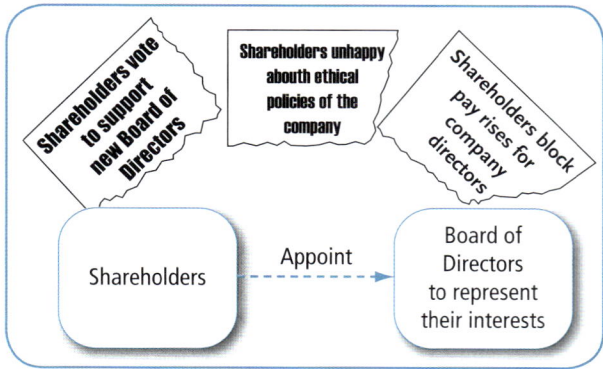

FIGURE 1.13 *Company directors have to satisfy shareholders*

are able to question company policy and can vote out the directors and take actions such as refusing to approve pay rises for directors.

Shareholders put funds into a company by buying shares. New shares are often sold in face values of £1 per share, but this is not always the case. Some shareholders will only have a few hundred pounds' worth of shares, whereas others may have thousands of pounds' worth.

The promoter or directors of the company can apply to the **Registrar of Companies** for permission to issue new shares. The amount that the Registrar agrees to is called the **authorised capital**.

The **issued capital** is the value of the shares that are actually sold to shareholders. A company may choose not to issue the full value of its authorised capital: it may hold back a certain amount for future issue.

Private companies tend to be smaller than public ones (discussed below) and are often family businesses. There must be at least two shareholders but there is no maximum number. Shares in private companies cannot be traded on the Stock Exchange, and often shares can only be bought with the permission of the board of directors.

Private companies may find it possible to raise more cash (by selling shares) than unlimited-liability businesses. The shareholders can also have the protection of limited liability.

Learning activity

The following task should be based on research carried out in your local town supported by knowledge that students in your group acquire from work experience and part-time jobs.

Make a study of a sole trader, partnership, private company and public company. Who owns it and who controls it? How much capital does it have? (If you can't find out the exact sum, give a breakdown of the main forms of capital it relies on, e.g. x per cent owner's capital, y per cent borrowing etc.) What are the advantages and disadvantages of this organisational form for this particular business organisation? As a group you could present the work as a newspaper feature using a desk top publishing package. The title of the feature could be 'Some interesting businesses in our local area'.

The main disadvantage compared with unlimited liability businesses are that they have to share out profits among shareholders and that they cannot make decisions so quickly. They cost more to set up.

A public company has its shares bought and sold on the Stock Exchange. The main advantage of being a public company is that large amounts of capital can be raised very quickly. One

FIGURE 1.14 *Companies have shareholders and directors*

disadvantage is that control of a business can be lost by the original shareholders if large quantities of shares are purchased as part of a 'takeover bid'. It is also costly to have shares quoted on the Stock Exchange.

In order to create a public company the directors must apply to the Stock Exchange Council, which will carefully check the accounts. A business wanting to 'go public' will then arrange for one of the merchant banks to handle the paperwork. Selling new shares is quite a risky business. The Stock Exchange has 'good days' (when a lot of people want to buy shares) and 'bad days' (when a lot of people want to sell). If the issue of new shares coincides with a bad day a company can find itself in difficulties. For example, if it hopes to sell a million new shares at £1 each and all goes well, it will raise £1 million, but on a bad day it might only be able to sell half its shares at this price. When a company is up and running, a cheaper way of selling is to contact existing shareholders inviting them to buy new shares. This is called a rights issue.

Sole traders, partnerships, and companies are in the **private sector** where the objective is generally to make a profit, although we have seen that other objectives such as high sales, growth and survival are important.

The other sector of the economy is the public sector. The **public sector** consists of organisations that the government is involved in on behalf of the people.

Public sector organisations have somewhat different objectives to private sector ones.

A **government department** like the Inland Revenue operates on behalf of the government and is staffed by civil servants known as revenue officers. Their job is to collect income and other taxes on behalf of the government, to collect repayments on student loans, and to make payments known as tax credits. Rather than

FIGURE 1.15 *The BBC is a public corporation*

seeking to make a profit they will want to collect taxes efficiently and make sure that taxpayers get a fair deal.

A **municipal enterprise** is a government enterprise on a local scale. It may have responsibility for looking after the local parks, or street lighting. The prime task is to provide an efficient local service to serve the local community.

A third type of public sector enterprise is the **public corporation**. There are not many of these left now but a good example is the BBC (British Broadcasting Corporation). The BBC has the task of providing a high quality news, information and entertainment service for the people of this country. It is currently funded by people paying television licences but this funding is under review. A government minister appoints the Chair of the BBC who then has a responsibility for making sure that the BBC acts independently and fairly in broadcasting programmes. A public corporation is concerned not only to run on business lines but also to provide a public service. This public service emphasis often conflicts with the objective of profit maximisation. The main differences between a public company and a public corporation are set out in the table opposite.

✱ DID YOU KNOW?

When you go to university and receive a student loan you will eventually have to pay this off bit by bit (provided that your income is more than a given threshold). Repayments are collected by the Inland Revenue.

PRIVATE SECTOR	PUBLIC SECTOR
Sole traders, partnerships, companies	Government departments, public corporations, municipal enterprises
Public/private partnerships	
(organisations that have both government and private funds and objectives)	

CONTRASTING PUBLIC CORPORATIONS WITH PUBLIC COMPANIES	
PUBLIC CORPORATION	**PUBLIC COMPANY**
Set up by Act of Parliament	Set up by issuing prospectus inviting public to buy shares
Owned by the government	Owned by shareholders
Run by chairperson and managers appointed by government	Run by management team chosen by directors representing shareholders
Aims to provide a public service as well as having profit-making objectives	Profit-making objectives

The range of functions carried out by businesses, and the part these functions play

When you start to work for a business you will usually find that you start off in a particular area of specialism which is termed a **function**. For example, working in a shoe shop you are most likely to work in the sales function. This will be the most important function in the shop, but there will be other functions such as the accounts department. If you work in a supermarket you may be involved in the sales function but you could also have a job in warehousing and packing. There will be a training department etc.

Some of the most important functions of a business are:

1 Production – responsible for making goods. This department is responsible for planning production schedules and for ensuring high quality standards.

2 Marketing – finds out what customers want through market research and then plans marketing activities such as advertising to attract customers.

3 Sales – whereas marketing is concerned with finding out what customers want, the emphasis in sales is on convincing the customer that products meet their needs and requirements.

CASE STUDY

Functions at McDonald's

Here is a list of business functions advertised by the McDonald's organisation:

* Administrative
* Accounting
* Air Travel
* Architecture/Construction
* Communications
* Corporate Tax
* Customer Satisfaction
* Distribution/Logistics
* Engineering
* Environmental Affairs
* Facilities Systems
* Franchising
* Government Relations
* Human Resources
* Information Services
* Insurance
* Legal
* Marketing
* Media Relations
* Product Development
* Purchasing
* Quality Assurance
* Real Estate
* Restaurant Operations
* Treasury

Outline the main functions of another organisation.

4   Finance and accounts – responsible for preparing budgets (financial plans), and for calculating the profit or loss made by various parts of the business, and the business as a whole. Creates financial reports such as the balance sheet showing the financial health of the business at a particular time, e.g. the end of the year.

5   Administration – responsible for creating and managing systems for keeping the business running smoothly.

6   Human Resources – responsible for people management in the company including hiring, firing and motivating.

7   Information Technology – creates the information systems that keep the business running smoothly, e.g. the development of a company website and intranet.

Until the late 1980s organisations relied very heavily on having large functional departments. This created tall organisational structures with lots of layers. Nowadays it is more common for organisations to concentrate on the functions which are most central to the organisations' activities, e.g. marketing in a marketing company,

Learning activity

Either by interviewing someone that works for a local business organisation, or using your own work experience, identify the main functions at your workplace.

production in a manufacturing company. Much of the work in non-core functions is then contracted out to other companies.

Today it is common practice for the various functions of a business to be more integrated. Often people are organised into **cross-functional teams**, so that it is possible to share experience, e.g. sales and marketing ideas, the accountant can explain budget implications of various decisions etc.

Organisation structures

An organisational chart is a way of illustrating how an organisation is organised. For example, Figure 1.17 shows how a printing firm producing textbooks might be organised.

There are other ways of structuring organisations, for example:

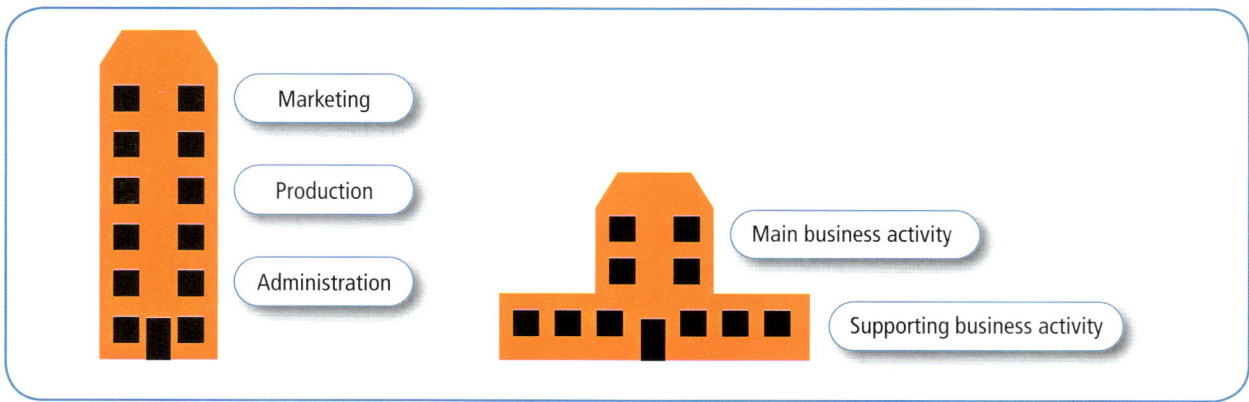

FIGURE 1.16 *The tall organisation v the flatter organisation*

Find out...

Using your own work experience or that of a friend or family member, provide an example of where you or they have worked in a cross-functional team. What were the benefits of working in this way?

1 By product or service

An organisation can be divided up according to the products supplied (e.g. in a supermarket into breakfast cereals, fruit and vegetables, toiletries) or the service (such as your local council's division into environmental services, parks, housing etc).

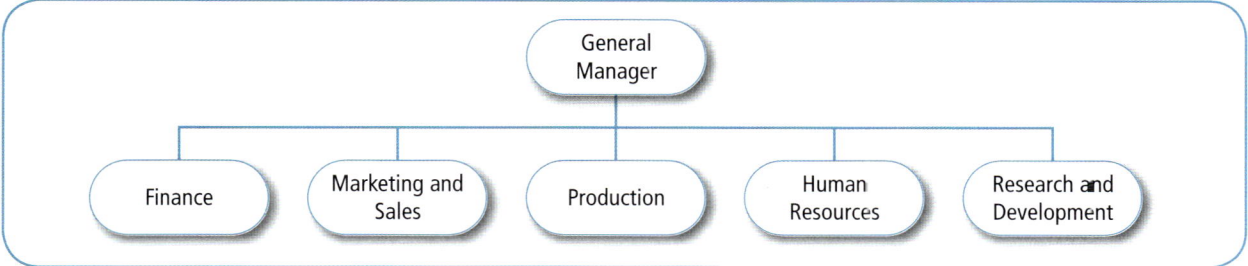

FIGURE 1.17 *The traditional organisation structure*

2 By customer

Often businesses are divided up to deal with different types of customers. For example, in banking there may be a department that deals specifically with business customers, and another with the general public.

3 By process or equipment

This is common practice in manufacturing in which a work area may be divided up into different types of machinery and activity. For example, in a printing company one department may be responsible for printing business catalogues, and another for magazines.

4 Matrix structures

A popular form of organisation structure today is the **matrix** which involves people working together on projects working as a team. A person

working on a project may be accountable to more than one team leader – the team leader of the department in which they work, and the project team leader.

The following grid shows a situation in which John Smith is working both on project 1 in a cross-functional team as well as in his own department (production).

Of course, we can add many more dimensions to the matrix structure according to the number of projects an individual is working on.

✳ DID YOU KNOW?

Henry Ford – the founder of the Ford motor car company – saw his organisation as a giant machine. Ford was at the head driving the machine and his workers were simply expected to follow instructions. His organisation had a top down model with Ford at the top.

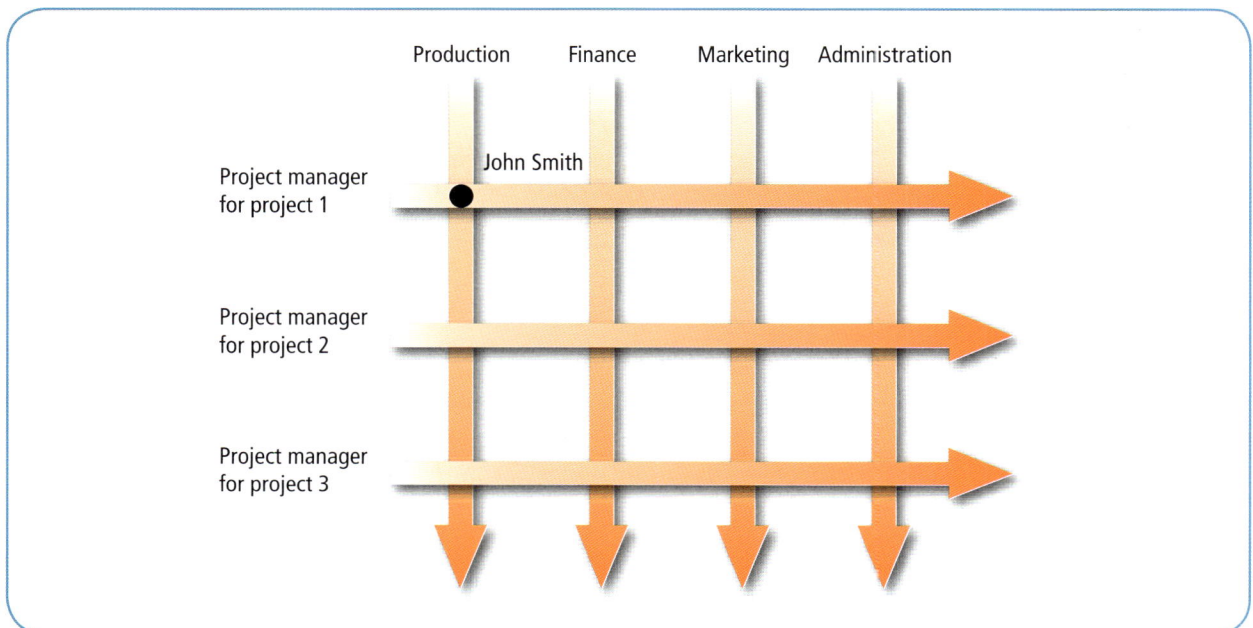

FIGURE 1.18 *A matrix organisation structure*

The roles of managers/supervisors and employees

Within an organisation there are various levels of management and supervision.

A **manager** is someone with responsibility – usually for others, for making various decisions, and for managing various resources.

For example, the job description of a marketing manager in a company might state that they:

* are *accountable* to their marketing director
* are *responsible* for staff in the market research function of the company
* are *responsible* for planning, organising and delivering market research campaigns
* have to create a market research budget and monitor that budget each month
* are *responsible* for making sure that the company keeps in tune with the changing needs of its customers.

You can see that management involves responsibility. The level of responsibility depends on the level of management.

Senior managers are responsible for long-term decisions made in a company, and major resources.

Middle managers are responsible for some medium-term decisions, and some important resources.

Junior managers are responsible for short-term decisions and have some responsibility for resources.

Supervisors also have an important role to play in an organisation and their responsibilities are often blurred with those of junior managers. Supervisors have responsibility for supervising a particular task or group of people.

Supervisors will often work with fairly tight boundaries. They have responsibility for making sure that:

* the right standards are met
* time deadlines are met
* people and other resources are supervised in an appropriate way.

Just because an employee is not a manager or employee does not mean that their work is any less important. Most employees have the potential to become supervisors and managers. Employees have a responsibility to meet legal requirements, and the responsibilities of the job set out in a job description. Today many employees are given additional responsibilities because managers recognise that individuals work best when trusted to do fulfilling work.

1.2 How businesses obtain employees

Businesses must plan to make sure that they have the right number of suitable employees for their needs.

The different qualities that business people look for

Examine the job advertisement below:

Superior Industries Ltd

ADMIN ASSISTANT

Due to expansion Superior Industries require an administrative assistant to help in their Customer Service department.

The successful applicant will possess excellent PC literacy and data entry skills and will be responsible for the management of customer orders for the business.

With an excellent telephone manner, you will be reliable and enthusiastic, well organised and a self starter and play a pivotal role in the day-to-day running of this busy but friendly department.

For further information and an application form please call xxxxx.

FIGURE 1.19 *A job advertisement*

> ### Learning activity
>
> Interview someone with a management role in a company. Assess whether their work is that of a senior, middle or junior manager. What are their main areas of responsibility? Who are they accountable to?

Although this post is not at a high level in the organisation it immediately becomes obvious that the company is looking for a number of qualities:

Existing skills: PC literate, database skills.

Personal qualities: Excellent telephone manner, reliable, enthusiastic, well-organised, self starter, willingness to take on responsibility.

Businesses need to be clear about the sorts of qualities that they are looking for when recruiting employees in order to attract the most suitable applicants.

They will need to consider carefully the sorts of:

* Competencies that they are looking for – i.e. what they expect applicants to already be able to do

* Knowledge required – what should applicants already know

* Skills required

* Attitudes required.

> **Learning activity**
>
> Select a job that you are familiar with. Make a list of the competencies, knowledge, skills and attitudes that you would expect someone to have to be appointed to work at that job in your business.

Reasons for recruiting staff

Superior Industries (advertisement shown in Figure 1.19) were looking to recruit because their business was growing. There are a number of reasons for recruiting new staff:

1 The growth of the business

For example, in recent years many companies have moved into e-commerce buying and selling through the Internet. They have therefore needed to recruit web page designers and other IT specialists.

2 Filling vacancies caused by job leavers

All businesses have a turnover of staff. For example, supermarket chains like ASDA and Sainsbury's constantly need to recruit checkout

staff, car park attendants and other employees. There will be a regular stream of people leaving their jobs, e.g. to go to college or university, who will need to be replaced.

3 Changing job roles

Modern work is constantly changing. Next year's jobs will require different skills to those that are required today. Businesses will therefore constantly create new opportunities and new jobs requiring new people.

4 Internal promotion

Most companies encourage their staff to take on more demanding and better paid posts within the business. New employees are required to replace those moving up the ladder.

Job descriptions, person specifications and advertisements for new staff

Organisations need to attract, recruit and retain the best possible people to fill the posts required and thus help a business to achieve its objectives.

Job descriptions

A **job description** will set out how a particular employee is to fit into the organisation. It will therefore need to set out:

* The title of the job
* To whom the employee is responsible
* For whom the employee is responsible
* A simple description of the role and duties of the employee within the organisation.

A job description could be used as a job indicator for applicants. Alternatively, it could be used as a guideline for an employee and/or line manager as to his or her role and responsibility within the organisation.

Job descriptions can be used by organisations to provide information for use in drafting a situations vacant advertisement and for briefing interviewers.

Job title

One of the most important parts of a job description is the job title. The job title should

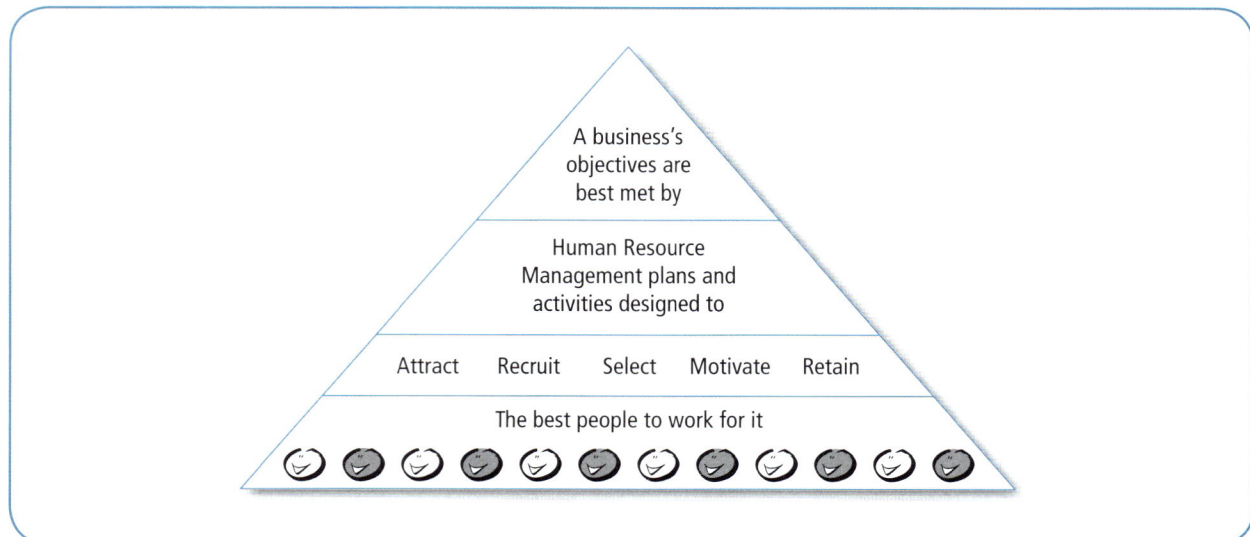

FIGURE 1.20 *Organisations seek the best people to achieve their objectives*

give a good indication of what the job entails. For example, you may hear people in organisations make statements such as: 'She's supposed to be the Managing Director, let her make the decision,' or 'Leave the word-processing of letters to the administrator, that's not your job.' I heard a conversation between a lecturer and a porter concerning the carrying of boxes which ended up with the remark: 'You're supposed to be a porter – get porting!'

When looking through job advertisements the first thing that job applicants will look for (apart from the salary) will be the job title.

From time to time job titles will change, often to give a slightly different feel to some jobs or to confer new status – the Principal of a college may become a 'Chief Executive', a dustbin man may become a 'Disposal services officer', a petrol pump cashier may become a 'Forecourt executive' and so on.

FIGURE 1.21 *A job title may be chosen to confer status*

Position within organisation structure

A job description will often establish where an individual stands in a particular organisation structure. This will mean that it can be clearly set out who the post-holder is accountable to, and who is accountable to him or her.

The position within an organisation will also give a clear idea of responsibilities. Job applicants will be interested to locate their position in order to work out whether their previous experience will be broad enough and to assess the kind of commitment they will be expected to make to the organisation.

Duties and responsibilities

A further important aspect of the job description will be that which sets out the duties and responsibilities of job holders.

Prior to setting out a job description an organisation may carry out an **analysis of the tasks** which need to be performed by a job-holder, and of the skills and qualities required.

If this is done carefully, then organisational planners will have a clear picture of how particular jobs fit in with all the other jobs carried on in an organisation. It also helps job applicants to get a clear picture of what is expected of them, and it helps job-holders to understand the priorities of their work (see Figure 1.22).

A **job analysis** is a study of the tasks that are required to do a particular job. Job analysis is very important in creating a clear job description. For example, the job of a trainee manager in a supermarket could be described under the following key headings:

* Title of post

* Prime objectives of the position

* Supervisory/managerial responsibilities

* Source(s) of supervision and guidance

* Range of decision making

* Responsibilities for assets, materials, etc.

FIGURE 1.22 *A job description helps the individual and the organisation*

✱ DID YOU KNOW?

One of ASDA's central values is to cut out waste of any kind. This value is stressed in job descriptions in which employees are instructed, for example, to 'Look for opportunities to reduce waste and put forward your ideas' and to 'Ensure stock is rotated correctly at all times'.

Learning activity

A large supermarket chain near to you (e.g. Sainsbury's, Morrisons, ASDA, Tesco) currently does not have enough shop assistants to meet the demands of customers, particularly at weekends. There are long queues at the tills, and it has become impossible to stack shelves neatly or to price all items accurately.

Set out a job analysis for a shop assistant, by answering the following questions:

1 What tasks need to be performed?

2 What skills and qualities are required?

3 How can the skills be acquired?

Person specifications

A person specification should do what the title suggests – specify (set out clearly) what attributes an individual needs to have to do a particular job well. The person specification goes beyond a simple description of the job, by highlighting the mental, physical and other attributes required of a job holder. For example, a recent Prison Service advertisement specified the following: 'At every level your task will call for a lot more than simple efficiency. It takes humanity, flexibility, enthusiasm, total commitment and, of course, a sense of humour.'

Armed with this sort of specification, those responsible for recruiting and selecting someone to do a particular job have a much clearer idea of the ideal candidate. At the same time those applying for a job have a much clearer idea of what is expected of them and whether they have the attributes.

The Human Resources department may therefore set out, for its own use, a 'person specification', using a layout similar to that shown in Figure 1.23.

Summary of job			
Attributes	**Essential**	**Desirable**	**How identified**
Physical			
Qualifications			
Experience			
Training			
Special knowledge			
Personal circumstances			
Attitudes			
Practical and intellectual skills			

FIGURE 1.23 *Layout for a person specification*

For example, a person specification for police recruits might include physical attributes related to the standard of physical fitness, qualifications including Advanced level or equivalents, etc.

The person specification can be used to:

✱ make sure that a job advertisement conveys the qualities that prospective candidates should have.

✱ check that candidates for a job have the right qualities.

Learning activity

Examine two job descriptions produced by an organisation (perhaps by the organisation that you work for or where you carried out your work experience).Explain how successful these job descriptions seem to have been in matching applicants with vacancies.

Create a person specification that would be suitable for selecting candidates for a job that you are familiar with.

Personal attributes and achievements

A person specification is concerned with identifying those people who have the right qualities to fit the jobs you are offering. For example, personal attributes for a member of the Paratroop Regiment might include physical toughness and alertness. The personal attributes of a teacher may include the ability to work well with others and to find out about the learning needs of pupils. The personal attributes of a shop assistant might include punctuality and smartness of appearance.

Personal achievements give a good indication of the existing abilities of given individuals. For example, someone who has achieved the Duke of Edinburgh Awards shows qualities of enterprise and initiative. Personal achievements can be good indicators of qualities such as the ability to work in a team, to help others, to persevere, etc.

Qualifications

Qualifications are another important ingredient in person specifications. For example, when recruiting a new Human Resources lecturer it would be essential to appoint someone with formal teaching qualifications, and some experience of work at an appropriate level in Human Resource management.

Qualifications are a good measure of prior learning. This has been simplified in recent years by the development of nationally recognised qualifications such as Applied Business courses.

The idea of a qualification is that it prepares you to do a particular job or activity. In creating job specifications, organisations will therefore need to consider the level of qualification required by a job holder.

Experience

There is a well-known saying that there is no substitute for experience. Someone with experience in carrying out a particular post or who has had particular responsibilities should be able to draw on that experience in new situations.

For example, an experienced lecturer has already taught, assessed, administered and carried out a variety of other duties in a college. A new lecturer has not had the same advantages.

We talk about the learning curve which results from experience. The implication is that the good learner will learn at a progressively faster rate as they draw on their experience. A person specification should therefore set out the required experience for a job-holder.

Competence

Competence is a word that is widely used today. Competence implies that a person has sufficient knowledge or skill to carry out particular tasks or activities. Most people would rather visit a competent than an incompetent doctor, or be taught by a competent rather than an incompetent teacher.

Person specifications should set out levels of competence required by a particular job-holder. Hairdressers, for example, need to show competence in a range of performance criteria that make up the elements of hairdressing work. A hairdresser would be foolish to take on a new stylist for dyeing purposes who had not first exhibited competence in mixing and applying hair dye.

FIGURE 1.24 *Competence is vital*

Job applications and curriculum vitae

We are now in a position to look at **job applications** and **interviewing**. First examine the two flow charts shown below which show the selection process for a job (a) from the employer's point of view, and (b) from the applicant's point of view:

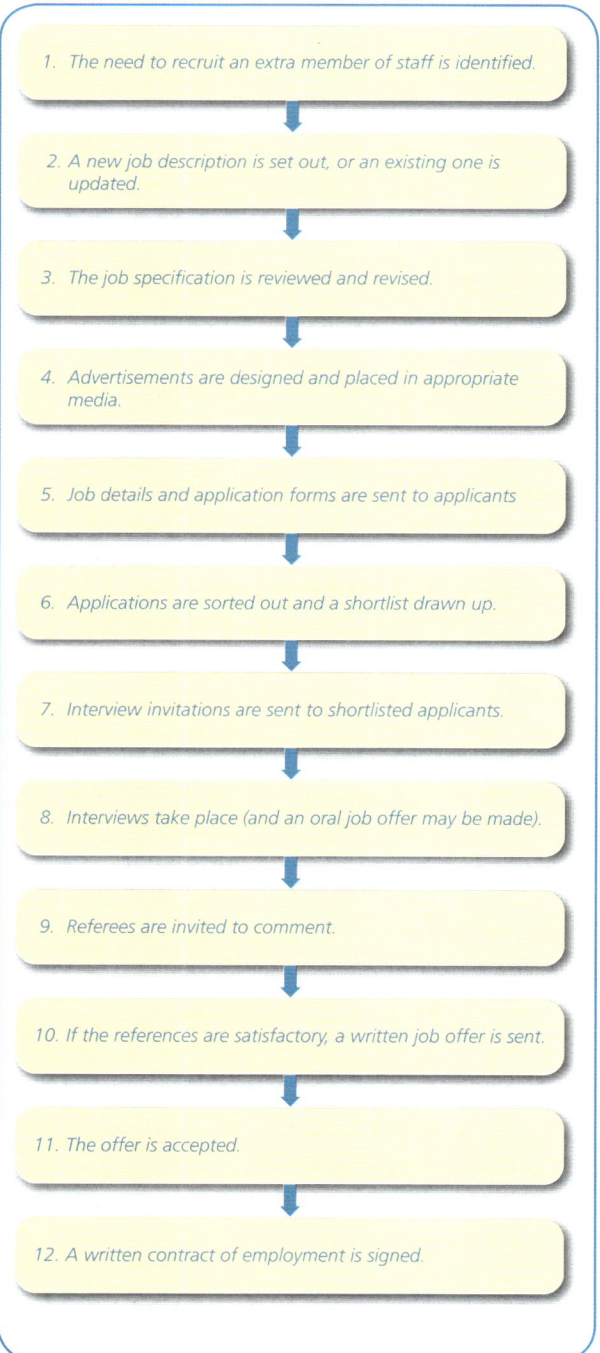

1. The need to recruit an extra member of staff is identified.

2. A new job description is set out, or an existing one is updated.

3. The job specification is reviewed and revised.

4. Advertisements are designed and placed in appropriate media.

5. Job details and application forms are sent to applicants

6. Applications are sorted out and a shortlist drawn up.

7. Interview invitations are sent to shortlisted applicants.

8. Interviews take place (and an oral job offer may be made).

9. Referees are invited to comment.

10. If the references are satisfactory, a written job offer is sent.

11. The offer is accepted.

12. A written contract of employment is signed.

FIGURE 1.25 *Job selection – the employer's schedule*

1. Evaluate different career choices, and narrow down your options.

2. Produce and update your curriculum vitae.

3. Ask three people to act as referees.

4. Photocopy your examination and other certificates.

5. See an interesting job advertisement and send for details.

6. Find out more about the organisation.

7. Send a short letter or e-mail asking for an application form.

8. Fill in the form and write a short letter supporting your application. Send copies of certificates and CV. Keep copies of all these documents.

9. If invited for interview, immediately telephone to confirm the arrangements.

10. Verbal acceptance of job.

11. Write a letter of acceptance and return the contract.

12. Make sure you know when and where you are expected to be on the first day.

FIGURE 1.26 *Job selection – the applicant's view*

Job applications

The following comments relate to how you should go about writing job applications. They are equally relevant in examining what businesses are looking for when they come to choose applicants. All students who are following this course will need at some stage to produce letters of application for jobs. It is important that you get this process right. Over the years we have seen many students applying for jobs. It is surprising how often there are two students who are almost identical in terms of qualifications, appearance and ability, but one is offered many interviews while the other receives only a few. Usually the difference is in the quality of their letters of application.

A letter should have a clear structure, with a beginning, a middle and an ending. It should state:

* your reasons for applying for the job
* the contribution you can make to the organisation
* how you have developed your capabilities through training and education
* the skills and knowledge you have acquired that would help you to do the job well.

The letter needs to be interesting – you are writing about (i.e. selling) yourself. It should contain just enough information to support your application form and CV (see below), highlighting the most relevant evidence. You will know that you are writing effective letters if they lead to interviews.

Here are some important rules to remember.

* Use good English with accurate spelling. Always check in a dictionary if you are unsure of the spelling of a word (use the spell checker on your computer)
* Use your own words rather than copying those in the advertisement
* Do not try to be too clever by using long words
* Keep the paragraphs short
* Try not to use 'I' too much
* Word process your work

* Follow the correct convention of addressing people. A letter beginning 'Dear Sir / Madam' should be ended with 'Yours faithfully', whereas one that begins 'Dear Mr Chanderpaul' should be ended with 'Yours sincerely'
* Keep a copy of what you have written.

Curriculum vitae

A **curriculum vitae** (usually called simply a CV) is a summary of your career to date. There are three stages you should follow when setting out your CV.

* assemble all the facts about yourself
* draft the CV
* edit the document several times

CASE STUDY

Applying for a post

The following letter was sent by an applicant for the post of trainee accountant with Great Western Trains.

1 **What strengths and weaknesses can you spot?**
2 **If you were to advise Charles Lawson on how he could improve his letter what comments would you make?**

21 Wade Park Avenue
Market Deeping
Peterborough
PE6 8JL

20th February 2005

Great Western Trains Finance Manager,
Room 109
East Side Offices
Bristol
BS3 9HL

Dear Sir/Madam,

I noticed in a national paper that you have a job available for a junior accountant. I am very interested in the post because I see it as presenting a good opportunity for me. I have always been very interested in rail accounts. I am also studing accounts at collage. I understand that on your accountancy training scheme there will be good opportunities for promotion. I am also studing a course in Applied Business. This is a very interesting course and I have had good reports from all my tutors on the course. As part of the course I am sing accounts. I have found the accounts to be the most exciting and interesting parts. I am also interested in train spotting.

I am working at the Anglia Co-operative Society. This is a part time post but it involves a lot of responsibility. I have to check the stock and make sure the shelves are well organised. I also have had EPOS training.

I am currently working on my cv and will send it to you next week. Many thanks for your interest in my application.

Yours Sincerely,

Charles Lawson

FIGURE 1.27 *Job application letter*

Curriculum Vitae

Name	Prakesh Patel
Date of birth	1.3.1986
Address	50 Palmerston Road, Reading, RG31 9HL
Telephone	01604 76321
Education and training	Waingels' Copse School Reading, Sept 1998 – July 2004
Qualifications (GCSEs)	Mathematics (B) English (B) Business Studies (A) French (B) Geography (B) German (A) History (B) Technology (B) All 2004
Interests and activities	Captain of school football team, house captain and prefect (2002–2004) Venture Scout, Gold Award Duke of Edinburgh. Member of Woodley Chess Club.

Referees:	Mr I. Marks Waingels' Copse School Denmark Avenue Woodley Reading RG3 8SL	Rev R. Babbage St Jude's Church Street Reading Reading RG4 7QZ

FIGURE 1.28 *An outline curriculum vitae (CV)*

Try to create a favourable impression (but always be truthful). Leave out negative statements about yourself. Do not be vague.

Always use a word-processing package with an impressive, yet conservative, font.

Assembling the facts

At the initial stage you are trying to get together as many relevant facts as possible about your career to date. It does not matter if you put down too many to start with – make a list of all your educational, work-based and leisure achievements, as well as training activities and courses you have been on. Make brief notes about each of these as well as about projects and assignments you have been involved in.

Drafting the CV

A CV should be divided into suitable headings and sub-headings, for example:

1 Name

2 Date of birth

3 Address

Learning activity

Produce your own up-to-date CV. Ask someone else to evaluate your CV against the following checklist:

* Have you given a good impression of your skills, knowledge, experience and personality?

* Are these set out in a concise and readable fashion?

* Do significant achievements stand out?

* Have you eliminated confusing terms, jargon and obscure abbreviations?

* Are all words spelt accurately, have you used correct grammar, and is the layout clear and organised?

* Does your CV have a good feel?

* Would the person reading it understand it easily?

4   Telephone number

5   Education and training

6   Qualifications

7   Other relevant achievements

8   Interests

9   References.

Remember that the key part of the CV is the career history, so the sections that go before should not be too long. For example, when dealing with training, list only the most important and relevant training courses, and then if necessary include some of the others under 'other information'.

When you set out your responsibilities and achievements, decide whether it is necessary to put some of them under sub-headings. It is normal practice to start your career history with your most recent job and work backwards in time, because employers are usually more interested in your recent experience.

If some of your experience is of a technical nature, try to present it in a way that can be read easily by the general reader (rather than only by a specialist).

Try to use dynamic words in your CV. Here are some good examples:

accomplished	achieved	conducted
completed	created	decided
delivered	developed	designed
directed	established	expanded
finished	generated	implemented
improved	increased	introduced
launched	performed	pioneered
planned	promoted	redesigned
reorganised	set up	solved
succeeded	trained	widened
won	work	wrote

The main legal and ethical responsibilities relating to discrimination and equal opportunities

There are a number of legal and ethical requirements which businesses must meet when obtaining employees to work for them. The Sex Discrimination Act (1975 and 1986) and the Race Relations Act (1976 and 2000) sought to encourage equal treatment of people and respect for people in the workplace.

The **Sex Discrimination Act** set out rights for both men and women. Unlawful discrimination means giving less favourable treatment to someone because of their sex or because they are married or single, and can be either direct or indirect. **Direct sex discrimination** means being treated less favourably than a person of the opposite sex would be treated in similar circumstances. For example, a policy to appoint only men to management positions is clearly illegal. Direct marriage discrimination means being treated less favourably than an unmarried person of the same sex. **Indirect sex discrimination** is less easy to identify. It means being unable to comply with a requirement which on the face of it applies equally to both men and women, but which in practice can be met by a much smaller proportion of one sex. For example, an organisation may be indirectly discriminating against women if access to certain jobs is restricted to particular grades which in practice are held only by men.

The Race Relations Act makes it unlawful to discriminate against a person, directly or indirectly, in the field of employment on the basis of race, colour or national origin. Direct discrimination means treating a person on racial grounds less favourably than others are or would be treated in the same or similar circumstances. Segregating a person from others on racial grounds constitutes less favourable treatment. Indirect discrimination consists of applying a requirement or conditions which, although applied equally to persons of all racial groups, is such that a considerably smaller proportion of a particular racial group can comply with it. Examples are:

✳ a rule about clothing or uniforms which disproportionately disadvantages a racial group and cannot be justified

✳ an employer who requires higher language standards than are needed for safe and effective performance of the job.

These laws seek to prevent discrimination in areas such as the recruitment and selection of staff. The European Union Equal Treatment Directive now makes it unlawful to discriminate on grounds of sexual orientation and religion or other belief. By 2006 age discrimination will also be unlawful.

In addition to the bare essentials of legal requirements organisations need to consider the ethical side of their recruitment and selection policies. **Ethics** is about doing the right thing consistently rather than compromising sometimes. What this means in effect is that good employers will go beyond the letter of the law to provide excellent opportunities for all their people.

Learning activity

Which of the following would be inappropriate questions to ask in an interview from an equal opportunities angle?

'Mrs Smith, I see you are married. Do you intend to start a family soon?'

'What will happen when your children are ill or on school holidays? Who will look after them?'

'Your hair is very long, Mr Smith. If offered the job are you prepared to have it cut?'

'Mr Smith, as you are 55 do you think it's worth us employing you?'

'Miss Smith, as a woman do you think you are capable of doing the job?'

'Do you think your disability will affect your performance in the job?'

'How do you feel about working with people from a different ethnic background from yourself?'

'As a man, Mr Smith, you will be working in a department consisting mainly of women. Are you easily distracted?'

'Miss Smith, don't you think your skirt is rather short?'

Find out...

The Equal Opportunities Commission site contains case studies and other materials on areas such as employment practice, equal pay and discrimination. Find it at www.heinemann.co.uk/hotlinks (express code 1130P, then go to Unit 1).

Types of interviews

There are a number of different types of interviews that take place in work situations that you need to be familiar with. The main types are:

1   **Job interviews**. These take place when an organisation is seeking to find the right person to fill a particular post. These interviews are discussed in the next section.

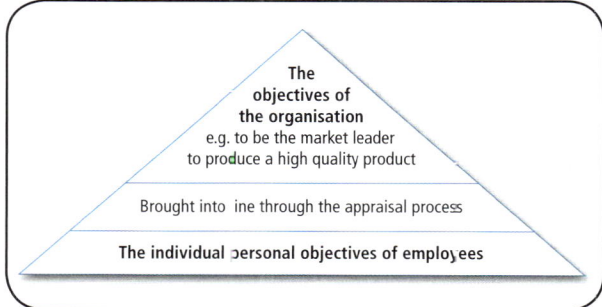

FIGURE 1.29 *Personal objectives and organisational objectives*

2   **Appraisal interviews** are an important means of bringing into line the objectives of the organisation and the individual personal objectives of the individuals that work for the organisation.

3   **Exit interviews** are used when people leave the organisation.

Appraisal interviews

Most organisations today operate some form of staff appraisal or staff development scheme.

Common stages of staff appraisal are as follows:

1   The line manager meets with the job holder to discuss what is expected. The agreed expectations may be expressed in terms of targets, performance standards, or required job behaviour.

2   The outcome of the interview is recorded and usually signed by both parties.

3   The job holder performs the job for a period of six months or a year.

4   At the end of the period, the job holder and line manager or team leader meet again to review and discuss progress made. They draw up new action plans to deal with identified problems and agree targets and standards for the next period.

Exit interviews

Exit interviews involve situations where an employee is leaving an organisation because:

* they are being made redundant, i.e. the job no longer exists

* they are being fired for disciplinary reasons

* they are retiring or have resigned.

One aspect can be to find out why the employee has decided to move on. This enables the firm to understand why employees are leaving and, where appropriate, adjust their activities to retain employees better.

An organisation that cares about its people will want to conduct such interviews in a way that maximises the development potential of the individual concerned.

CASE STUDY

Advice for holding an appraisal interview

The following advice was given to members of staff carrying out appraisal interviews in a large UK company:

1   Give the appraisee a copy of the company's objectives, and a record of the previous year's appraisal at least two weeks before an appraisal takes place.

2   Ask the appraisee to provide you with details of their aims, aspirations and targets in written form at least one week before the interview to provide a basis for discussion.

3   Start the meeting by outlining the company objectives, and ask the appraisee to evaluate their own performance in meeting targets set in the previous year.

4   Don't make judgements. Use prompts like 'What do you see as being your major achievements?' 'How successful do you think you have been in meeting your targets?' 'What new targets do you have for the coming year?' 'What do you see as being your major training and development needs?'

5   Once the appraisee has outlined answers to the questions above, focus them on establishing new targets. Ask whether these targets are manageable. Ask them to consider how their personal aspirations fit with the objectives of the company.

1   **Why do you think that appraisors were asked to carry out the appraisal using the format described above?**

2   **What do you see as being the main strengths and weaknesses of the format outlined above? What improvements would you like to see?**

SUITABLE CANDIDATES	POSSIBLE CANDIDATES	REJECTS
Those that meet all or most of the relevant criteria.	Those that meet some of the relevant criteria and may show some exciting characteristics that could make them worth a chance.	Those that meet very few of the criteria.

FIGURE 1.30 *Sorting candidates for a shortlist*

Shortlisting procedures, job interviews and assessment methods

Shortlisting

Shortlisting involves drawing up a list of the most suitable applicants from those that have applied for a post with an organisation. Usually a small group of people will be trusted with the task of drawing up this list. Armed with a job specification, and other sets of criteria, it is possible to reject candidates who do not meet the required criteria.

It is helpful to sort applications into three piles – suitable, possible and rejects (see Figure 1.30).

A basic principle of equal opportunities is that clear criteria should be set up prior to selection, and that these criteria should be used in the first instance to select those candidates that are suitable to interview.

Learning activity

As part of your studies you should practise being the interviewer and the interviewee using the outline set out below. Record interviews using video recording equipment, and discuss in a group what makes a good interviewee/ interviewer, and what makes a good job interview. Useful things to look out for are:

* the effective use of body language, and eye contact,

* the completeness of answers given to questions (rather than answering 'Yes' or 'No')

* whether interviewees listened to questions and gave appropriate responses.

Planning and carrying out job interviews

Carrying out practice job interviews is a helpful way for students to understand the dynamics of interview situations, what firms are looking for when carrying out interviews, and the characteristics of a good interviewer/interviewee.

Opening the interview

Generally speaking, interviewers should try to make the interviewee feel relaxed. For example, they might ask the interviewee about his or her journey to the interview on that day: 'Where have you come from?' 'Did you find it easy to get here today?', etc.

Of course, there are exceptional times when interviewers deliberately set out to make the interviewees feel uncomfortable to see how they react, for example by putting them on a wobbly chair or placing them at a lower height than the interviewer's chair.

However, the important thing to remember is that modern business organisations are not run like some sort of secret police. Generally the interviewer should find some means of making the interviewee feel comfortable, so that the interviewee can show his or her best side.

When there are several interviewers a starting point might be to introduce the interviewee to each of the panel in turn.

Asking questions

The next stage is to ask the interviewee a set of predetermined questions. The questions asked

Learning activity

Create a score sheet to be used in an interview situation. Relate the requirements to the job specification.

Post: Junior Retail Manager

Candidate's name: Linda Booth

Requirements	Score 1–5 1 = Poor 5 = Excellent	Notes
Tidy appearance	3	*Untidy hair*
Intelligence	5	*Answered questions quickly and with good attention to detail.*
Punctuality	1	*Turned up 2 minutes late for interview.*
Etc	etc	etc

FIGURE 1.31 *Part of an interviewer's score sheet*

should relate to the person specification and job description. Remember that you are looking for a candidate who is best able to meet the organisation's requirements. The interviewer will have a copy of the candidate's application form and curriculum vitae. Interviewers will normally want to make notes to check how each interviewee meets the job requirements.

For example, they may have a sheet like that shown as Figure 1.31 in front of them. By setting out a score-sheet it is possible to compare candidates' responses to questions and behaviour in the interview situation.

Interviewing requires a considerable amount of intelligence and inventiveness. When candidates answer your questions you may feel that you need to ask them a little bit more in order to get a more complete answer. Follow on questions are very important here. Some follow on questions may be planned in advance, while others may need to be developed on the spur of the moment.

For example, an interview for the job of a shelf stacker in a supermarket may proceed as follows:

Interviewer: Have you had experience of shelf stacking in a supermarket before?

Interviewee: Yes, I worked at Waitrose doing it for three months.

Interviewer: (Follow on question). Can you tell me exactly what you were responsible for doing in your shelf stacking job? (And why you left it!)

Without follow on questions an interview can pass very quickly with little being found out about the true strengths (and weaknesses) of job applicants.

Using body language

People do not communicate with each other just through words. They also communicate through their **body language**. An interviewer who wants to draw the best out of candidates for a job will use appropriate body language. The interviewer should be seated at the same height as the interviewee with a good frontal or open posture. The interviewer should not cross his or her arms or make threatening gestures such as pointing a finger or banging a fist down on the table. He or she should smile and use clear eye contact.

Closing the interview

The usual way of closing an interview is that, when the interviewer or interviewing panel have finished their list of questions, they will ask the interviewee if there is anything he or she would like to ask. When this is completed the interviewer will say something like: 'Thank you very much for coming to the interview, I hope you have a safe journey back. You will be hearing from us by...' The interviewer will clarify the procedures through which the interviewee will be informed of arrangements, and explain how any administrative task such as claiming for expenses should be done.

Giving feedback

Often candidates for a post will be given feedback on how they performed in the interview situation. They should be told about their strengths and weaknesses and the reasons why they were or were not chosen for the post. This feedback should be seen as a positive process concerned with the ongoing development of the interviewee.

Interviewee techniques

Interviews can be nerve-racking. In a short space of time the candidate must convince the interviewer that he or she is the person the organisation needs.

FIGURE 1.32 *Wear appropriate clothes for an interview*

	INTERVIEW ASSESSMENT					
Factors	Rating					Remarks
	A	B	C	D	E	
Appearance Personality Manner Health						
Intelligence Understanding of questions						
Skills Special skills Work experience						
Interests Hobbies Sports						
Academic						
Motivation						
Circumstances Mobility Hours Limitations						
OVERALL						

A = Exceptional   B = Above average   C = Satisfactory
D = Below average   E = Unsuitable

FIGURE 1.33 *Interview assessment form*

Preparing

Both the interviewer and the candidate need to be prepared. The candidate can prepare by practising answers to the questions likely to be asked, possibly with the help of a friend who takes the role of the interviewer.

It must be remembered that interviews are a two-way activity. The candidate has a chance to ask questions and find out if the organisation and the job are suitable. Questions can, for example, be asked about training, promotion prospects and social facilities.

There are all sorts of things that you can prepare before an interview. For example, you may want to try out the clothes that you will wear to the interview beforehand, perhaps by wearing them to some sort of public occasion.

There is nothing worse than feeling uncomfortable in the clothes you have chosen for an interview. Many people like to plan the route they will take to get to the interview, even doing a dummy run beforehand.

You may like to prepare yourself by thinking about the kinds of things that interviewers will be look for in you. Figure 1.33 shows an interview

DO	DON'T
Find out about the firm before the interview	Be late
Dress smartly but comfortably	Smoke unless invited to
Speak clearly and with confidence	Chew gum or eat sweets
Look at the interviewer when speaking	Answer all questions 'yes', 'no' or 'I don't know'
Be positive about yourself	Be afraid to ask for clarification if anything is unclear
Be ready to ask questions	Say things which are obviously untrue or insincere

FIGURE 1.34 *Interview checklist*

assessment form that gives you some useful indications of the qualities that are looked for in many job holders.

The checklist shown in Figure 1.34 should also be helpful in giving you some useful preparatory advice for interviews.

Showing confidence

It is important for interviewees to appear confident but not over-confident. You should be confident in your own abilities. One of the most important attributes to have in the interview situation is enthusiasm. An enthusiastic person will tend to radiate confidence. Candidates who appear hangdog and timid will be viewed in a poor light, particularly for posts that require some degree of responsibility and initiative.

Body language

At an interview it is important for you to adopt the right body language. Look alert and eager. Look the questioner in the eye. Avoid nervous movements, and try not to cross your arms in a defensive position. Try not to threaten the interviewer by pointing your finger or making violent movements. Sit up straight and try to look

FIGURE 1.35 *Appropriate body language*

Learning activity

Study the following pictures which show a person who turned up for an interview for a part-time shelf filler's post.

In each case explain why the body language is inappropriate.

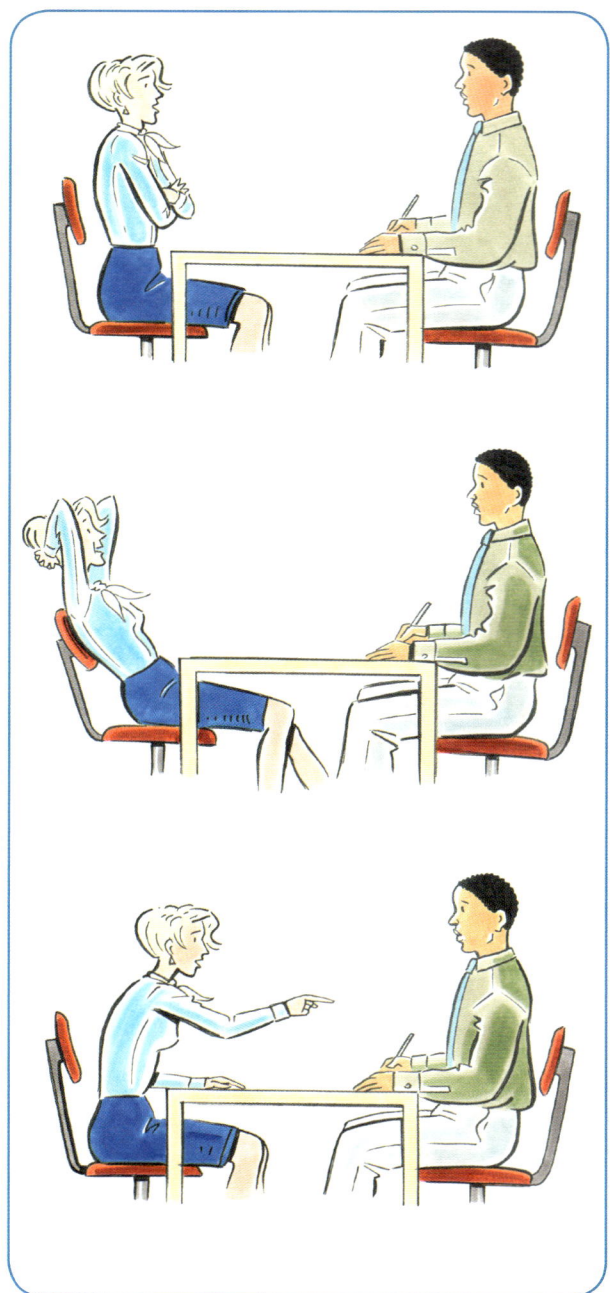

FIGURE 1.36 *Inappropriate body language*

confident and at ease – not apathetic and too laid back.

Do not give brief one-line answers, but try to expand on your answers so that the interviewer can see you at your best. Smile, and at all times try to appear interested and enthusiastic about what is being discussed. You do not have to let yourself be pushed around by an aggressive interviewer – be assertive by standing up for yourself, without taking it to the extreme by becoming heated and argumentative.

Listening to questions

When you are being interviewed, listen carefully to the questions that you are asked. If you do not understand a question or have not heard it clearly, it may be helpful to say, 'Please could you repeat that question?'

Responding to questions

When answering questions you will need to expand on points rather than giving a simple yes/no or a short answer. Try to give detailed and

---

Learning activity

It is often the first few minutes of an interview that the panel make up their minds about which candidate to appoint. A recent study reported that the person who is first on the interviewer's list is three times less likely to be hired than the last name on the list.

In groups, carry out mock interviews for one of the following posts.

1 A post that you are familiar with from work experience.

2 A post as a part-time shelf filler for Marks & Spencer.

3 An alternative post that members of your group agree on because you have sufficient knowledge of the post, and can get hold of materials such as job descriptions, job specifications etc.

Before the interviews take place the interviewing panel will need to establish the qualities they are looking for in the successful applicant. The interviewing panel will also need to establish a set of questions. The same questions need to be asked of each applicant if the interviews are to be fair.

The applicants will each need to produce a CV and a written application. They will also need to research the nature of the organisation and the post.

After the interviews, all interviewers and interviewees should fill in an evaluation sheet containing the following questions:

✳ How did you feel about the interview?

✳ How do you consider the interview went?

✳ What impression do you think that you gave?

✳ What do you think of the interviewers'/ interviewees':

   ✳ planning and organisation

   ✳ preparation for the interview

   ✳ performance at the interview?

Individual students should prepare an appraisal form for analysing their own strengths and weaknesses in the interview situation. This should be a very helpful process because it encourages you to be objective in your self-criticism. You can then use the form to reflect on your performance. Prepare the form before the interview takes place either by watching a video showing you interviewing or being interviewed, or simply by recalling your thoughts and feelings.

Aspect of performance	Rating				
	Very good	Good	Fair	Weak	Very weak
Eye contact					
Body language					
Appearing confident					
Answering questions					

FIGURE 1.37 *A self-appraisal form*

clear responses. Remember that the inverviewers are judging you against certain criteria. Try to think about what those criteria might be and prepare full answers which enable them to give you high scores.

Asking questions

When given the opportunity ask a small number of relevant questions. Don't ask questions that simply involve the repetition of what you have already been told. If you are not sure whether you want the job or not, ask questions that will help you to make an informed choice.

Be clear and concise

Good verbal communication involves asking and answering questions in a clear and concise way. The person who is straightforward, interesting and direct will often sway an interview in a positive way.

Other assessment methods

Many jobs today involves some form of **psychometric or aptitude testing** to find out whether individuals have the right sorts of personalities or dispositions to carry out particular types of work. A psychometric test is a way of assessing an individual's personality, drives and motivations, often by means of a paper and pencil questionnaire – or online test.

For example, one of the dimensions the psychometric test might draw out is an individual's willingness or ability to work in a team situation, or to handle stress.

A number of organisations place a great deal of emphasis on these tests because they believe they are reliable indicators of the sociability / personality of individuals, and that they are useful predictors of whether individuals will fit into the organisation.

Learning activity

Obtain a psychometric test that is used for selection purposes. Try out the test. What does it claim to show about your personality and disposition? Do you agree?

Evaluating recruitment and selection processes

Recruitment and selection can be a very costly process for a business. It takes a great deal of time to set up the process – involving deciding on what the jobs that are to be recruited for will entail, advertising, sifting through applications, checking which applications best meet the criteria set down for the post, interviewing candidates and, finally, selecting the best candidate for the post.

There is considerable scope along the way for waste and inefficiency. For example, when a job advertisement attracts 100 applicants there will be considerable waste when reducing the list down to six. If you get your procedures wrong you may eliminate some of the best candidates right from the start and end up with six who are barely

Learning activity

Produce an attractively laid out four-page booklet setting out good practice for recruiting and selecting applicants to fill posts in a specific organisation. You may want to base the work on the organisation in which you have carried out your work experience or had a part-time job. Alternatively relate your work to recruiting part-time shelf fillers at your local Marks & Spencer store.

The booklet should consider:

1 Creating an effective person specification, and job descriptions.

2 Creating job advertisements.

3 Complying with the legal and ethical requirements, e.g. Equal Opportunities laws.

4 Shortlisting.

5 Interviewing to get the best candidates.

6 Any other areas that you consider relevant.

Once you have developed your material you will be well placed to evaluate the recruitment and selection processes in different businesses. Using your own experience of being recruited and selected to work in a particular job, how did the process you experienced compare with the good practice guidelines that you have drawn up?

satisfactory. If you end up choosing an unsuitable candidate for the job, the company will suffer from having a poorly motivated person, who may make mischief within the organisation before walking out on the job and leaving the company to go through the expense of replacing him or her yet again.

Training staff

Training includes all forms of planned learning experiences and activities designed to make positive changes to performance and other behaviour. You can train an individual to develop new:

* knowledge

* skills

* beliefs

* values

* attitudes.

Learning is generally defined as 'a relatively permanent change in behaviour that occurs as a result of practice or experience'.

There are a number of training methods and activities which are described below.

Induction

Induction is the process of introducing new employees to their place of work, job, new surroundings and the people they will be working with. Induction also provides information to help new employees start work and generally 'fit in'.

As well as following naturally from recruitment and selection, induction should also consider the initial training needs either on joining a new organisation or on taking on a new function within it. As well as dealing with the initial knowledge and skills needed to do the job, in the case of a new organisation, it should also

FIGURE 1.38 *An induction pack*

deal with the structure, culture and activities in the organisation. The new recruit will typically be given an induction pack that introduces him or her to the organisation.

Mentoring

Mentoring involves a trainee being 'paired' with a more experienced employee. The trainee carries out the job but uses the 'mentor' to discuss problems that may occur and how best to solve them.

This approach is used in many lines of work. For example, it is common practice for trainee teachers to work with a mentor who is responsible for their early training and development. The student teacher will watch the mentor teach before starting his or her own teaching. The mentor will then give ongoing guidance to the student teacher on how best to improve his or her performance. The mentee will take any problems

and difficulties he or she is facing to the mentor to seek advice.

Coaching

Coaching involves providing individuals with personal coaches in the workplace. The person who is going to take on the coaching role will need, first, to develop coaching skills and will also need to have the time slots for the coaching to take place. The coach and the individual being coached will need to identify development opportunities that they can work on together – ways of tackling jobs, ways of improving performance, etc. The coach will provide continuous feedback on performance and how this is progressing.

Of course, coaching does not just benefit the person being coached; it also aids the coach's own personal development. It is particularly important in a coaching system that:

Learning activity

Study the pictures below and see if you can match the coach and the person they helped to develop.

FIGURE 1.39 *Can you match the coach with the star?*

* the coach wants to coach the person and has the necessary coaching skills

* the person being coached wants to be coached and has the necessary listening and learning skills

* sufficient time is given to the coaching process

* the organisation places sufficient value on the coaching process.

Some of the best sportspeople in this country have improved their skills and abilities by working closely with a coach they respect (Figure 1.39).

Apprenticeships

One of the great strengths of the British industrial system was the existence of a range of apprenticeship schemes, many of which no longer exist. With the apprenticeship scheme, the apprentice learnt by working for a more skilled craftsperson. The apprentices had to work for a number of years to master their trades.

Apprenticeships were once widespread in skilled work and, when the apprentices had learnt their trades, they were able to set up on their own and so bring in higher wages, employing apprentices on their own. During the early years of the apprenticeship wages might be quite low, and then rise as the apprentice became more skilled.

In recent years, the government has developed a Modern Apprenticeship scheme that enables young people to combine learning on the job with college-based courses. These schemes are subsidised by the government, which gives employers a greater incentive to take on apprentices. A modern apprenticeship is made up of a:

* A National Vocational Qualification (i.e. nationally recognised job-related qualification)

* Key skills

* A technical certificate.

Provided an individual starts the Modern Apprenticeship before they are 25 they will receive government funds. The length of time to complete the apprenticeship varies and the qualification is at both a Foundation and Advanced level.

In-house training and external training

In-house training is where an organisation has its own training department. External training is where employees are sent on external courses, or are trained in other ways, away from the organisation. In-house training can take place on the job or off the job within the company, but external training always takes place off the job.

CASE STUDY

Apprenticeship at Audi

Audi the car manufacturer has a well-organised apprenticeship and training scheme in this country to develop high quality people. Audi training centres are designed to develop the right skills. The following chart shows progression for technicians at Audi.

1 **What other fields that you are familiar with provide the opportunity for apprenticeships?**

2 **What might attract an individual to take a Modern Apprenticeship?**

3 **Carry out a web search to find out the range of Modern Apprenticeships on offer.**

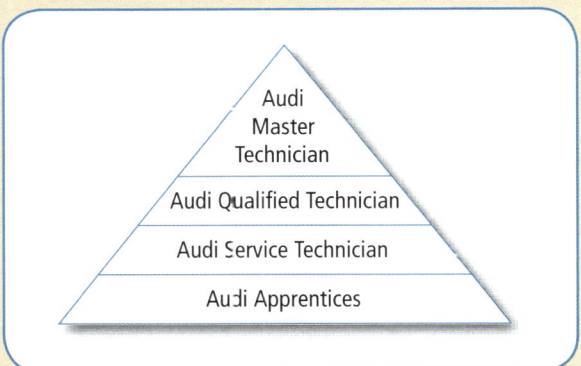

FIGURE 1.40 *Progression for technicians at Audi*

Nestlé provides two kinds of OJT. The first is for trainees. These training sessions are generally short and are geared towards new arrivals and those starting a job within a company.

The other is for current employees. Every Nestlé employee continues to receive training throughout his or her time with the company. The process is a constant and systematic communication of knowledge from executive levels down, and includes every level of management.

1 Why do new trainees require OJT ?
2 Why do existing employees need OJT?
3 Why is management important in delivering this training?

On-the-job training

On-the-job training (OJT) takes place when employees are trained while they are carrying out an activity, often at their place of work. There are four main advantages to this approach:

1 Participants can gain a thorough knowledge of the organisation.

2 There can be no substitute for hands-on experience in developing skills.

3 It allows the trainee to engage in productive, paid work and it can be carried out without the need for structured, permanent training facilities.

4 OJT is also a useful means of testing a trainee's knowledge and competence for any given task.

Off-the-job training

Off-the-job training, as its name suggests, takes place away from the job. This can be either internally within a company or externally using outside trainers. Many large companies will engage in a great deal of both off-the-job and on-the-job training.

Nationally recognised training structures

Most businesses take advantage of nationally recognised training schemes and qualifications. For example, **Modern Apprenticeships** allow young people to combine further education with on-the-job training. **Local Education Councils (LECs)** help to provide training for people in a particular area, to make the unemployed and others more employable.

Investors in People

Many organisations in all sectors now pride themselves in meeting the **Investors in People Standard**.

To achieve the Standard, an organisation needs to demonstrate that it does the following:

INVESTORS IN PEOPLE

FIGURE 1.41 *Investors in People is a nationally recognised standard*

Plan – develop strategies to improve the performance of the organisation, from business goals to leadership strategies.

Do – implement those strategies, taking action to improve the performance of the organisation.

Review – evaluate and adjust those strategies, measuring their impact on the performance of the organisation.

Being an Investor in People means that the organisation is likely to be seen more favourably by prospective employees, customers and other stakeholders. To achieve the Standard, an organisation is assessed by an independent assessor who gathers evidence (verbal, written and observed) that all requirements of the Standard are met. The assessor's recommendations are approved by a panel of business peers and the organisation is recognised as an Investor in People.

Learning activity

Interview someone who has been involved in setting up the systems that have enabled an organisation to gain Investors in People status. What were the main policies and practices that needed to be put in place to meet the standards?

Find out...

To find out more about Investors in People go to www.heinemann.co.uk/hotlinks (express code 1130P, then go to Unit 1).

Individual Learning Accounts

The current government's **'New Deal'** for the unemployed provides subsidised employment and support for young people to continue in full-time education and training. The creation of **Individual Learning Accounts** encourages individuals to save towards the costs of additional training.

Individual Learning Accounts are part of government policy to encourage everyone to engage in lifelong learning. An individual puts up a small sum of money towards a training or education course. The LEC then puts up a much larger sum of money towards the scheme. The Learning Account is then opened, and the trainee can go to a registered trainee with their account and sign on for training. The scheme is available for anyone in the 18–65 age range.

1.3 How businesses motivate employees

Having obtained and trained their staff, businesses will seek to keep these staff happy in their work.

Legislation that protects the well-being of employees

As a bare minimum, employees will need to comply with legislation about:

* **Hours of work:** As a member state in the European Union the UK must comply with EU regulations. The **Working Time Regulations** set out that workers aged 18 and over are entitled to four weeks' holiday a year, to work no more than six days out of every seven, to have a 20-minute break every six hours, and to work no more than an average of 48 hours a week.

* The **Employment Act 2002** provides employees with the right to leave from work in line with EU regulations. Employees are entitled to maternity and paternity (two weeks) leave before, during, and after the birth of a child. Employees who adopt a child are also eligible to 26 weeks' paid leave followed by 26 weeks' unpaid leave.

Learning activity

Carry out an internet search using the key words 'maternity leave', 'UK' and the current year, e.g. 2005. What are the latest entitlements of mothers in this respect?

Carry out another search using the key words 'Minimum Wage' 'UK' and the current year to find out what the present level is.

* **Minimum wage**: Before the minimum wage was introduced, well over a million workers were employed in jobs which paid less than the rate set. Many of these workers would have been young people in part-time or casual jobs with no permanent contact. The minimum wage is raised from time to time to guarantee a fair return for the most disadvantaged.

Pay and non-financial incentives

From a management view, a payment system should:

1 Be effective in recruiting the right quantity and quality of labour.

2 Be effective in retaining labour over the required period of time – it is expensive to have to keep advertising for and training new employees.

3 Keep labour costs as low as possible in order to maintain the competitiveness of a business.

4 Help to motivate staff and encourage effort. Careful thought needs to be applied to structuring pay systems in a way that encourages motivation and performance.

5 Be designed to allow for additional rewards and benefits.

The sum paid for a normal working week is termed a **basic wage** or **salary**. Many employees receive other benefits in addition to their basic wage, either in a money or non-money form. The main ways of calculating pay are outlined below. Sometimes elements of these methods are combined.

Flat rate

This is a set rate of weekly or monthly pay, based on a set number of hours. It is easy to calculate and administer but does not provide an incentive to employees to work harder.

Time rate

Under this scheme, workers receive a set rate per hour. Any hours worked above a set number are paid at an 'overtime rate'.

Piece rate

This system is sometimes used in the textile and electronics industries, among others. Payment is made for each item produced that meets given quality standards. The advantage of this is that it encourages effort. However, it is not suitable for jobs that require time and care. Also, many jobs particularly in the service sector produce 'outputs' that are impossible to measure.

Bonus

A bonus is paid as an added encouragement to employees. It can be paid out of additional profits earned by the employer as a result of the employee's effort and hard work, or as an incentive to workers at times when they might be inclined to slacken effort, e.g. at Christmas and summer holiday times.

Commission

This is a payment made as a percentage of the sales a salesperson has made.

Output-related payment schemes

Output-related schemes are the most common method used to reward manual workers. Most schemes involve an element of time-rates plus a bonus or other incentive.

> **Learning activity**
>
> The wages department of a large manufacturing organisation is deciding on the most appropriate payment systems in the following situations. What advice would you give them? If you have done work experience in a manufacturing company you may want to relate the reward system outlined to the company where you did your placement.
>
> They want to provide a financial reward system:
>
> 1 For sales people that rewards them according to the number of sales they make.
>
> 2 For production line staff that encourages them to be careful in their work.
>
> 3 For production line staff that discourages them from slacking off just before the Christmas period.

FIGURE 1.42 *Is the police force a suitable case for performance-related pay?*

In recent years the emphasis in a number of organisations has shifted towards performance-related pay. Based on performance appraisal techniques, such schemes have been adopted in a wide range of occupations, including the police force, universities, insurance and banking. Evidence indicates that up to three-quarters of all employers are now using some form of performance appraisal to set pay levels.

Managerial jobs are most affected by performance-related pay. Today managers' performance is increasingly assessed against working objectives. Individual objectives can be set by reference to company goals. An individual may be set broad objectives known as accountabilities. Shorter-term goals may be attached to each objective. Scoring systems are then worked out to assess performance against objectives, and these distinguish levels of attainment, e.g. high, medium or low.

One way of rewarding performance is to give a bonus if certain targets are met. Another is to give increments as targets are met, with the employee progressing up an incremental ladder each year.

1 **Give a brief definition of performance-related pay.**
2 **Do you think it is appropriate to use performance-related pay in the police force? How would performance be measured?**
3 **Give examples of jobs where performance-related pay might be appropriate and ones where it definitely would not be appropriate.**

Standards are set in many ways, varying from casual assessment to detailed work study based on method study and work measurement.

* **Method study** sets out to determine what is the most effective way of carrying out particular tasks.

* **Work measurement** takes place in three stages:

1 The time taken to perform a task is measured.
2 The effort of an individual worker or work-group is rated.
3 The work carried out is assessed and compared with the standard rate.

A standard allowable time is set according to the two stages. The worker's pay is then determined according to the success of the third stage.

Non-financial rewards

In addition to financial rewards so-called **fringe benefits** are provided including:

* Pension schemes
* Subsidised meals or canteen services
* Educational courses
* Opportunities for foreign travel
* Holiday entitlements
* Crèches
* Assistance with housing and relocation packages
* Discount and company purchase plans (i.e. cheap purchases of company products)
* Telephone costs
* Discounts on insurance costs

* Private healthcare, dental treatment, etc.
* Time off (sabbatical)
* Sports, leisure and social facilities.

There are a number of reasons for giving non-financial rewards including:

1 They can often be provided to employees free of tax, which benefits both the employer and the employee.

2 Some benefits can be provided cheaply through economies of scale, e.g. a works canteen offering cheap meals.

3 Some benefits are needed to improve employee performance, e.g. healthcare and hairdressing on site.

4 Some companies may be able to offer discounts on their own products and thus at the same time increase their sales.

5 The provision of certain benefits may help to create long-term commitment to the company, e.g. a crèche on site, a company pension scheme, company cars, etc.

Conditions of work and internal promotion

When you start work an important determinant of how happy you are in your job is the conditions in the workplace. One aspect of the conditions is the physical environment, for example:

* are you working in a bright, clean and well-lit environment?
* is the temperature suitable for work (not too hot or too cold)?
* is the workplace safe?
* other physical conditions.

The other important aspect is the 'culture' of the organisation. The culture relates to the relationships and typical ways of interacting and

✻ DID YOU KNOW?

The term HR refers to Human Resource management. This is an approach which involves welcoming the contribution that people can make to an organisation. However, some people are cynical about this approach particularly when HR managers end up sacking people. In these cases HR is said to stand for Human Remains!

✻ DID YOU KNOW?

From the 1970s right through to the 1990s when Liverpool Football Club was so successful, many of its managers were former backroom staff. This encouraged the backroom staff to be loyal to the club with excellent results.

doing things in the organisation. Different types of organisations have different cultures.

Promoting people within an organisation (internally) is another good motivating tool, because employees then see that they can develop themselves within the organisation.

The importance of motivating individuals

Motivation is the strength of commitment that individuals have to what they are doing. There are several theories which help us to think about motivation.

Maslow's hierarchy of needs

Maslow identified a hierarchy of needs split into five broad categories. He suggested that, although it is difficult, if not impossible, to analyse

FAVOURABLE CULTURES	UNFAVOURABLE CULTURES
Warm and welcoming	Unfriendly
Encouraging	Discouraging and based on fear
Welcomes initiative	Have to do what you are told

FIGURE 1.43 Organisational cultures

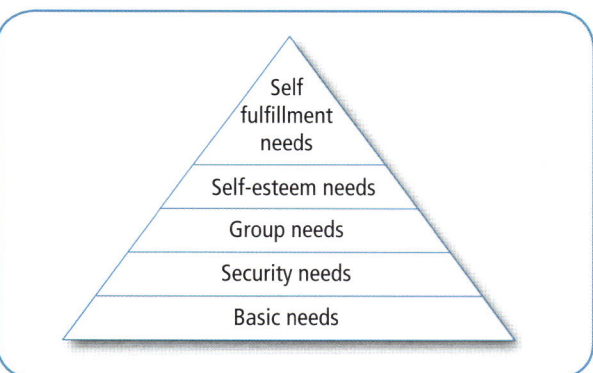

FIGURE 1.44 *Maslow's 'hierarchy of needs'*

individual needs, it is possible to develop a hierarchical picture of needs, split into categories.

Basic needs

Basic needs are for reasonable standards of food, shelter and clothing, and those other items that are considered the norm to meet the needs of the body and for physical survival. This base level of need will be attained at work from receiving a basic wage packet that helps the employee to survive – for example by receiving the minimum wage.

Security needs

Security needs are also concerned with physical survival. In the workplace, these needs could include safety, security of employment, adequate rest periods, pension and sick schemes, and protection from unfair treatment.

Group needs

Group needs are concerned with an individual's need for love and affection (within a group). In groups there are always some people who are strong enough and happy to keep apart. However, the majority of people want to feel that they belong to a group. In small and medium-sized organisations (up to 200 people) it is relatively easy to give each member of the group a feeling of belonging. However, in large organisations individuals can lose their group identify, becoming just another number, a face in the crowd. Managers therefore need to think about how they can organise their people into teams so as to meet group needs.

Self-esteem needs

Self-esteem needs are based on an individual's desire for self-respect and the respect of others.

Employees have a need to be recognised as individuals of some importance, to receive praise for their work and to have their efforts noticed and rewarded.

Maslow placed self-fulfillment at the top of the hierarchy of needs. Self-fulfillment is concerned with full personal development and individual creativity. In order to meet this need, it is important for individuals to be able to use their talents and abilities fully.

Maslow argued that individuals first have to have their lower-level needs met; however, if

✱ DID YOU KNOW?

The Chinese philosopher Confucius said that 'The person that finds a job they like never does a day's work in their life.'

Learning activity

Which of Maslow's needs do you think the following are looking to satisfy at work? How might managers go about seeking to meet these needs?

1 Simon is working part time in a supermarket to save up enough money to go back to university with. He is prepared to work long hours, providing his total pay is good. He is not interested in taking on responsibilities, but wants to work in a safe environment.

2 Pritesh is a graphic designer who recently graduated from art college. Ideally he would like to do something which allows him to express his artistic talent. He feels that his current job working in an advertising agency does not allow him to express himself. He works in a junior role in the company copying work that has been created by senior designers.

3 Gillian has recently been promoted to the post of supervisor in the food processing plant where she works. This has meant a rise in salary enabling her to take out a mortgage to buy a house and put down a deposit on a new car. The supervisor's post gives her the status she desires and she likes her working environment and the relationship she has with colleagues.

they are not to experience frustration it is also important for their higher level needs to be met. Frustrated employees are likely either to develop a 'couldn't care less approach' or to become antagonistic to working life. If employees are to become committed to work these higher level needs must be met. Self-fulfillment at work creates the complete employee, the person who enjoys work and feels a direct involvement in it.

Herzberg's theory of motivators and dissatisfiers

Herzberg carried out research on 200 engineers to find out what motivated them at work. He made a distinction between things that move people, which he referred to as KITA (kick in the ass), and factors that motivate people.

He argued that if he kicked his dog, this would get the dog to move (out of fear), but it would not motivate the animal.

When we are motivated we do something because we want to do it. In other words it provides an intrinsic (internal) reward.

Herzberg identified nine factors which he referred to as 'dissatisfiers' and when these factors reached a certain level they would cause employee absenteeism, poor levels of output, resistance to change, obstruction, and other negative actions.

The **'dissatisfiers'** are:

* dominating or unpredictable company policy and administration
* low pay
* poor working conditions
* confrontational relationships between different levels in the organisation
* unfriendly relationships within the chain of command
* unfair management and supervision
* unfair treatment of employees
* feelings of inadequacy
* impossibility for development of the individual.

By reducing these dissatisfiers you can reduce negative feelings but they are not the real motivating drives.

In contrast, Herzberg identified five motivating factors which relate to the content of jobs. He called these 'satisfiers'.

The **'satisfiers'** are:

* recognition of effort and performance
* the nature of the job itself – does it provide the employees with appropriate challenges?
* sense of achievement
* assumption of responsibility
* opportunity for promotion.

Herzberg suggested that jobs could be given more meaning if they included elements of responsibility and a more creative use of an individual's ability, as well as opportunities to achieve.

McGregor's Theory X v Theory Y

Douglas McGregor divided managers into two main types.

Theory X managers tend to have the view that:

* The average person naturally dislikes work and so will avoid it when possible. Management therefore needs to emphasise high levels of production, incentive schemes to encourage effort, and to discourage time wasting.
* Because people naturally dislike work, they need to be pushed, threatened and driven to get things done.
* The average person likes to be told what to do and to avoid responsibility; they have little ambition, and therefore require 'managing'.

Theory Y managers have a contrasting view, and believe in trusting employees to take on responsibilities. The Theory Y manager believes that:

* Work is a natural activity which people can enjoy. Managers need to create the right conditions in which work is enjoyable.

* External control is not the only way to manage people. Employees who identify with the organisation's objectives will be motivated to work hard.

* The most significant reward that will motivate people is self-fulfillment (see Maslow). Managers therefore need to identify opportunities for employees to fulfill themselves while working to meet company objectives.

* The average human being learns, when given the opportunity, to accept and to seek responsibility.

* Many people can contribute to a business's objectives when given the chance.

* People's potential is rarely achieved in the workplace.

McGregor saw the potential to make organisations far more effective by unleashing the people who work for them.

Moss Kanter's ideas on empowerment

Rosabeth Moss Kanter argues that we can empower people by giving them greater responsibility in the organisation.

FIGURE 1.45 *Rosabeth Moss Kanter*

Empowerment involves passing power and responsibility down in the organisation, so that good ideas can bubble up to the surface from below. Empowered individuals enable an organisation to be more successful by coming up with lots of good ideas. In turn empowered people are motivated people.

1.4 How people are influenced at work

Managers and employees are affected not only by internal issues such as the conditions of work and levels of motivation, but also by external issues.

Environmental issues

Today we are more aware than every before of **environmental issues**. The Rio Treaty of 1992 marked a turning point in which governments, businesses and other groups recognised that we have a joint responsibility for our common environment.

The Kyoto Climate Change Treaty of 1997 recognised that businesses and governments should work together to limit harmful effects that are caused by pollution and environmental

Learning activity

Kyoto provides a useful topic for discussion. Currently Britain is on track to meet its targets. The United States has not signed up to the Treaty and is currently producing more pollution than the rest of the world put together. Developing countries like India and China do not have to abide by the Treaty. Is this fair? Should Britain comply with a treaty that the world's biggest polluters are ignoring?

degradation. The Treaty set out that governments should work together to limit the creation of greenhouse gases.

Treaties like Rio and Kyoto put pressure on business and the individuals that work for businesses. For example, the Rio Treaty set out Agenda 21 which is a list of actions for the 21st century. Part of Agenda 21 was the creation of Local Agenda 21s in which groups of businesses and local government in different parts of the country set out environmental action plans. For example, local councils have targets for recycling glass, paper, cardboard and other wastes.

The government has created a series of laws governing how businesses must operate, for example in how they handle waste. For example, dangerous wastes should not be put in waste containers with ordinary waste. Businesses must use special drains for clearing away harmful liquids which must not be mixed with other liquids such as rain water.

People who work for businesses are trained in methods of waste disposal. Wherever possible materials should be reused and **recycled** rather than being disposed of.

Many businesses have created environmental management systems. These systems involve:

* Auditing (listing) all business activities that have an environmental impact.
* Creating plans and policies for environmental management.
* Creating systems for environmental management.
* Training staff to manage these systems.
* Setting targets for environmental improvement.
* Creating reports which monitor the success of the business in meeting these targets.

Every employee in a business has a responsibility for environmental management, and must be familiar with guidelines and good practice in:

* Recycling
* Disposing of wastes
* Caring for the environment.

Social and ethical issues

Business organisations need at all times to do the 'right' thing rather than to get involved in questionable activities. Business **ethics** is concerned with behaving in a moral way.

CASE STUDY

Corporate social responsibility at Manchester United

Corporate social responsibility is the process of organisations taking responsibility for the wider community. Manchester United recognise that the success of the organisation is not only based on success on the field of play and profitability but also the impact the business has on the quality of life in communities and in the environment. Manchester United focuses its efforts on three main areas:

* sport
* health
* education.

Internationally Manchester United joined forces with UNICEF, the United Nations children's charity, in a partnership aimed at improving the lives of disadvantaged children in the world's poorest countries. Over a million pounds has already been raised. In addition the club works with the charity to raise awareness of children's issues such as the exploitation of children in the workplace.

Nationally the club supports a range of charities such as the Prince's Trust, designed to help 15–25 year olds to develop new skills.

FIGURE 1.46 *Manchester United supports the KIO initiative against racism*

The club works with unemployed people to get them back to work through education and training. It collaborates with Kick It Out (KIO) to nominate one game per season as Anti-Racism Day of Action.

Locally the club supports a number of initiatives. For example, the Football in the Community scheme offers coaching sessions to children and youngsters throughout the Manchester area. The club arranges educational-based activities in conjunction with schools and the local education authority.

In addition the club works to improve the local environment by:

* increasing the percentage of rubbish sent for recycling
* using more green supplies
* more environmentally friendly marketing material.

Of course, cynics might argue that businesses' commitment to social responsibility is partly fuelled by a desire to gain a good reputation which is good for their business. The more people who think that Manchester United is a great club, the more they are likely to buy the shirts and merchandise and go to matches.

1 Why is it important for business organisations to show a commitment to wider communities?
2 Explain how another organisation meets its commitment to international, national, and local communities as well as the environment.
3 Do you think that businesses have a genuine commitment to corporate social responsibility or is this a smokescreen for making as much profit as they can?
4 Can you give examples of situations in which what appears to be corporate social responsibility is really profiteering?

In responding to social and ethical issues organisations need to take account of industry **codes of practice** setting out good standards of behaviour. In addition it is also important to listen to stakeholder groupings.

For example, stakeholder groupings that help to shape Manchester United's social and ethical policies include:

* The government, which seeks a more responsible football industry

* The Premier League

* Supporters Associations

* The local community

* The shareholders.

Another important area to recognise is organised pressure groups, who campaign on specific or several related issues.

For example, Friends of the Earth claims to be 'the UK's most effective environment group'.

Another good example of pressure group activity is the work of children's charities in lobbying mobile phone companies to create controls which bar access of children to 'adult content' such as pornography and gambling on mobile phones and through internet connections.

Legal and self-regulatory constraints and issues

There are a number of other influences that determine the sorts of decisions that managers, supervisors and other employees are able to make in the workplace.

Some of these influences are legal, i.e. they results from laws made by the European Union or by government in this country. Other influences are self-regulatory, i.e. an industry creates its

---

CASE STUDY

Friends of the Earth

An advertisement from Friends of the Earth reveals how the organisation works:

Friends of the Earth

'Who really makes the big decisions about our future? Too often, it's the fat cats and the faceless business executives. In the search for ever bigger profits, many companies just don't think about the terrible side-effects of what they are doing.

Support Friends of the Earth and we'll work hard getting government to pass laws to make sure the likes of Shell, Asda Wal-Mart and the Royal Bank of Scotland get their filthy hands off our future.

We're not anti-business and we're only too happy to give praise where it's due. But Friends of the Earth believe passionately that a healthy, unpolluted world is too precious to squander for quick profits.

If you agree, please support us today with a regular gift of just £3 a month. We really are only as powerful as the people who support us.'

1 **What do you see as the important messages here for businesses?**
2 **How do you think that socially responsible businesses should respond to these criticisms?**

own rules about how firms should behave in the industry.

Competition law

A number of laws have been passed in this country to seek to ensure that firms compete fairly with each other. The Office of Fair Trading (OFT) is an independent organisation set up by the government and is responsible for making sure that markets work well for customers. Markets operate well when businesses work in open and vigorous competition with each other. The OFT's powers come from consumer and competition legislation, e.g. The Competition Act 1998, designed to ensure that businesses compete fairly; it outlaws certain types of anti-competitive behaviour. The OFT has strong powers to investigate businesses suspected of anti-competitive behaviour, and can impose tough penalties on wrong doers.

Find out...

Search for the OFT website at www.heinemann. co.uk/hotlinks (express code 1130P, then go to Unit 1) to see the range of OFT activities.

Consumer protection

There is a wealth of consumer protection law designed to protect the consumer from unfair business dealing, including laws concerning trades descriptions, sale of goods, food safety, weights and measures.

Trade Descriptions Acts, 1968 and 1972

These laws make it illegal to give false or misleading descriptions of goods, services, accommodation or facilities.

The Sale of Goods Act, 1979

This law sets out that:

* the seller must have the right to sell their goods (i.e. it is not stolen property)

* the goods must fit the description provided

* the goods should be of satisfactory quality

* the goods should be fit for the buyer's purpose (e.g. a bed should not break when you are sleeping on it)

* when a sample is provided the remainder of the goods should be the same as the sample.

Supply of Goods and Services Act, 1982

There are provisions so that:

* the supplier must carry out the service with reasonable care and skill

* the service must be performed within a reasonable time

* a reasonable price must be charged.

Food Safety Act, 1990

This sets out that businesses which handle food must take all reasonable precautions when manufacturing, transporting, storing, preparing and selling food items. In 1999 the government set up the Food Standards Agency to monitor the food industry.

Consumer Protection Act, 1987

This sets out regulations for certain potentially harmful products such as flammable items and poisonous substances.

Weights and Measures Act, 1985

This requires traders to provide standard measures of fluids and weights of substances. It has been followed up by legislation requiring information about weights and measures to be displayed on packaging.

The work of trade unions

Today many unions see themselves as working in partnership with government, employers and workers towards common goals, including a safe, secure, harmonious working environment for all employees regardless of their differences. There are a number of benefits to being a member of a trade union.

In a unionised workplace:

1 Average earnings are around 8% higher.

2 The average trade union member receives 29 days annual holiday compared with 23 days for non-unionised workers.

3 Unionised workplaces have health and safety officers to ensure employers keep work safe.

4 Unions help workers to gain compensation for injuries, illness at work and other matters.

5 Unionised workplaces are more likely to have in place parental policies that are more generous than the legal minimum.

6 Workers in unionised workplaces are more likely to receive job-related training.

7 Workers in unionised workplaces are more likely to have an equal opportunities policy in place.

8 Trade union members are only half as likely to be dismissed as non-union ones.

9 Black and Asian trade union members earn 32% more than their non-unionised colleagues from similar ethnic backgrounds.

10 Trade unions support each other.

Unions are involved in negotiating the best possible working conditions for their members and for workers in general. Sometimes trade unions will work together to negotiate with management on behalf of a whole category of workers within an organisation. This is known as collective bargaining. This gives a great deal of power to the union. Unions typically prefer to solve disputes by negotiation. However, when all else fails the action taken is known as industrial action and includes:

* a strike involving all members
* selective strike action
* action short of strike action such as just working to the rules of the job
* refusing to work overtime or unsociable hours.

Trade unions are not just concerned with resolving conflict and disputes, they also help to provide lots of benefits for members such as educational courses, pension and insurance schemes, and many other benefits.

Employment protection

The **Employment Act of 2002** set out a number of rights of employees in the workplace to modify previous Employment Acts. Employees are entitled to receive a written statement of the main terms in their contract of employment within two months of starting work.

The terms which must be included are:

* The names of the employer and employee
* The date employment began
* Pay, hours, overtime, holiday and sick pay entitlements
* Pension terms
* Workplace and mobility clauses (circumstances in which workers may be required to change their location and/or do different work)
* Job title and description of duties
* Notice entitlement for both parties
* Disciplinary and grievance procedures.

Employees are also entitled to an itemised pay slip setting out deductions, and are also entitled to the minimum wage.

* Conditions for handling the dismissal and discipline of workers must be set out in every contract of employment, and there is a clear code as to how such matters should be handled.
* Rules are set out for handling employee grievances.
* Maternity leave has been improved. Fathers are also entitled to a period of parental leave.
* There is a statutory period of leave allowed for employees who adopt a child.
* Flexible working conditions apply to parents with a child under the age of 6 or a disabled child under 18 and who have been continuously working for over 6 months. They can apply for flexible working conditions to help with child care arrangements.

Health and safety

Employers are required by law to provide a safe and healthy working environment for their employees. In addition employees are required to work in a safe and responsible manner. Employers are required to provide appropriate health and safety training and information to employees. The Management of Health and Safety at Work Regulations require the employer to do a risk assessment to identify the best way to make premises safe. There needs to be a written health and safety policy setting out the systems and procedures that have to be in place for ensuring the health and safety of employees, visitors and customers of a business.

The BusinessLink and Health and Safety Executive (HSE) websites will help you to carry out a health and safety risk assessment in a workplace and to draw up a health and safety policy. Search for them at www.heinemann.co.uk / hotlinks (express code 1130P, then go to Unit 1).

UNIT ASSESSMENT

INVESTIGATING PEOPLE AT WORK

Specimen paper

Answer all the questions

To find a boyfriend/ bet on the next Rooney hat-trick/ play games with friends elsewhere in the country, press the red button on your remote now. The rise of interactive TV means that people increasingly have the option of dating, gambling and gaming without leaving the couch.

YooMedia, which owns Dateline and a string of other services in these areas, is expert at expanding them as offerings on interactive TV platforms such as Sky. It has also positioned itself to win government contracts to put health advice on interactive television if the technology really catches on. However, YooMedia might well find that people don't take to interactive TV as fast as it hopes, or that, if they do, competition will suddenly flare up.

You can buy shares on the Stock Exchange in YooMedia. Many of its services are profitable so it seems like a good stock to buy for investors interested in high-tech shares.

1 Describe one business objective that YooMedia might have. Describe another business objective of a business that you have studied during your course. (4 marks)

2 Explain why a particular stakeholder grouping would support the objective you identified for YooMedia. Contrast this with why another stakeholder grouping might support the objective you identified for an organisation you have studied. (4 marks)

3 Who are the owners of YooMedia? (1 mark)

4 What benefits is YooMedia likely to have from being a public company? (5 marks)

5 How would a company like YooMedia raise money for expansion? Compare these methods with those of another organisation that you have studied as part of your business course. (10 marks)

6 How does YooMedia stand to benefit from its public sector contacts? (3 marks)

7 Why would it be important for YooMedia to have a strong marketing function? (3 marks)

Total for this section: 30 marks

YooMedia is looking to recruit a new junior sales manager with responsibility for winning international custom. The sales manager will be responsible for a small sales team of 10 staff operating initially in European Union member countries. The sales manager will need to have had previous selling experience in an international field. This is a new post.

8   What sort of details would you expect to find in the job description for the new sales manager? (4 marks)

9   How do these details differ from those included in a job description for a business organisation that you studied as part of your course? (4 marks)

10 What purposes might the job description be used for in the organisation that you studied as part of your course? (4 marks)

11 Why might YooMedia also create a person specification for the post? (4 marks)

12 Explain one piece of legislation designed to prevent discrimination that would be taken account of by Human Resource managers when designing a job advertisement. (5 marks)

13 How might psychometric testing be helpful in the selection process for the sales manager at YooMedia? What sorts of characteristics might the psychometric testing be looking for? (6 marks)

14 Why might YooMedia choose to train the sales person externally rather than in-house? (4 marks)

15 Explain how either coaching or training has benefited a specific individual or group of employees in an organisation you studied as part of your course. (4 marks)

Total for this section: 35 marks

YooMedia is a new and exciting company to work for. The management team is determined to attract and retain high quality employees with appropriate skills such as good IT skills, the ability to communicate well with others and to operate in team situations.

16 Describe one possible payment method that the company might use to encourage sales staff to work hard. Contrast this method with payment schemes that you have come across in organisations that you studied during the course. (6 marks)

17 Explain one non-financial incentive that you are familiar with from studying another business and which YooMedia might offer its employees. Explain how this would work. (5 marks)

18 Senior managers believe that it is important to motivate staff at YooMedia.

    i   What is meant by motivation? (2 marks)

    ii Use the work of one important motivational theorist to explain how managers might be able to achieve high levels of motivation at work. Illustrate your answer by reference to an organisation you studied during the course. (7 marks)

Total for this section: 20 marks

Employees are affected not only by internal issues such as the conditions of work and levels of motivation, but also by external issues.

19 What initiatives might managers take to make sure that employees are aware of the importance of reducing waste? Illustrate your answer by reference to an organisation that you have studied. (5 marks)

20 How might managers seek to motivate employees to give a high priority to reducing waste? (5 marks)

21 Identify one pressure group and explain how its actions might affect YooMedia. (5 marks)

22 Why might employees working for YooMedia seek to join a trade union? (5 marks)

23 Describe one piece of consumer protection legislation that will limit the actions of YooMedia. (5 marks)

Total for this section: 25 marks

Total for paper: 110 marks.

The following marking scheme provides you with examples of how you can develop your answers to score high marks. However, there are many other ways of answering questions that will help you to meet the criteria. Please note that while you can score marks for describing and identifying points, higher marks are achieved for relating your answers to the context of the case study, and for using higher order skills such as analysis and evaluation. The mark shown for each question is the maximum that can be achieved.

1   For describing a business objective of YooMedia you can score up to 2 marks. One for naming the objective, the second for further description. E.g. An objective of YooMedia might be to make a profit (1 mark) e.g. by seeking to sell services such as Dateline by achieving revenues in excess of costs (1 mark). (Other objectives might include to be the market leader, to increase sales, to develop an international presence etc.) Naming a business objective of a business where you did your work experience will enable you to score 1 mark (e.g. to increase sales, to build up a brand image etc). You score a further mark for describing this objective in greater detail.

2   Here you score 1 mark for naming a stakeholder group (e.g. shareholders, employees, customers, etc). You score a second mark for explaining why it would support the objective you identified in question 1. E.g. shareholders would support the objective of making a profit because this enables them to benefit from increased dividends. You can then score a further 2 marks for naming another stakeholder group that would support the business objective that you identified for the company that you did work experience in (1 mark) and for showing that this is a different motive from the one you identified for the stakeholder grouping for YooMedia (1 mark).

3   1 mark for listing this as the shareholders.

4   Here you will score up to 3 marks for identifying and explaining a benefit. E.g., as a public limited company YooMedia will be able to raise more capital (1 mark) by selling shares that are traded on the Stock Market (1 mark) enabling it to put more capital into advertising, marketing, and other aspects of expansion (1 mark). You can score up to 3 marks for developing other benefits such as having limited liability, developing a wider market presence, being able to employ specialist managers and directors, etc.

5   Here you can score up to 6 marks for identifying sources of capital that would be appropriate for YooMedia. (If you simply make a list of sources of capital without relating them to YooMedia the most you will be able to score is 3 marks). E.g. YooMedia could sell shares in their company (1 mark) giving them access to a pool of capital to develop the YooMedia brand. (1 mark) they could take out a loan from a bank (1 mark) enabling it to use these funds to buy capital equipment with interest being paid back on the loan (1 mark), etc. You can score up to 4 other marks for showing how a business where you did work experience raised money for expansion. If you simply list these you can score up to 2 marks only. However, if you compare these with YooMedia's sources of capital, and explain how these sources of capital relate specifically to your organisation you can score all 4 marks.

6   Here you can score 1 mark for explaining what a public sector contract is, namely a contract from a government owned or funded organisation. You can then score up to 2 marks for developing a reason why YooMedia can benefit from these contracts. E.g. you can show that the government is a widespread user of information channels (1 mark) so that government contracts are worth a lot of money through repeat and new contracts (1 mark).

7   You will score 1 mark for describing the benefits of having a good marketing function e.g. marketing helps a company to find out what customers want and need and then to provide them with it. You will score a further 2 marks for explaining the importance of marketing in the context of YooMedia e.g. it is important to find out what users of Dateline and other services are looking for (1 mark), in order to create the right sorts of facilities for them to access at the right times and in the right places (1 mark).

8   Up to 2 marks for each appropriate point that would appear on a job description e.g. who they are responsible to, who and what they are responsible for, etc. An additional 2 marks for aspects of a description that relate to the job of a sales manager for YooMedia e.g. description of where YooMedia salesperson would be working from and what countries they would be responsible for, and description of how their work would fit into YooMedia's sales operation (2 marks).

9   In answering this question you will get up to 2 marks for each developed explanation of how details of the job description for a sales manager differed from those in an organisation that you studied as part of your course. E.g. the description of a sales manager might include an outline of the materials and resources that they would be responsible for, whereas a job description that you might have studied for an assembly line worker might have included much less responsibility.

10 Up to 2 marks for describing appropriate purposes in the context of an organisation that you worked for. E.g. the description of a supervisor at Marks & Spencer was used as part of the recruitment process being sent out to job applicants (1 mark) so they knew what the job entailed (1 mark). Or the supervisor was able to use the job description when they had a dispute with managers (1 mark) about what their responsibilities involved (1 mark).

11 Here you can score up to 4 marks for explaining reasons why YooMedia might additionally create a person spec as well as a job description. You score 1 mark for answering in the context of YooMedia, 1 mark for explaining in the context of the salesperson's job. You could then score additional marks for showing that e.g. the person specification is more useful in job interviewing than the job description, by setting out essential and desired qualities (1 mark) which can be checked off by YooMedia interviewers to get the best person for the post (1 mark).

12 To answer this question you need to choose an appropriate piece of legislation e.g. Race, Sex, or Disability Discrimination Acts. You score 1 mark for naming the Act. You can score up to 2 marks for each developed point relating to how HR managers would take account of the Act when designing a job advertisement. E.g. the Sex Discrimination Act sets out that job advertisements must not indicate or imply (1 mark) that members of a particular gender group (1 mark) will be unfairly disadvantaged or treated less favourably (1 mark) as a result of the way a job is described or offered in a media advertisement (1 mark).

13 You can score 1 mark for explaining what a psychometric test is, i.e. a test to identify personality traits of an individual that are relevant to an organisation like YooMedia. You can score up to 3 marks for developing an argument as to why YooMedia would want to use psychometric testing, e.g. a psychometric test will enable Yoomedia to recruit and select with greater accuracy (1 mark) individuals who have appropriate personality characteristics for working in a dynamic enterprise (1 mark) and help to weed out unsuitable candidates (1 mark) You can score up to 2 marks for identifying personality characteristics that would be appropriate for YooMedia e.g. the ability to work in a team, the ability to think outside the box etc.

14 Here you can score 1 mark for explaining the difference between training on-the-job or in some other inhouse approach at YooMedia, and through external off-the-job training with an external agency. You can then score up to 2 points for each benefit to YooMedia that would encourage them to train externally, e.g. it enables the individual to draw on a wider range of skill/knowledge than available within YooMedia (1 mark), and that external training gives the individual a break from their work which acts as a motivating incentive, (1 mark) etc.

15 Here you can score up to 2 marks for describing the benefits of either coaching or training within the context of your work organisation e.g. training enabled individuals to learn new skills (1 mark) which enabled them to take on more responsibility (1 mark). You can score up to a further 2 marks for evaluating the benefits, e.g. the training and coaching acted as a motivational tool (1 mark) and was seen as a way in which they could develop their careers (1 mark).

16 You can score up to 3 marks for describing a payment method that YooMedia could use to encourage sales staff to work hard. You can only score 1 mark for describing a payment method. You can score 3 marks for doing so in the context of YooMedia. E.g. YooMedia could offer sales staff a bonus based on the sale of a new service to a new client. (1 mark). The bonus would act as an incentive to encourage staff to go out and sell (1 mark), it would also be a means of rewarding the most effective staff (1 mark). You can score up to 3 marks for contrasting this with another organisation that you've studied. E.g. you could show that another organisation uses a reward system linked to appraisal (1 mark). This approach may be seen as more effective because targets are agreed between the salesperson and the sales manager (1 mark) so that sales targets can be set which are seen as being reachable and appropriate (1 mark).

17 You can score up to 2 marks for describing a non-financial incentive in the context of an organisation you have studied. E.g. you may show that a well known retailing organisation rewards loyal employees by offering them the opportunity to be promoted to supervisors' positions (1 mark) where they would be given more responsibility within the organisation (1 mark). You can then score up to an additional 3 marks for evaluating the merits of such an approach in showing how it would work. E.g. promotion to a supervisor's position gives an individual something to strive for (1 mark) that would give them more personal fulfilment (1 mark) enabling them to achieve some of the higher levels of personal satisfaction that Maslow and Herzberg alluded to (1 mark).

18 i Here you can score up to 2 marks for providing an appropriate definition of motivation and expanding on it. E.g. you might argue that motivation is something that comes from inside the individual (1 mark) and is based on a desire and willingness to achieve given goals at work and elsewhere (1 mark).

ii Here you need to identify one motivational theorist e.g. Herzberg, Maslow or McGregor (1 mark). You can score a further 2 marks for describing key features of their work accurately. (2 marks) However, to score an additional 4 marks you will need to show how these theories can be applied to a specific organisation in order to create a high performance workplace. Each developed point will be worth 2 marks.

19 You can score up to 2 marks for listing initiatives that managers might employ for minimising waste, e.g. by publicising the costs of wastes through company communications on noticeboards (1 mark), and by developing work practices that seek to eliminate waste (1 mark). To score an additional 2 marks you will have to relate these initiatives to an organisation that you studied on your course.

20 You can score up to 3 marks for each well-developed argument as to how managers can motivate employees to reduce waste. Each answer must combine the concept of motivation with that of waste reduction. E.g. managers might develop training courses about waste management which identify the benefits to the individual, and the company (1 mark) this would enable employees to appreciate that waste reduction at work will lead to greater company profits and hence wages (1 mark), a more prosperous and efficient business would be able to offer a more securing working future for individual employees.

21 Here you can score 1 mark for identifying a pressure group and then up to 2 marks for developing arguments which show how the actions of this group may impact on YooMedia. E.g. you might show that a children's charity like Childline may be worried about the activities of companies like YooMedia. They may be worried that children may be exposed to dangers resulting from access to the Internet and exploitation by unscrupulous adults. Childline may then put pressure on the government (1 mark) to pass legislation that limits the activities of YooMedia in terms of who they can offer their services to. (1 mark) Childline could also alert the media to some of YooMedia's activities (1 mark) leading to adverse publicity for the company (1 mark).

22 You can score 1 mark for explaining what a trade union is – ie an association of employees who by joining together in a union are able to put pressure for their collective and individual interests to be looked after. You can then score a further four marks for identifying individual benefits of a trade union. E.g. It puts pressure on employers to provide better wages (1 mark) and improved working conditions (1 mark). The union will represent individual members in disputes (1 mark). A union also provides benefits such as subsidised health care, insurance, and discounts on shopping with various companies (1 mark)

23 You can score 1 mark for identifying a piece of consumer legislation. (e.g. Trade Descriptions Act), up to 2 marks for describing the limitations of this Act, and a further 2 marks for describing the limitations in the context of YooMedia.

UNIT 2

Investigating business

This unit contains four parts:

2.1   Business planning

2.2   Managing business activities

2.3   Financial management in business

2.4   The use of software to aid decision-making

Introduction

In this unit, you will find out about how businesses are planned and managed. An important part of this process is the management of people and other resources. Managers need to develop systems which enable them to control the business and its activities. Managers will need to check the performance of the business in meeting objectives. By regularly checking business performance, managers are able to take appropriate steps to keep the business on track. You will find out about the importance of financial management in obtaining the right sorts of short-, medium- and long-term finance for the business as well as how to check the solvency and profitability of the organisation.

As part of your learning, you will obtain, use and assess information drawn from businesses.

What you will learn in this unit

* Why businesses plan and the importance of planning

* Important steps in setting up a business

* Planning to acquire resources and to monitor performance

FIGURE 2.1 *Richard Branson's Virgin PLC is well known for detailed planning and for efficiently bringing together a range of suitable resources to deliver good business results. Virgin uses modern ICT and e-commerce applications.*

- ***** The relationship between planning and business objectives
- ***** Key elements in business planning such as marketing, finance and production
- ***** The types of resources used in business
- ***** The importance of quality control, quality assurance and total quality management
- ***** The importance of monitoring and reviewing business performance
- ***** The need to manage and measure financial performance
- ***** Ways of measuring the 'financial health' of a business
- ***** Key financial statements (balance sheet and profit and loss account), cash flow forecasts, budgets, and break-even analysis
- ***** The use of software to aid decision-making
- ***** The use of spreadsheets, word processing and database software
- ***** Specialist software and the use of the Internet
- ***** The importance of e-commerce
- ***** The main legal and corporate issues associated with using ICT in a business environment.

2.1 Business planning

Central to the work of any business – large or small, existing or newly set up, in the public or private sector – is planning. Without planning there is no way to judge if the business is likely to achieve its objectives. In this chapter we are concerned with how and why businesses plan.

There are a number of key reasons why organisations produce a business plan:

1 To provide a clear sense of direction for owners and managers so they know where they are going

2 To provide a means for managers and other interested parties to check on progress in meeting targets

3 To provide a means of controlling the business, i.e. keeping to plan

4 To help raise finance. Outside parties such as banks need to be able to see that an organisation is well planned if they are to have confidence in it (e.g. to provide loans).

The importance of enterprise and innovation to business

When people say 'enterprise' or 'individual initiative' they automatically think of a small business, usually a service or creative business. Big companies, particularly those engaged in manufacturing, are just 'there' – no-one quite knows how.

The fact is that with very few exceptions, every big company began as a small company, often with one enterprising individual at its head.

William Morris began by mending bicycles in a back street garage in Oxford, and built up a major motor manufacturing company.

William Lever started work in the family shop when he was sixteen, and then decided that he could make soap as well as anyone else. Result… Unilever is now one of the world's great companies.

> *** DID YOU KNOW?**
>
> One of George Bush's famous 'foot in mouth' quotes is 'The problem with the French is that they don't have a word for entrepreneur' – of course, the word entrepreneur is a French one!

More recently, Anita Roddick started up The Body Shop from a small shop in Brighton and went on to pioneer one of the great 'alternative businesses' of the modern age.

Patak's, the leading supplier of authentic Indian foodstuffs worldwide, was set up by L.G. Patak on his arrival from Kenya in this country. He started out by selling samosas from home to raise sufficient capital to buy his first small shop in north London. The business expanded with the introduction of other products, including pickles and chutneys, as orders from small shops, housewives and students flooded in and Patak's fame spread.

Small may be beautiful, but in business the great thing about being small is that one day you may become big, as illustrated by Patak's and The Body Shop.

Enterprise does not stop once a business starts. No business can begin without enterprise but no matter how big it becomes, no business can continue without enterprise. Nor, for that matter, can any other kind of human activity, commercial or charitable.

Being enterprising involves the following characteristics:

* Coming up with original ideas (e.g. Anita Roddick's natural products)

* Willingness to take a risk (e.g. Jack Cohen investing most of his money in buying stocks to resell on his market store)

* Being energetic and willing to work hard (e.g. L.G. Patak who worked long hours to build his business).

All of the above characteristics help to get a business off the ground. However, many small

FIGURE 2.3 *Anita Roddick – an enterprising business woman who started a great company from small beginnings*

businesses do not flourish because they have not planned effectively. For example, they:

* have failed to secure the finance required to ensure the development of the business

* have not carried out enough market research to find out what consumers want

* have not planned carefully when cash will come into the business to cover outgoings

* have failed to look at the legal requirements which are essential to setting up in business

* had other planning failures – can you think of some?

We use the term entrepreneur to describe someone who brings together the various resources required to run a business, and takes a risk in doing so. Patak, Roddick, Morris and Cohen were all entrepreneurs and in recent years have been joined by new names such as Martha Lane Fox and Brent Hoberman – the founders of LastMinute.Com which will provide you with a range of last minute services including tickets to a Norah Jones concert or a last minute holiday in the sun.

Innovation is another important aspect of setting up in business. Innovation is all about producing new solutions to problems. A good example of an innovative idea is Google, the Internet search engine that was recently developed by entrepreneurs Larry Page and Sergey Brin working from a garage. Google's major innovation was searching out web pages according to their popularity and interrelationship, not just according to key words. The results are therefore more likely to be what the customer wants. However, Google and LastMinute.Com would not have survived without careful business planning and detailed

organisation, enabling them to dominate their respective market places.

Another example of innovation is Dyson. James Dyson is an enterprising and energetic designer. One of his first innovations was the ball barrow as an improvement on the traditional

FIGURE 2.4 *The ballbarrow and the dual cyclone are winning innovations*

Learning activity

Carry out some research into local examples of enterprise. Methods of doing the research include: studying the local paper to find examples of new businesses that have recently set up with an interesting or innovative idea, or talking to friends and relatives to see if they can suggest an example of a local person or group that has come up with an enterprising idea. For example, at the University where the authors work a researcher came up with the original idea of putting flavourings into crisps.

If you can identify a local exciting entrepreneur, then why not arrange to interview them to find out how they first developed their idea and what were the biggest hurdles they had to overcome to turn their good idea into a working business.

wheelbarrow. Later he hit upon the idea of creating a dual cyclone vacuum cleaner. The idea came to him when he was visiting a factory and saw an industrial cyclone in operation. He realised that if he could reduce the scale of the cyclone it would provide a brilliant way of vacuuming up dirt and other materials in the home. He tried hundreds of prototypes before perfecting the Dyson Dual Cyclone. Today everyone is familiar with the product which comes in a range of attractive designs.

The legal implications of starting in business

There are a number of legal implications involved in planning to set up in business:

1 Choosing a business name

A business that is a private company must have Ltd after its name. If it is a public company, like Marks & Spencer, it must be followed by PLC. The registrar of companies will not register a business name if it is already registered. A business name will not be registered if it is offensive or implies the provision of sexual services.

2 Setting up a business

A sole trader can simply set up by choosing an appropriate name and registering for VAT if the annual turnover exceeds a set limit. Partnerships are typically set up by registering a Deed of Partnership with a solicitor. Setting up a company is more regulated.

A private limited company must:

* have at least two members, one of whom must be a director
* have at least £1 worth of capital
* obtain a certificate of incorporation before starting trading
* produce a set of audited accounts within 10 months of the end of its financial year.

A public limited company must:

* obtain a certificate of incorporation and a certificate to trade before starting trading

* have a minimum starting capital of £50,000
* produce a set of audited accounts within seven months of the end of its financial year
* register a memorandum of association stating that it is a PLC
* have at least two directors and two members
* have a qualified company secretary.

Companies must be registered by law. Registration involves filing two documents.

The Memorandum of Association outlines:

* The name of the company
* The address of the registered office of the company
* The amount of the liability of the members
* The authorised capital
* The company objectives.

The Articles of Association concern the internal administration of the company and cover:

* Rules about meetings
* Voting rights of shareholders.

The Articles also include a list of directors and information on other internal matters. A shareholder might want to examine the Articles to find out how their company is run.

A company must have a Board of Directors. These directors may be fee-paid trustees who represent the shareholders, or senior executives who work full-time for the company. There must be at least one executive in a company but usually there are several, e.g. a company accountant, a marketing executive etc.

Companies are not required by law to have a chairperson but most do because they need someone to run the annual meeting. The managing director is the senior executive director of a company.

Directors owe a duty of care to the company not to act negligently when managing its affairs. Directors are typically experts in a particular field such as accountancy or law, and so a high standard of care is expected of them.

Other legal implications of setting up in business are that the business will need to:

* Abide by health and safety legislation.

* Comply with equal opportunities legislation. For example, it must give equal pay to work of equal value. It must also comply with legislation preventing discrimination.

* Abide by employment legislation related to hours worked, payment of the minimum wage, contracts of employment and dismissal and redundancy matters.

* Have appropriate insurances, e.g. employer's liability in case of accidents involving employees, public liability to protect against accidents involving customers and members of the general public on company premises, and product and other forms of liability insurance.

* Abide by consumer protection and competition legislation.

* Comply with other legal requirements.

Learning activity

Interview a senior business manager or owner of a small business. What are the main areas of legislation that they must keep on top of in running the day-to-day activities of the business?

* DID YOU KNOW?

In December 2004 the BT Group was found to have unlawfully misused confidential customer information to try to stop its customers leaving for competitors. The part of BT that runs telephone networks was warning BT retailing when customers intended to switch. This allowed BT Retail to try to 'save' the customer by offering them new deals. The case illustrates the way in which legal requirements seek to create a level playing field for businesses to compete (in this case, rivals of BT Retail were being unfairly disadvantaged).

Sources of advice and support for business

There are a number of sources of advice for people wishing to set up in business. Some of these are government sources, while others are private sources.

Government sources

Currently the government's Department of Trade and Industry provides a range of support for business through grants, loan guarantees and subsidised consultancy.

Grants are sums of money provided by the government for specific activities, e.g. for research purposes.

Loan guarantees are where the government will guarantee to pay back certain loans that a business might take out.

Subsidised consultancy is where the government provides part of the sum of money a business has to pay out for advice from third parties.

Typical areas of government support include:

* Succeeding through innovation: providing practical support for the key stages of innovation or research and development into new products

* Achieving best practice: helping businesses to become more efficient, competitive and profitable

* Regional investment: encouraging investment in specific areas of the country to promote economic regeneration.

The Small Business Council advises the government on small business issues. It is made up of 24 members, 22 of whom are small business owners.

Unemployed people can find out about setting up a small business from their local Jobcentre. Young people can get further help with starting a business under the New Deal. Parts of the UK have been designated as 'Employment Zones' and in these areas people can get advice on getting a business off the ground from the Department of Work and Pensions.

The government has created a new fund to encourage entrepreneurship in disadvantaged communities and groups.

The Ethnic Minority Business Forum advises the government on the needs of ethnic minority businesses.

New businesses (particularly those using new technology) can get help with premises and management from the UK Business Incubation Centre or from one of the 50 UK Science parks.

There are regional schemes to help small businesses, supported by the European Structural Funds. They are normally administered by government offices and delivered through organisations such as local Business Links (and their equivalents).

Private sources

There are also many private sources of aid for business. Most banks have arrangements to help customers in new and small businesses. You can also get business advice from professional accountants, solicitors and independent advisors.

Young people wanting to set up a business can find advice and guidance from the Prince's Trust and 'Livewire' sponsored by Shell UK Ltd.

To find out more, search for these useful websites at www.heinemann.co.uk/hotlinks (express code 1130P, then go to Unit 2):

* The Federation of Small Businesses
* Young Enterprise UK
* Business Link – practical help and advice for business
* Young entrepreneur site
* Scottish Enterprise
* The Prince's Trust
* Shell LiveWire

FIGURE 2.5 *Livewire helps young people setting up in business*

Learning activity

Produce a short brochure using a desktop publishing package. Research the work of an organisation that supports young people in setting up a new enterprise of their own. The brochure should outline the work of this organisation and give a case study of a young person who has been able to benefit from the support of this organisation.

The importance of planning

If a business is to acquire the resources that it needs to carry out ongoing activities then it will need to show clear evidence of good planning. Having created plans, the business is then able to monitor how well it is doing and identify any corrections that need to be made.

When you create a business plan, you need to be able to show that:

* You have a clear sense of where you are going. We call this direction – hence the term 'directors of a company'. A short mission statement will set out the purpose of the organisation.

* You have clear targets and objectives to work towards

* You have created structured plans to enable you to get where you want to go

* In business the concept of focus is an important one. A plan should not be vague it should be focused. Managers need to

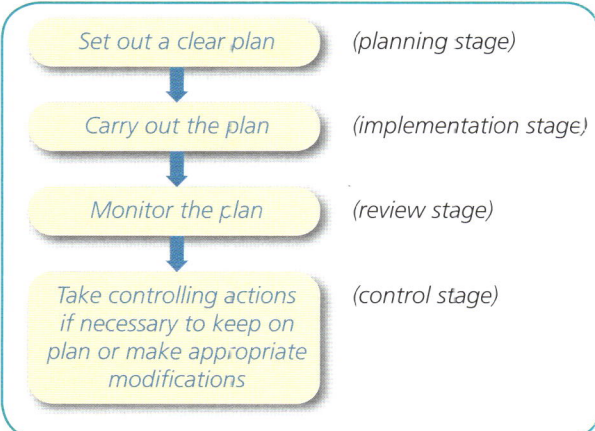

FIGURE 2.6 *Creating and using a business plan*

understand the plan and communicate it in a focused way

* A master plan can be broken down into a number of sub-plans. These plans should all be carefully integrated and well focused.

A business plan is very important in helping the organisation to gain resources because:

* Providers of capital, e.g. shareholders, have more confidence in a well-planned business

* Banks and other providers of finance will often want to examine plans to make sure that they are well structured and based on accurate calculations

* By having a well-organised plan it is also possible to monitor performance. For example, one part of a business plan will be budgets. Budgets are plans for the future that are set out in numbers.

FIGURE 2.7 *The Chief Executive and the bank manager both appreciate a business plan*

Learning activity

Working in a small group, identify a good idea for a business.

Establish an appropriate mission for the organisation and a set of objectives. Then identify six areas of the business that it would be appropriate to create plans for (you do not need to produce these plans at this stage).

For example, Superior Holidays might budget to make the following sales over the next twelve months. The budgeted costs of making the sales, e.g. supplying catalogues, answering phone calls, etc. are shown (see Figure 2.8).

However, in the real world events don't always turn out as planned. For example, sales may be less than expected in the first three months of the year. Costs may be higher than expected, for example:

	Jan	Feb	Mar
Sales (000s)	18	20	23
Cost of sales (000s)	17	21	21

FIGURE 2.9 *Superior Holidays actual sales and costs*

By examining the plan, managers are able to take actions to try and improve performance. For example, to improve sales they can increase advertising activities or lower prices. To reduce costs they may lay off staff or produce fewer brochures.

Planning therefore supports a cycle of monitoring and improvement, as shown in Figure 2.11.

The process of monitoring can be applied to any form of plan. For example, an action plan is a very useful method of planning. It sets out actions that need to be taken, by who, and by what time (see Figure 2.10).

BUDGET: SALES AND COSTS OF MAKING SALES FOR SUPERIOR HOLIDAYS												
	Jan	Feb	Mar	Apr	May	Jun	Jul	Aug	Sep	Oct	Nov	Dec
Sales (000s)	20	25	25	30	35	40	40	45	40	35	30	55
Cost of sales (000s)	15	20	20	25	30	30	30	40	30	30	25	45

FIGURE 2.8 *Superior Holidays sales and costs budget*

ADVERTISING ACTION PLAN FOR SUPERIOR HOLIDAYS		
ACTION POINT	**WHO RESPONSIBLE**	**DATE OF COMPLETION**
Decide on budget	John Christopher	1st March
Discuss creative brief with client	Rupinder Kaur, Meenum Mandal	15th March
Create designs	Meenum Mandal, John Francis	30th March
Show designs to client	John Francis, Rupinder Kaur	1st April
Client to provide feedback	Client to liaise with Rupinder Kaur	10th April
Create final designs	Meenum Mandal	21st April

FIGURE 2.10 *An advertising action plan for Superior Holidays*

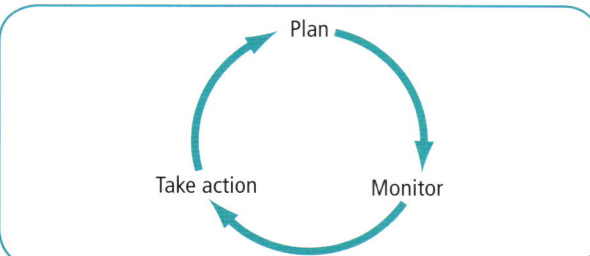

Learning activity

Create an action plan for an activity that you are involved in with other group members. The action plan should set out:

1 A list of actions to be completed

2 A list of who is responsible for performing these actions

3 A list of criteria for assessing when the actions have been successfully completed.

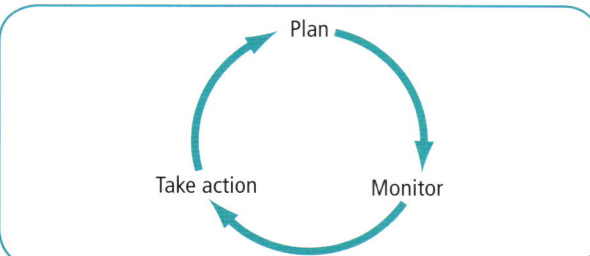

FIGURE 2.11 *The process of monitoring*

Business objectives and planning

A business plan should be seen as the means by which a business achieves its objectives.

For example, supposing that a business has established the following objectives for next year:

1 To increase its share of the market from 10% to 15%

2 To improve staff IT skills

3 To increase profit margins from 20% to 25%.

A well-organised plan can be developed to achieve these targets. The plan should:

* provide a clear strategy, setting out the steps that need to be taken

* the strategy should be easy to communicate by means of the plan

* the achievement of the plan should be able to be checked by an ongoing monitoring process

* a master plan should be able to be broken down into sub-plans for various functions and operating units within the organisation.

We can show how the overall plan can be broken down into relevant components. For example, a marketing plan should set out how the marketing objective will be met, e.g. through advertising and promotional activities. The IT skills objective can be achieved through a human resources and training plan setting out how and when training activities will be carried out to make sure that all staff are given the required training opportunities.

Budgets can be set out planning how the profit objective will be achieved, e.g. by setting out budgeted sales and costs.

Key elements in business planning

A well-constructed business plan will help a business owner:

* to manage and control a business well

* obtain finance (e.g. from a bank)

* make accurate forecasts of future cash flows and profits.

Cash flow forecasts set out the timing of cash flows into a business and cash payments made by the business. It is essential that the business has enough cash flowing into the business to meet pressing needs for cash e.g. to pay bills, wages, etc.

Profit forecasts set out how much profit the business expects to make and when. It is essential that a business makes a profit to cover the risk of running that business. The business that only just covers its costs is taking too big a risk.

FIGURE 2.12 *Business plans and objectives*

The contents of the business plan

A business plan (for a small business) should be clearly set out under the following headings:

1	Contents page	A contents page is useful in any kind of report that is more than two or three pages long.
2	The owner	This section should give some information about the owner (or owners), including their educational background, what jobs they have done, and their interests. This section should include the names and addresses of two referees – people of some status who will vouch for the character of the business owner.
3	The business	This should set out the name and address of the business. There should then be a detailed description of the product or service being offered, how and where it will be sold, who is likely to buy it, and in what quantities.
4	Business aims and objectives	It is important to set out aims and objectives so that those reading the plan can see how well focused the business is.
5	A SWOT analysis	A brief analysis setting out the internal strengths and weaknesses of the business and the external opportunities and threats. This section should show how the business is seeking to build on its strength, minimize weaknesses, take advantages of opportunities and reduce the threats.
6	The market	This section will describe the market research that has been carried out and what it has revealed. It should give details of prospective customers – how many there are, how much they are prepared to buy, and what price they are willing to pay. It should also give details of the competition. It s useful to draw a few charts showing details such as the total size of the market and the expected market share of the new business.
7	Advertising and promotion	This section should give information about how the business will be publicised to potential customers. It should also give details of like y advertising costs.
8	Premises and equipment	This section should show that the owners have considered a range of locations before choosing the best site. It should also give details of planning regulations (if appropriate). Costs of premises and the equipment needed should also be set out.
9	Business organisation	This should state whether the enterprise will take the form of sole trader, partnership, private or public company.
10	Costings	A guide to the cost of producing the product or service should be set out and the prices that will be charged to cover these costs. A calculation of gross profit can be calculated by taking away the cost of sales from sales revenue.
11	Profit forecasts	Profit forecasts should be set out for the first year in detail, as well as expected profits for the first five years.
12	Cash flow forecasts	This should set out the expected incoming and outgoings over the first year. These will be approximate figures.
13	The finance	This should set out details of how the finance for the business is going to be raised. How much will come from savings? How much needs to be borrowed?
14	Expansion	This final section gives an indication of future plans. Does the business want to keep on producing a steady output or is a dramatic expansion possible? Will the business increase its product range? What kind of competition is likely to emerge and how will the business deal with it?

Key elements of the business plan are the marketing, finance, and production plans.

The marketing plan should set out:

* Marketing objectives related to such aspects as market share, awareness of brands and products by consumers, growth of the market etc.

* The marketing environment, e.g. plans to compete against rivals, plans to manage changing social trends and so on.

* Market research – to find out what customers want and need and then to develop plans to give them what they want.

* The marketing mix, i.e. the mix of product, price, promotions, and place (i.e. distribution channels).

For example, a young entrepreneur offering a web design service to local businesses may have the objective of becoming the web designer of choice for at least 50% of the main local business areas in a town. A further marketing objective might be to increase the size of the total market by 10% a year. The plan would set out who the main rivals are and their key selling points. The plan would show how the web design business would offer a better product and service than the competition. The marketing mix would examine aspects of:

* details of the product/service

* prices charged

* how the business would be advertised and promoted

* where the business's activities would be bought and sold, e.g. by working directly at clients' premises.

The financial plan would set out:

1 A forecasted profit and loss statement

2 Break-even calculation

3 Cash flow forecast.

The profit forecast shows expected profit after the running costs of the business are deducted from the value of sales.

The break-even is the point where income from sales covers all costs. It shows the number of items the business has to sell to cover costs. These items can be products or services e.g. sandwiches (products) or cinema film viewings (services).

The cash flow forecast sets out the sums of money the business expects to come in and go out of the bank account each month.

The production plan should be closely tied to the marketing and financial plans.

The production plan needs to be created so as to enable the organisation to satisfy customers. Marketing-oriented production involves making the types of goods that customers want, when they want them. Production methods are therefore designed with the consumer in mind. Production and marketing departments will work with financial budgets which will be regularly monitored. Efficient production techniques will enable the business to go well beyond the break-even point to produce profit forecasts which yield high returns to business owners.

MARKETING PLAN	FINANCIAL PLAN	PRODUCTION PLAN
Study the market environment	Set out profit forecasts	Decide what to produce
Carry out market research	Identify the break-even	Decide how to produce
Clarify your marketing objectives	Set out a cash flow forecast	Decide when to produce
Set out a marketing mix	Set out marketing and production budgets	

FIGURE 2.13 *Marketing, financial and production plans should be closely tied together*

Create an outline structure for a business plan for an organisation that you are familiar with or one that you would consider setting up. At this stage you simply need to create a list of headings, rather than filling in the details. Use a word processing package to create your outline for the plan. At a later stage you can fill in the details.

2.2 Managing business activities

Having made plans, businesses must check whether their actual performance is meeting their planned performance. To do this, managers and staff will monitor, review and control the activities of their business.

FIGURE 2.14 *Managing business activities*

CASE STUDY

Planned performance in a Quick Service Restaurant

FIGURE 2.15 *Performance should be monitored against a plan*

The senior manager of a Quick Service restaurant has a busy working life. Customers have high expectations of receiving a friendly service, combined with convenience and good value for money. Employees expect to be properly trained, to have clear job descriptions and instructions about what they are expected

to do. The local community that live within the neighbourhood expect to live in a clean litter-free environment. Suppliers expect to be given clear and precise orders that arrive on time.

The managers are also accountable to their regional manager and to Head Office.

1 What do you think would be the key results areas for the senior manager of a Quick Service Restaurant?
2 How do you think these results could be monitored?
3 Give three examples of situations in which the manager might find that results were falling below the performance standard required.
4 What controlling actions could be taken in each situation to get back on plan?
5 What do you think that the manager should do if he or she found it impossible to achieve the planned results?

The role of the manager

There are a number of ways of looking at management, three of which are described below.

Management through people

Management has been described as 'getting things done by other people'. Although this sounds like the manager is avoiding responsibility, this misses the point about good management. A good manager is someone who motivates others and gives them clear guidelines to work to. For example, Anita Roddick – the founder of The Body Shop – is often quoted as someone with good management skills. She set up a business with a focus on natural ingredients, waste minimization and recycling in cosmetics. She was then able to inspire lots of independent business owners who worked on a franchise system to work hard for the brand.

Arsene Wenger, the Arsenal manager, is another example of someone who 'gets things done by others'. He provides inspiration and the systems for his team to work to.

Management – what managers do

Another way of examining management is in terms of what managers do. For example the mnemonic 'POSDCORB' is often used to describe what managers do:

P Planning – creating paper-based and other plans with objectives, actions and measurements for checking that the business is on target

O Organising – creating systems and deciding who does what in an organisation and how plans will be put into practice

S Staffing – placing the right people in the right posts at the right time

D Decision-making – deciding what will be done and communicating these decisions clearly

C Co-ordinating – co-ordination involves
O bringing together in the right sequence and
R at the right time the appropriate resources and parts of the plan. Co-ordination lies at the heart of successful management.

B Budgeting – making plans which involve the use of numbers (often financial plans) and then controlling the budget to keep it to plan.

Management of resources

Another way of looking at management is in terms of the resources that need to be managed, which include:

* People
* Finance
* Time
* Physical resources, e.g. plant, machinery, and materials
* Information.

In her famous book *Managers and their jobs*, Rosemary Stewart identified the following work that is carried out by managers. It was based on studying managers at work. Managers typically:

FIGURE 2.16 *Wenger and Roddick are good at getting things done by others – are you?*

Study the work of a manager e.g. within your school/college or at work.

1 To what extent does the manager 'get things done through other people'?

2 Analyse the work of the manager in terms of POSDCORB.

3. What are the key resources that the manager manages?

* Work long hours. The number of hours worked increases with seniority and with more general rather than specific functional responsibilities.

* Are highly interactive. A typical day contains several hundred brief interactions. Working on one item for more than half an hour is very rare. As rank increases, the number of interactions increases, but the fragmented nature of the job remains.

* Have to cope with highly variable tasks. Managers have to cope equally well with paperwork, meetings, telephone calls, visits, ceremonial functions etc.

* Communicate mostly by word of mouth. About three-quarters of communication is verbal. Many managers actually prefer verbal data such as hearsay, gossip or general feelings. Such data are immediate, accessible and can be acted upon before it is too late and gossip becomes fact. Information by post or written reports comes very much in second place in informing the manager what is going on (note that Stewart's work was carried out before the age of e-mail).

* Use lots of contact points to gather information. Managers continually exchange verbal information with others. Most of this occurs within the organisation although as rank increases the number of verbal information points outside the organisation also increases. Information is traded across all levels of the hierarchy, with superiors, peers and subordinates.

Types of resources used by businesses

We can now look at some of the main resources managed by managers – human resources, physical resources and financial resources.

Human resources

The prime concern of people management at work was at one time 'manpower planning'. This involved getting the right number of people in the right number of jobs at the right time.

In the early nineteenth century people were seen as a resource to be manipulated. Frederick Winslow Taylor developed an approach to managing people known as 'scientific management'. This involved trying to find the best way of getting people to work efficiently, e.g. by studying their movements at work to cut out waste.

The Ford Motor Company's approach characterised scientific management, where the production line ran like a giant machine. The workers had simply to keep up with the machine.

However, in the 1920s experiments were carried out in America which identified a 'human relations' approach to work. A team of experimenters at the Hawthorne Electrical Company, led by Elton Mayo, had been trying scientific approaches to improving work efficiency, for example, turning the lights up and down to find the best lighting to get the highest output. However, they found out that whatever they did to the lights work levels increased. They discovered that the workers were responding to

* DID YOU KNOW?

F.W. Taylor was known as 'speedy Taylor' because he set out to speed up the rate at which work was completed. He thought that he could create a science of work to find out the single best way that particular tasks could be carried out. Some companies today use a sort of scientific management approach in which they have studied all the processes involved in carrying out a particular operation to make it as simple and quick as possible. For example, it is argued that Quick Service Restaurants are based on a scientific management approach.

The following figures relate to a confectionery plant that employs two types of production line employees – skilled employees and unskilled employees.

The firm currently employs 10,000 employees – 8,000 of them are skilled and 2,000 are unskilled. The manpower planners have created an employment budget for the next four years.

YEAR	2005	2006	2007	2008
Required number of skilled employees	8,000	8,500	8,500	8,800
Required number of unskilled employees	2,000	2,200	2,400	2,200

The firm has calculated that each year it will lose the following numbers of employees:

Year	2005	2006	2007	2008
Skilled leaving the company	500	520	540	560
Unskilled leaving the company	600	650	650	700
Unskilled graduating into the skilled category	400	420	420	420

FIGURE 2.17 *Employment budget for a confectionery plant*

1 Using the figures given above calculate:

* The number of new skilled employees that will need to be recruited externally in each year.

* The number of unskilled employees that will need to be recruited externally each year.

2 An external consultant has suggested that the company spends more money on training its unskilled workforce. What do you think of this suggestion?

Whilst manpower planning is very important, it is the part of people management that is very mechanical (machine-like). What is more important in managing people at work is the human side of things – hence the term Human Resource Management (HRM).

1	Scientific Management	Early 19th century. Involved treating employees as part of the machine. Look for the best way of maximizing their output.
2	Human Relations	1920s onwards. Understanding that if you take an interest in your employees they will work harder for you.
3	Personnel management	Up to the 1990s. Approach which valued people and looked for ways of encouraging them to help an organisation to meet its objectives.
4	Human Resource Management	Modern approach in which managers seek to find out what motivates and drives employees. It involves identifying the needs and aspirations of employees so that employees can fulfil themselves in their work while at the same time working to help the organisation meet its objectives.

FIGURE 2.18 *The development of Human Resource Management (HRM)*

the interest shown in them by the researchers. They hit upon the idea that if workers were made to feel important and valued then their motivation would increase. Since that time the new human resource approach has dominated thinking.

Indeed, in the modern world Human Resource Management has gone one step further, as illustrated in Figure 2.18.

There are a number of ways in which managers can help to motivate people using an HRM approach, including:

1   Appraisal – regular performance reviews at which the employee is given the opportunity to discuss their hopes, aspirations and training needs and in which the appraiser can clarify the objectives of the organisation or a relevant part of that organisation. Appraisal makes it possible to review current performance and to establish future targets.

2   Job enrichment – identifying ways in which employees' work can be made more rewarding and interesting.

3   Job enlargement – giving employees a wider selection of responsibilities and activities to carry out.

4   Employee involvement (EI) – providing more opportunities for employees to become involved in decision making processes.

5   Linking pay and rewards to performance.

Management of physical resources

Physical resource management includes the management of premises, machinery and equipment, materials and other stocks.

While these activities are particularly important in manufacturing plants they are also relevant in services.

Learning activity

Which of the activities in Figure 2.19 do you see as fitting more closely with a scientific management or a human resource management approach?

FIGURE 2.19 *Scientific Management or Human Resource Management?*

CASE STUDY
Fish and chips and hairdressing

FIGURE 2.20 *Managing business activities*

The manager of a fish-and-chip shop needs to make sure that the premises are in an appropriate location for customer parking. The premises must meet health and safety and fire regulations. The premises need to be kept clean and well decorated. The fish and potato frying equipment must be to industry standard and be regularly cleaned, with proper electrical testing. The potatoes and fish which are the basic ingredients must be bought regularly and waste handled in an appropriate way. The right sort of packaging material needs to be used (newspaper is no longer acceptable). It is essential to keep appropriate stocks to meet customer demand.

Managing a hairdressing business has very similar requirements. There must be ease of access to the premises, which must meet fire regulations and health and safety checks. Appliances such as hairdryers and dyeing equipment must meet industry standards. It is essential to regularly re-order new chemicals, shampoos etc.

What are the main similarities and the main differences in managing a fish-and-chip shop and a hairdressing salon?

The management of the production process can be broken down into the 'five Ps of production':

* product
* plant
* process
* programme
* people

1 The product
It is essential to provide a good or service that clearly meets the needs of consumers and that can be provided at the right place, at the right time and for the most attractive price.

2 The plant
The location, size, design, safety and layout of the plant are all important. Managers need to think carefully about how parts and materials are to be delivered and how finished goods will be transported away from the plant. The layout should make it easy to co-ordinate the various activities that will take place there. Time and costs involved in transferring goods, materials, information and people should be kept to a minimum.

Managers must also make sure that plant and equipment are properly maintained. A maintenance department may include electricians, plumbers and joiners, as well as many other skilled workers. The effectiveness of the maintenance department can be judged by the number of breakdowns and accidents at work. Safety is vitally important.

3 The process

Different organisations will have different sets of operations depending on the nature of the product they make, the type of plant and equipment employed and many other factors. Process management sets out to:

✱ Identify the key processes of business activity. If these are carried out properly it will be possible to maximise customer satisfaction thus leading to better financial performance.

✱ Develop a detailed understanding of how processes work.

✱ Identify who in the organisation is involved in these processes.

✱ Seek ongoing improvements in the management of these processes.

✱ Put in motion an ongoing cycle of continuous process improvement.

4 The programme

Programming is mainly concerned with timetabling the use of resources. To meet orders successfully, the organisation will need to plan and control activities carefully. Successful programming involves purchasing, stock control and quality control.

5 The people

The success of any production process will depend on the people involved. The quality of people depends on how much is invested in them and how motivated they are. Training and development are vital.

Stock control

In an ideal world, in which businesses know demand well in advance and suppliers always meet delivery dates, there would be little need for stocks. In practice, demand varies and suppliers are often late, so stocks act as a protection against unpredictable events.

Organisations hold stocks in a variety of forms:

✱ raw materials

✱ work-in-progress

✱ finished goods

✱ plant and machinery spares.

The aim of any stock control system is to provide stocks that cater for uncertainties but are at minimum levels thus making sure that costs are kept low without reducing service to customers.

CASE STUDY

Lean production

Lean production is a means of organising people and physical resources in a highly efficient way. It is an approach that has been used widely in Japan and is today used in a lot of British manufacturing plants such as the Jaguar plant near Birmingham.

Lean thinking involves identifying exactly what your customers want and then providing them with it in the most efficient way. The objective is not just to reduce costs but also to simplify processes. Lean thinking focuses on what the customer needs at a specific price at a specific time.

In order to create value, the next step is to identify the value stream or to set out all the actions required to bring a particular product from concept to completion. By doing this many types of 'muda' (waste) will be identified.

By cutting out 'muda' you can concentrate simply on those activities that create value. Organisations can be re-organised into product teams which focus on the customer. This enables companies to let customers pull the product from them as they need it, rather than pushing products on to a market that does not necessarily want them.

For example, at Castle Bromwich, the Jaguar production line runs at the speed which enables finished cars to come off the line just in time to meet customer demand. All along the production line, teams of workers work in problem-solving circles to identify 'muda' and to cut it out. What this means is that the employees work smarter rather than harder. By working smart they work at value-creating activities rather than wasting time on muda. The physical layout of the factory has been reorganised to cut out all those activities that are wasteful. For example, supplies and stores are kept away from the manufacturing area as much as possible because they get in the way. Parts and supplies are brought in when they are needed by a worker pressing a buzzer to call for them.

FIGURE 2.21 *Jaguar uses lean techniques to manage resources*

1 How is lean thinking based on customer needs?
2 How does lean thinking involve reorganising the physical plant and restructuring processes?
3 Why is it essential to cut out waste?
4 How does the elimination of waste help the customer?
5 Identify an area of work that would benefit from lean thinking.
6 Show how muda can be removed from this area of work.
7 How can you reduce muda in organising your work on your business course?

PROBLEMS OF LOW STOCKS	PROBLEMS OF HIGH STOCKS
Difficult to meet orders	Increased risk of stock going out of date
Possible loss of business	Increased risk of stock theft and other loss
Loss of goodwill	High storage costs
Ordering needs to be frequent and handling costs rise	Stocks tie up money

FIGURE 2.22 *Problems caused by incorrect stock levels*

Balancing stock levels is essential. Having too little or too much stock can be harmful to a business. High stock levels mean that cash isn't being generated quickly enough through sales, whereas low stock levels might result in not being able to meet orders.

Figure 2.22 shows the impact of having the wrong stock levels and the modern approach is 'Just-in-time'.

In contrast to a Just-in-time approach, we can have a 'Just-in-case' approach where an organisation holds a buffer stock.

This approach can be helpful to make sure there are large enough stocks.

A minimum stock level is established – stocks should not fall below this.

Stocks are re-ordered when the existing stock falls to the re-order level.

When new stocks arrive this will take the stock situation back to the maximum stock level.

The re-order quantity is the quantity that will be supplied when stocks have fallen to the minimum level and brings the stock level back up to the maximum stock level.

CASE STUDY

Just-in-time (JIT)

Just-in-time approaches to holding stock are very important in modern industry. Just-in-time is a very simple idea:

* Finished goods are produced just in time for them to be sold, rather than weeks or months ahead.
* The parts that go into a finished product arrive just in time to be put together to make the final product, rather than being stored (at some cost) in a warehouse. With a JIT system, a factory or other workplace is re-organised so that people are grouped together around the products they produce.

1 What do you see as being the main benefit of a JIT system?
2 Can you see any potential drawbacks?

Try out the following activity. Divide the class into two equal groups. One group of students should be given 20 car templates (see Figure 2.23) and some glue. The job of the group is to make 20 completed cars. They must be of a high quality.

The other group of students must be divided into four: one group to assemble the final car using glue, one group to cut out windows, one group to distribute parts to final assembly and one group to cut out wheels. The final assemblers must call for parts just in time to assemble them. When the activity is completed the quality of the cars produced by both groups and the time taken to make them must be assessed. An analysis should be carried out of the efficiency of the Just-in-time approach.

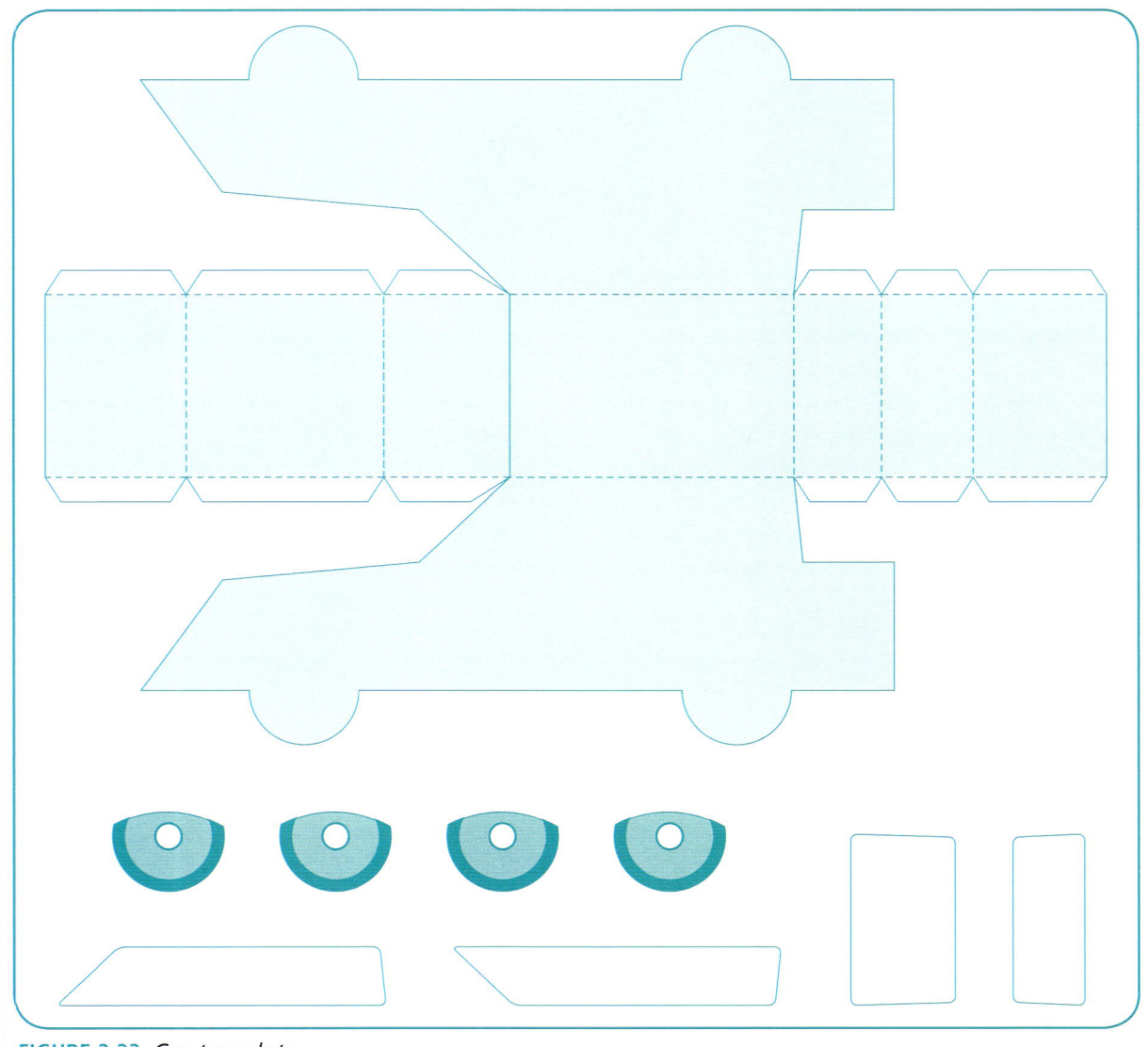

FIGURE 2.23 *Car template*

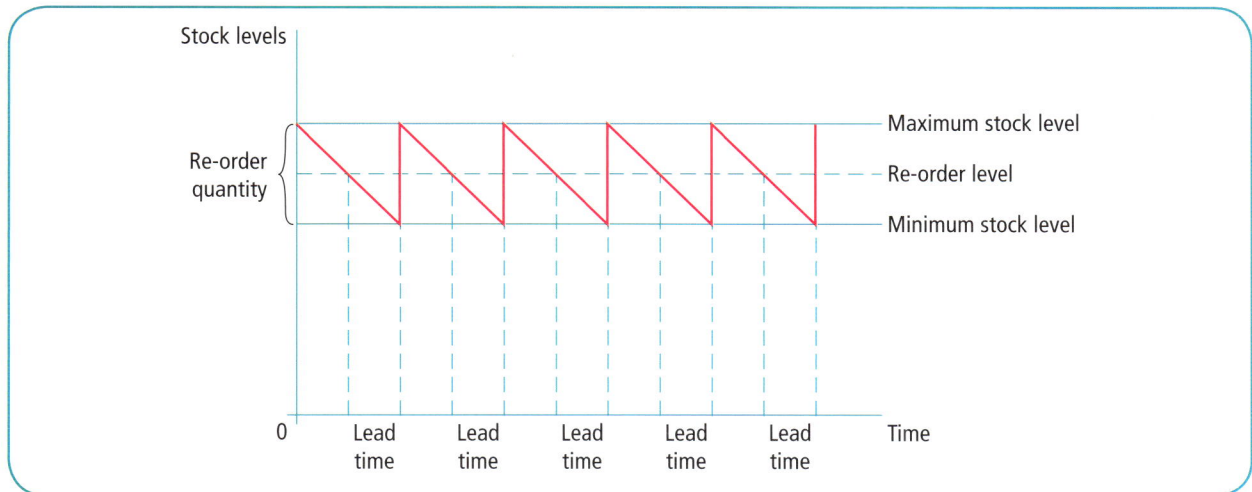

FIGURE 2.24 *Lead time*

The lead time is the time that is taken between the re-ordering of the stock and the arrival of this new stock (see Figure 2.24).

Managing financial resources

Another important managerial responsibility is that of obtaining finance for a business or part of a business. Each year individual managers will need to bid for funds. Typically this involves arguing the case for levels of funding that are appropriate to the activities that need to be carried out. For example:

* a course manager in a school or college will need funds to manage a course

* a production manager in a factory will need to bid for funds to buy new machinery and equipment and to purchase stocks of raw materials.

At an organisation-wide level, financial managers will have responsibility for securing funds for the business to enable it to operate well.

Learning activity

What other examples of needs for funds can you think of? Use your work experience and part-time job experience to generate ideas.

Organisations have available to them a number of sources of finance, including:

* individuals

* organisations providing venture capital

* banks and other financial institutions

* suppliers

* government

* profits retained in the business.

In deciding what types of finance to draw on financial managers need to consider:

* the length of time for which they need the finance

* the cost of raising the finance in one way rather than another.

ORGANISATIONS MAY NEED:	
Long-term finance	e.g. to purchase other businesses or buildings
Medium-term finance	e.g. to update machinery, equipment and fittings
Short-term finance	e.g. to buy new stocks, to pay wages etc

FIGURE 2.25 *Types of finance*

Owner's capital

This is raised from individual owners of a business, from partners or shareholders. This type of capital is raised when starting up a new business venture or when expanding a business.

When issuing shares, careful consideration needs to be given to the need to pay a dividend (share of the profit) to shareholders. The amount of dividend paid is decided by the Board of Directors of the company. A good thing about raising finance from shareholders is that the company is not legally obliged to pay a set return each year (as it has to with loans). However, if the company keeps asking shareholders for more funds they will lose confidence in the company.

Venture capital

Venture capital companies such as 3i provide finance in return for an equity (ordinary) shareholding in the company and an element of control. This is a quick and relatively cheap way for a new business to raise capital but it may not want to lose some control to the venture capitalist.

Profit retention

One of the most important sources of finance for a business is from profits that have been put back in. Initially, profits are subject to corporation tax, payable to the Inland Revenue. Then a proportion of what is left is distributed to shareholders as dividends. Finally profits can be ploughed back into expansion.

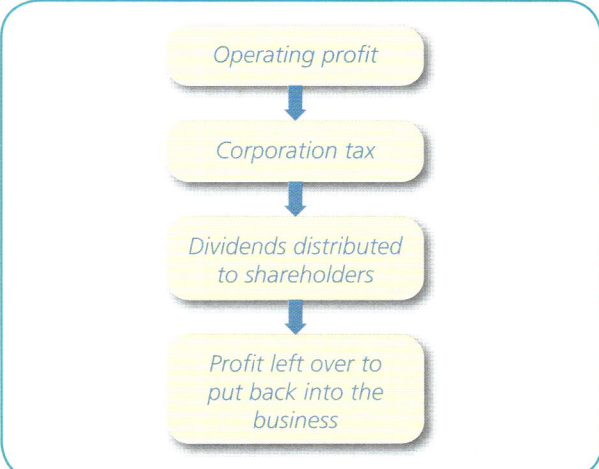

FIGURE 2.26 *Profits are an important source of finance for a business*

Borrowing

The charge made for borrowing money is termed interest. The longer the business borrows money the greater the rate of interest charged.

1 Bank loans are taken out for a fixed period, repayments either being in instalments or in full at the end of the term. Banks generally provide funds on a short- to medium-term basis, with relatively few loans over more than ten years in duration. As well as the interest payment there may be an arrangement fee.

2 Debentures are certificates issued by companies acknowledging their debt. The debt is paid at a fixed rate of interest and the certificate sets out the term of repayment at the end of the period of debts. Debentures can usually be traded on the Stock Exchange.

3 Bank overdrafts are the most frequently used form of short-term bank finance and they are used to ease cash flow problems. Arrangements are made between the customer and the bank to include an agreed limit on an account beyond which the customer will not draw. Interest is calculated on the level of the overdraft on a daily basis. Often a bank will make a special charge for arranging an overdraft. A bank can take away the customer's right to use an overdraft if they think it is being abused.

Hire-purchase

Hire-purchase (HP) allows a business to use an asset (e.g. photocopier, computer) without having to find the money immediately. A finance house buys the asset from the supplier and retains ownership of it during the period of the hire-purchase agreement. The business pays a deposit and then further payments to the finance house, as set out in the agreement. At the end of the HP agreement, ownership of the asset is passed to the business. The repayments made by the business are in excess of the cash price of the item. The difference is the finance charge to the finance house.

Leasing

Leasing an asset provides similar benefits to hire-purchase, in that a leasing agreement with a finance house (lessor) allows the business (lessee) to use an asset without having to buy it outright. However, leasing does not give an automatic right to eventual ownership of the asset. It is a very popular form of finance for company vehicles, office equipment and factory machinery.

The lessee benefits from not having to put up large sums of capital to be able to use assets and they can exchange the asset for a more modern version when technology changes. The lessor is also usually responsible for the maintenance of the item.

Mortgages

A commercial mortgage is a loan secured on land and buildings and can either be used to finance the purchase of the property or to provide security for a loan applied to some other purpose. It is a long-term financing arrangement typically from 10 to 30 years. Repayments include a considerable interest rate.

Sale and leaseback

This involves a firm selling its freehold property to an investment company and then leasing it back over a long period of time. This releases funds for other purposes.

Suppliers

Suppliers are a valuable source of finance for many businesses. Just as the business may give credit to its own customers, the firm may be able to negotiate credit terms with its suppliers. Credit terms are typically 30 days from date of supply or the end of the month following a delivery, i.e. 30 to 60 days.

Factoring

When a business is owed money and needs cash urgently it can sell off part or all of this debt for collection by a third party – a factoring company.

Government loans

Businesses can acquire loans and grants from the government for various purposes depending on circumstances. Some of these grants and loans may come from European Union sources, others from UK national government, and others from local government. National Lottery funds can be obtained in some circumstances. Typical purposes might be funds for helping with government schemes such as Modern Apprenticeships and job creation schemes. Other grants may be for building development and machinery purchase, particularly in areas of economic decline.

Learning activity

You are the financial manager of an organisation that is opening a petrol station on a new city bypass. Refer to Figure 2.27 and match the organisation's financial needs with the possible sources of finance available.

NEEDS	POSSIBLE SOURCES OF FINANCE
✳ Land and buildings: £500,000	✳ Hire-purchase or leasing
✳ Shopfittings: £50,000	✳ Bank loan for two years
✳ Petrol pumps: £100,000	✳ Commercial mortgage
✳ Stocks of petrol and retail items: £75,000	✳ Bank overdraft
✳ Computer terminal: £6,000	✳ Trade credit
✳ First few weeks' wages: £8,000	✳ Owner's capital: £100,000

FIGURE 2.27 *Finance needs and sources*

We have seen that business organisations use a range of methods of finance. If you are a financial manager in the following organisations what type of finance would you use in each case?

1 A school wishes to replace its existing photocopier with a more elaborate version which they want to pay for over a period of time.

2 The Queen's Medical Centre wishes to build a new hospital wing on vacant land close to its existing site in Nottingham.

3 Prakesh Patel needs a new computer system costing £7,500 for his business. Identify two ways of financing the purchase and state the circumstances in which either would be most appropriate.

4 A medium-sized company wants to expand its factory building. The cost will be £1m. Identify two ways of financing the expansion and state the circumstance in which either would be more appropriate.

5 A small firm is temporarily having problems with its cash flow. Identify two ways of financing any shortfall it might currently have in its cash requirements and state the circumstances in which either would be more appropriate.

The role of quality control, quality assurance and total quality management

Quality can be defined as:

* continually meeting agreed customer needs
* what it takes to satisfy the customer
* fitness for purpose.

Consumers make purchases when they feel that their need for quality is being met.

There have been three main stages in the development of quality in business, as shown in Figure 2.28.

Quality control

Quality control is an old idea. It is concerned with detecting and cutting out components or final products which fall below set standards. This process takes place after these products have been made. It may involve considerable waste as defect products are scrapped. Quality control is carried out by Quality Control Inspectors. Inspection and testing are the most common methods of carrying out quality control.

Quality assurance

Quality assurance occurs both during and after the event and is concerned with trying to stop faults from happening in the first place. Quality assurance is concerned with making sure that products are produced to predetermined standards. The aim is to produce goods with 'zero defects'.

Quality assurance is the responsibility of the workforce, working in cells or teams, rather than an inspector (although inspection will take place). Quality standards should be maintained by following steps set out in a quality assurance system.

Total Quality Management (TQM)

Total Quality Management (TQM) goes beyond quality assurance. It is concerned with creating a

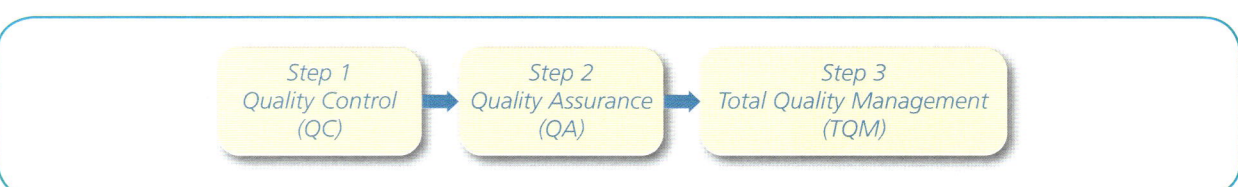

Step 1
Quality Control
(QC)

Step 2
Quality Assurance
(QA)

Step 3
Total Quality Management
(TQM)

FIGURE 2.28 *The evolution of quality in business*

Can you think of examples of businesses that operate with a Total Quality Management approach:

* in the hotel business

* in providing air travel

* in retailing

* in the entertainment industry

* elsewhere.

quality culture so that every employee will seek to delight customers. The customer is at the centre of the production process.

A company that believes in TQM will seek to provide customers:

* with what they want

* when they want it

* how they want it.

TQM involves moving with changing customer requirements and fashions to design products and services which meet and exceed their requirements. Delighted customers will pass the message on to their friends.

Quality Circles

A lot of the early work on the development of Quality was done by Dr W. Edwards Deming working as a consultant to Japanese companies after the Second World War. In a total quality system, TQM takes place at every stage of an organisation's operations and is the responsibility of all employees. Emphasis is placed on quality chains, i.e. links between groups and individuals involved in operations. The concept of 'customer' extends to include the 'internal' customer. Internal customers are people inside the company receiving products (usually unfinished) or services from their colleagues also in the company.

Deming developed the idea of the Quality Circle. Quality Circles are made up of small groups of employees engaged in any sort of problem

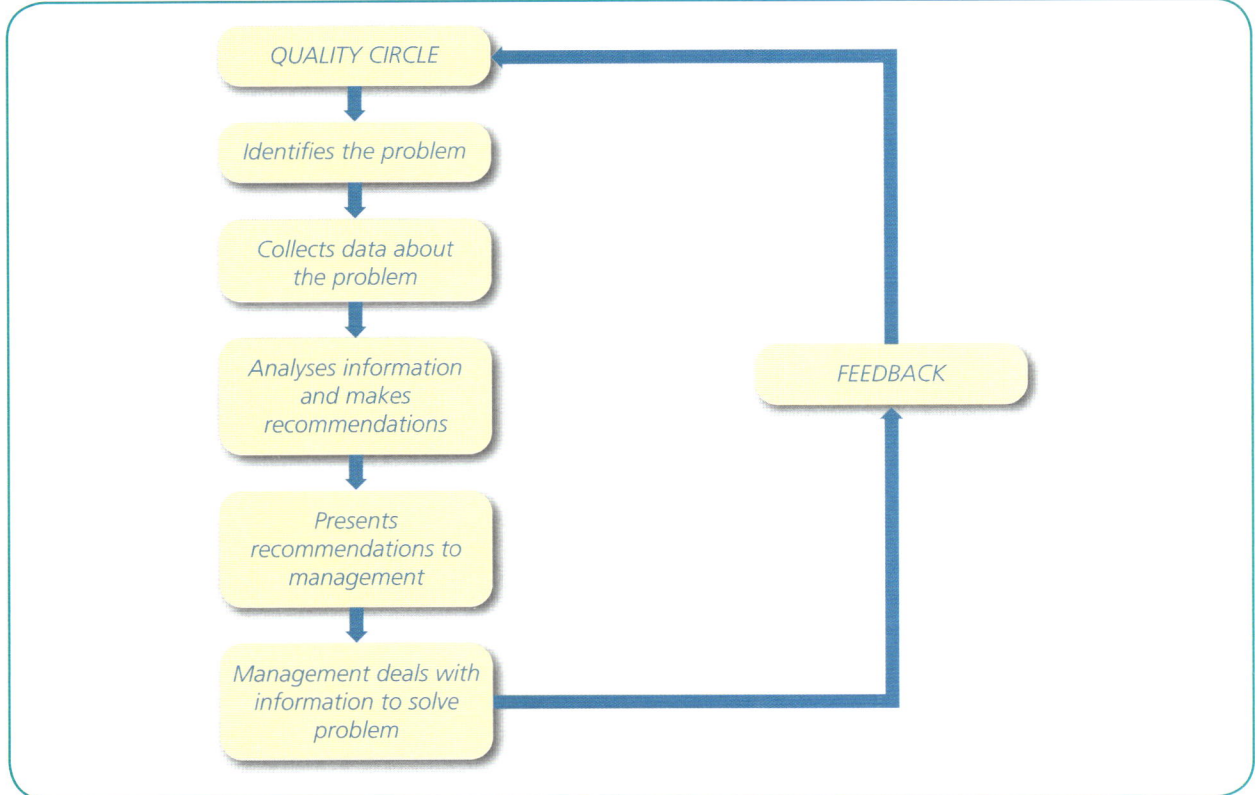

FIGURE 2.29 *The function of a Quality Circle*

Learning activity

How was quality managed in an organisation in which you carried out work experience or in which you have a part time job?

affecting their working environment, for example, safety, production methods, efficiency. They are a means for employees to improve their working life by putting forward their points of view on day-to-day quality issues. Quality Circles may meet once a week or more frequently. Each circle has a leader and operates as shown in Figure 2.29.

A great benefit of Quality Circles is that an organisation can use specialists who know and understand their jobs and problems related to them to solve problems without having to call in management consultants. Because these circles are supported by top managers, the members of them feel that they are trusted and valued. This increases motivation and the links between managers and employees.

The importance of monitoring and reviewing business performance

Managers need to monitor and review the performance of a business in order to make improvements. The act of monitoring and reviewing performance gives the manager control, as illustrated in Figure 2.30.

Control involves the measurement and correction of performance. Control and planning should go hand in hand. Many writers on management theory argue that the two cannot be separated. They can be seen as the twin blades of a pair of scissors.

FIGURE 2.31 *Planning and control should always go together*

In order to monitor and review business performance it is necessary to have standards against which to judge this performance.

Such standards include:

1. The solvency of a business
2. Profitability

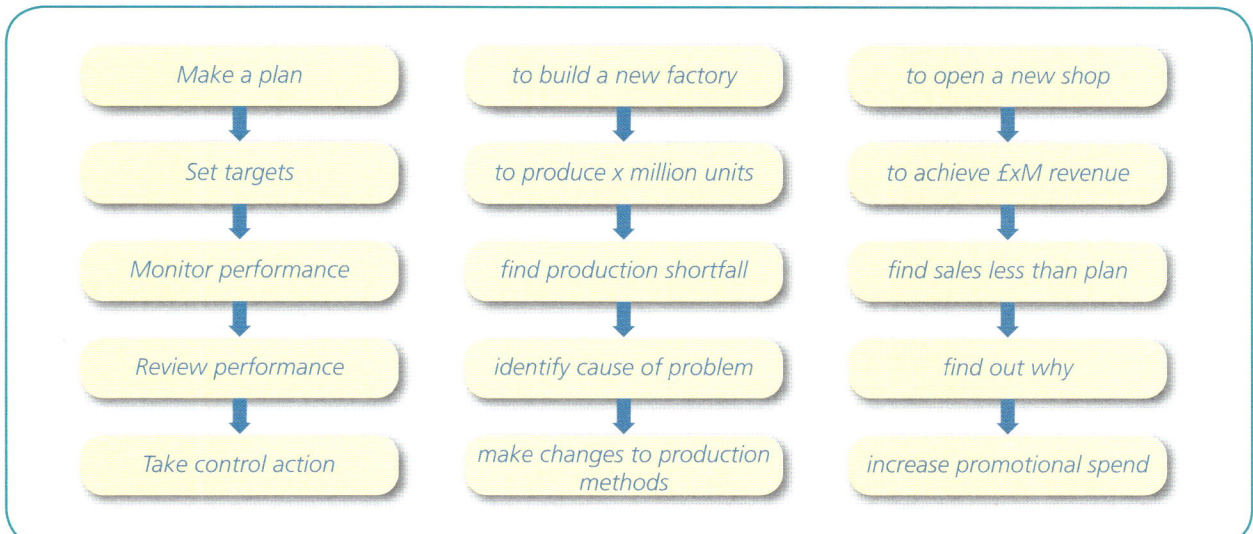

FIGURE 2.30 *Management control by monitoring and reviewing performance*

FIGURE 2.32 *The cross-channel business is very competitive*

In the period 2003–2004 the cross channel ferry section of P&O carried 10 million passengers but it still made a loss of £25 million in the first half of 2004. These losses seemed likely to increase. After reviewing this situation managers decided to take the following actions:

✳ Cut 1,200 jobs
✳ Sell off one third of the fleet
✳ Reduce the number of routes from 11 to 7.

1 Can you identify a news story where a company has taken management control actions after reviewing its profit performance?
2 What had happened to profits?
3 What control actions were taken?

---

3 Complying with laws
4 Identifying areas for improvement.

1 The solvency of a business

Solvency is concerned with whether a business has access to enough cash to pay outstanding demands. For example, if a business knows that in any quarter it will have to pay out £10,000 for wages, raw materials and other short-term costs, it must make sure that it can quickly get hold of £10,000 to meet these demands. A solvent business is one that can always meet demands for short-term payments. Cash flow forecasting is an important management tool for controlling solvency. It involves forecasting cash incomings and outgoings from a business.

2 Profitability

Businesses need to make a profit if they are to survive. Managers will therefore establish profit targets for coming periods. Actions can be taken to make sure these profits are achieved, e.g. by creating an appropriate pricing or advertising policy as well as having a quality product. If profits fall short of expectations then managers will need to take appropriate control actions as illustrated by the P&O case study.

Learning activity

Identify one situation where there is a legal change that affects business. Identify the sorts of actions that managers might need to take in this situation to make sure that the business complies with the law.

3 Complying with laws

Managers also have responsibility for making sure that their business complies with relevant laws, e.g. with regard to Health and Safety at Work, Equal Opportunities, Environmental Protection, Competition Policy, Data Protection etc.

4 Identifying areas for improvement

Managers have a general responsibility for identifying all areas where there is room for improvement in business performance.

✳ DID YOU KNOW?

There are around 460 loss-making companies listed on the London Stock Exchange and some of these are fairly well-known companies. Some organisations make losses because of a sudden change in their business environment. For example, the events of 11th September 2001 suddenly hit the aviation industry.

Record sales for Tesco this year

Price of petrol hits record high

£1 in every £3 of grocery retail sales is made by Tesco

Manchester United keep players' wage costs at under 50% of the value of sales

Manchester United continue to lead British football clubs in the profit stakes

Oil giants BP and Shell make record profits in the history of British companies

FIGURE 2:33 *The kind of headlines you might see in the financial pages of a newspaper*

2.3 Financial management in business

Look at the financial pages of any newspaper and you will see the extent to which external confidence in the management of a large business is determined by its financial performance. Shareholders and other external stakeholders keenly await information on financial performance of the business. If you are working for the business, your work will contribute to this financial performance and you may have a role in recording the financial transactions of the business. Even the smallest transaction will be audited so that the final accounts accurately represent what the business has been doing during the year. Public confidence in a business and the confidence of all employees will rely upon good accounts.

Every business has to meet internal and external reporting requirements to show its financial health and to meet legal and other requirements. The following people need financial information about the performance of a business:

* Internal users – groups within the organisation, such as managers.
* External users – groups outside the organisation, such as shareholders and creditors.

Every business environment is competitive, which by its very nature means that in this rapidly changing world in which organisations exist, some will inevitably perform better than others. Where a business does well, there are many rewards and benefits for individuals and organisations affected by its actions. On the other hand, if a business has a bad year or does not do well, there is a similar knock-on effect with a range of consequences for individuals and organisations that may be affected in a range of ways by its poor performance.

Every individual or organisation likely to be affected through the successes, failures or actions of a business will therefore have their own areas of concern. To clarify their concerns, they will have information needs and requirements. They will want facts, knowledge and understanding about how the actions of that organisation affect either their own circumstances or the circumstances of the organisation for which they work.

The importance of profitability and liquidity (solvency)

Profitability

Some businesses make losses over a considerable time as it is difficult to generate revenues to cover expenses. For example, with new high-tech companies or drug companies it may take years to generate revenues.

Despite their lack of profits, many investors like loss-makers, mainly because there is always a chance of a turnaround and the shares may be cheap.

Why do we assume that all businesses will be profitable?

Is it possible to identify a sector in which few businesses are profitable?

Why might an investor wish to buy shares in unprofitable companies?

In order to make judgements about business activities, individuals require accounting information from an accounting system. Accounting acts as an information system by processing business data so that those parties either interested in or affected by the business can be provided with the means to find out how well or badly the organisation is performing.

Business data are the inputs for the accounting system. The output is financial information. Financial information can then be fed to those who require such information.

Accounting information may be used both within and outside an organisation. It involves providing important data that may form the basis for decisions. In order to clarify what we mean by accounting information, it is perhaps best to explain what we mean by accounting:

Accounting is concerned with identifying, measuring, recording and reporting information relating to the activities of an organisation.

We can break each of these activities down into the following:

* Identifying – This involves capturing all the financial data within a business related to how it is performing. For example, this would include all information about the sales of goods to customers, data about the payment of expenses (such as wages and rent) and also information about the purchase of any stock, as well as data about the purchase of new vehicles and machinery.

* Measuring – Money, in the form of pounds and pence, is used as the form of measurement of economic transactions. In the future, the form of measurement might change to become euros. For accounting purposes, instead of saying a business had sold 10 cars in a week, which may be meaningless if you do not know the value of the cars, it may be useful to specify the value of the cars. For example, 10 cars valued at £15,000 would mean a turnover during the week of £150,000.

* Recording – Accounting data and information must be recorded into either handwritten accounting books or into a suitable computer package, such as a specialised accounting package or a spreadsheet.

* Communicating – The reporting of financial information may take a variety of different forms. For example, although some financial information may be required and extracted from the accounts weekly, such as sales totals, there are standard financial statements (such as profit and loss accounts and balance sheets) that have a set format for reporting the activities of organisations.

It is important that throughout this accounting process the accounting information is:

* Reliable – free from errors and bias
* Comparable – accounting information should be comparable with information from other organisations
* Relevant – accounting information should relate to many of the decisions that have to be made about the business
* Understandable – information should be capable of being understood by those at whom it is targeted.

Financial and management accounting

The process of accounting can be divided into two broad areas: financial accounting and management accounting.

Financial accounting

This is concerned with the recording of financial transactions and the preparation of financial reports to communicate past financial performance.

Subject to accounting regulations, financial accounting ensures:

* that reports/statements follow a standard approach
* a broad overview of the whole business using totals
* information to a particular date
* general statements and reports
* information in monetary terms and values.

Management accounting

Management accounting involves looking to the future using a knowledge of past performance, where relevant, to aid the management of the business.

In management accounting reports are only for internal use so no restrictions are necessary. This sector of accounting:

* uses information extracted from parts of the organisation where it is used to help with a particular decision

* will look at future performance as well as at past perfomance
* produces reports with a specific decision in mind
* may have non-financial information such as stocks.

Following the financial reports in any newspaper will reveal that one of the key newsworthy areas constantly emphasised by the press is profits. For example, 'Eurostar' might be 'rocked by profit warnings' or 'Somerfield to retreat to the high street'. Profits are a key indicator when judging business performance. It is the first point of reference for many organisational stakeholders.

It is all very well saying that sales have risen, productivity is soaring and the organisation is growing. However, shareholders and providers of capital will always ask the question: 'But have you been making a profit?'

Learning activity

Which of the following would fall into the realms of financial accounting and which would be management accounting?

* Recording transactions from source documentation.
* Calculating what the profit is likely to be over a range of outputs for the launch of a new product.
* Producing financial statements to show what has happened to the business during the past year.
* Advising a business on its tax liability.
* Creating a budgetary system to improve control over the costs within a business.
* Setting the prices of products or services.

* DID YOU KNOW?

The UK insurance industry is the largest in Europe and the third largest in the world.

Liquidity (solvency)

The words 'liquidity' or 'solvency' mean 'to be able to meet financial obligations'. A business becomes 'technically insolvent' when it has sufficient assets to meet all its financial obligations but insufficient time to convert these assets into cash. It is 'legally insolvent' if it is in a situation of permanent cash shortage.

A number of users of accounting information will want to check regularly on the solvency of business organisations. For example, owners and shareholders will want to know their money is 'safe'. In this respect they will want to look at the distribution of assets and liabilities a company has. In other words they will want to know what a business owns and what a business owes. For example, the company may have money coming in at 'some time in the future'. However, unless it has money coming in now, tomorrow and the next day, it may face cash flow problems that make it 'technically insolvent'.

Lenders of money to organisations want to know their loans will be repaid and that interest will be paid at regular intervals. Employees and other stakeholders in organisations will want the security of knowing the organisation is solvent.

Managers will want to know the extent of solvency so that they can restructure assets and liabilities into an appropriate form. For example, they will want to manage their assets in a way that enables them to pay bills as and when they arrive in the organisation, without being too liquid and having too much cash or cash not doing anything. Solvency is a base-line for ongoing business operations.

When auditors carry out a periodic audit of an organisation's accounts, one of the key areas they would need to emphasise would be how solvent the organisation is.

Assets, liabilities, expenses and revenues

Assets

Assets are things that an organisation owns, as well as other items that may be owed to the business. The word 'asset' appears frequently in a balance sheet, which provides a statement of what an organisation owns and owes at any fixed point in time. Assets in a balance sheet are normally set out in what is called an inverse order of liquidity. This means items that may be easy to convert into cash quickly, and are therefore liquid, appear at the bottom of the list of assets. By looking down the order it is possible to gauge the ease with which successive assets can be converted to cash, until we come to the most liquid asset of all, cash itself.

Assets can be divided into fixed assets and current assets.

Fixed assets tend to have a life-span of more than one year. They comprise items that are purchased and generally kept for a long period of time. Examples of fixed assets would be premises, machinery and motor vehicles. When a business buys fixed assets it does so by incurring capital expenditure.

Current assets are sometimes called 'circulating assets' because the form they take is constantly

Learning activity

Explain what the word 'asset' means.

A small bakery has the following assets. Try to put them into an inverse order of liquidity, with the least liquid at the top and the most liquid at the bottom:

✱ cash in the tills

✱ bread in the shops

✱ a bakery van

✱ the baker's oven

✱ supplies of flour

✱ money in the bakery's bank account

✱ money owed to the bakery by firms

✱ the baker's premises.

Identify (with reasons) which of the following items should be considered as a current asset of a newsagent:

* the fixtures and fittings of the shop
* cash in the tills
* money in the bank
* money owed by the newsagent to the suppliers
* money owed by customers for newspaper bills
* the delivery bicycle
* stocks of newspapers in the shop.

changing. Examples of current assets are stocks, debtors, money in the bank and cash in hand.

For example, a manufacturing business holds stocks of finished goods in readiness to satisfy the demands of the market. When a credit transaction takes place, stocks are reduced and the business gains debtors. These debtors have bought goods on credit and therefore owe the business money; after a reasonable credit period payment will be expected. Payments will have to be made on further stocks so that the business has a cash cycle. 'Cash' or 'bank' changes to 'stock' then to 'debtors', back to 'cash' or 'bank' and then to 'stock' again.

Liabilities

Liabilities include anything that an organisation owes and are usually set out either as current liabilities or long-term liabilities, depending upon their duration.

Current liabilities are debts a business needs to repay within a short period of time (normally a year). These liabilities include creditors, who are suppliers of goods on credit for which the business has been invoiced but not yet paid. They may also include a bank overdraft that is arranged up to a limit over a time period and is, technically, repayable on demand. Other current liabilities may include any short-term loans and any taxes owed.

Working capital is always an important calculation for an organisation as it shows how easily the business can pay its short-term debts. Working capital is the ratio of current assets to current liabilities.

$$\text{Working capital ratio} = \frac{\text{current assets}}{\text{current liabilities}}$$

It is important for an organisation to maintain a sensible ratio. The level of ratio depends on the type of business and the likelihood that funds will be required quickly to meet liabilities (e.g. creditors demanding quick repayment). For most businesses a ratio of 2:1 is regarded as a sign of careful management, but some businesses have lower ratios.

Working capital is important because it provides a buffer: to 'keep the wolf from the door'. Many businesses have suffered the consequences of having too many of their assets tied up in liquid assets.

A long-term liability is sometimes called a deferred liability as it is not due for payment until some time in the future. By convention, in a set of accounts this means longer than one year. Examples for a sole trader could include a bank loan or mortgage.

As we saw earlier, capital is provided by the owner of the business and is therefore deemed to be owed to the owner by the business. The balance sheet keeps an updated record of the amount owed by the business to the owner.

During a year's trading the owner's capital may be increased by the inflows of profits (profits for the period) and decreased by outflows of drawings (money or other assets taken out of the business for personal use). Having taken these into consideration, a new capital figure is calculated at the end of the year. So the balance sheet shows how the capital has increased (or decreased!) since the last balance sheet was prepared. For a company, capital will appear as shares and the profits are called dividends.

✱ DID YOU KNOW?

UK domestic energy consumption increased by 32% between 1970 and 2001 and by 19% between 1990 and 2001 alone.

Expenses

Almost all business activities involve some element of cost and most managers have to deal with costs on a day-to-day basis. Expenses are fundamental, from the early development of a business, through to the controlling and monitoring of expenditures. Information about expenses and costs help an organisation to:

* create short-term, medium-term and long-term plans

* control an organisation's activities

* decide between alternative strategies.

Every organisation incurs expenses and a range of overheads. These might include:

Rent of premises
Gas
Electricity
Stationery
Cleaning costs
Insurance
Business rates
Depreciation (loss in value of an asset through wear and tear)
Bad debts (people owing the business money who fail to pay)
Interest on loans
Advertising costs
Sundry expenses
Motor expenses
Accountancy and legal fees.

Revenues

Most revenue for a business organisation will come either from sales or from fees charged to customers. The sales figure can be derived by looking at the selling price of the units sold, against the number of units sold. Some organisations receive income from sources other than sales. This is known as non-operating income. This may include rents received on any

CASE STUDY

Understanding how to manage working capital

Working capital is often considered to be the portion of the capital that 'oils the wheels' of business. It provides the stocks from which the fixed assets help to produce the finished goods. It allows the salesforce to offer attractive credit and terms to customers, which creates debtors.

Organisations that do not have sufficient working capital lack the funds to buy stocks and to produce and create debtors.

The dangers of insufficient working capital are therefore clear to see:

* A business with limited working capital will not be able to buy in bulk and could miss out on any opportunities to obtain trade discounts.
* Cash discounts will be lost as the business will avoid paying creditors until the last possible opportunity.
* It will become more difficult to offer extensive credit facilities for customers. By shortening the credit period, customers may well go to alternative suppliers.
* The business will be unable to innovate. Limited finances will hinder its ability to develop new products or improve production techniques.
* The business's financial reputation as a good payer may be lost.
* Creditors may well take action. As capital becomes squeezed, a business will be forced to finance its activities by overdrafts and trade credit. A point could well be reached where its future is dependent upon the actions of creditors.
* Overtrading could take place. This is where a larger volume of production or orders take place, without sufficient working capital to support it. This then leads to a complete imbalance in the working capital ratio.

As a result of problems with working capital, there are a number of options. These may include the following:

* Reducing the period between the time cash is paid out for raw materials and the time

cash is received from sales. This helps to provide funds for regeneration. However, although the improved efficiency of the cash cycle may improve working capital, actions taken may be unpopular with creditors.

* Fixed assets (such as land and buildings) may not be fully utilised, or space may be used for unprofitable purposes. Space could be rented, sold or allowed to house a more profitable operation so that cash flow could be improved. A business's cash flow might be improved by selling assets and leasing them back, although this may commit an organisation to heavy leasing fees.

* A company could review its stock levels to see if these could be subject to economy measures. If the stock of raw materials is divided by the average weekly issue, the number of weeks' raw materials held in stock can be calculated. The problem with this is the business might then lose out on trade discounts or have problems obtaining supplies.

* Many businesses employ a credit controller to manage cash flow and control the debtors. A credit controller will vet new customers and set them a credit limit, ensure that credit limits are not exceeded and encourage debtors to pay on time. Credit controllers are often caught in a conflict with sales staff, who wish to offer attractive credit terms, and the accounts department, who want debtors to pay quickly and so increase their working capital.

* As we have seen, the use of cash budgets can be an important control mechanism that can be used to predict the effects of future transactions on the cash balance of a company. Cash flow forecasting or cash budgeting can help an organisation to take actions to ensure cash is available when required.

* A number of short-term solutions are available to increase working capital. Companies might extend their overdraft or bring in a factoring company to buy some of their debtors and so provide them with instant finance. It might be possible to delay the payment of bills, although this obviously displeases creditors.

When a business can no longer pay its debts it may go into liquidation. This may be ordered by a court, usually on behalf of a creditor. This may then be followed by receivership, where independent accountants supervise the sale of the different parts of the business. But, sometimes, while struggling to survive and meet the demands of creditors, a white knight appears on the scene to launch a rescue bid and save the business.

1 Why do organisations have to manage their working capital?
2 Describe one problem that arises if an organisation fails to manage its working capital properly.
3 What are the likely effects upon the business of insufficient working capital?

properties that the business owns, profits from the sale of assets such as cars, as well as income from other areas such as investments.

Constructing financial statements

Final accounts are usually produced once a year by a firm of outside auditors or accountants. As well as helping the owners of a business to revise and fine-tune their business strategies, they provide a broad picture of how an organisation is performing and may be presented to the Inland Revenue and lenders of money, such as banks.

Profit and loss account

As the trading account is usually linked together with the profit and loss account, with the trading account appearing above, they are sometimes collectively called 'the profit and loss account'.

The trading account can be likened to a video giving ongoing pictures of an organisation's trading activities. For many business organisations, trading involves buying and selling stock. The difference between the value of the stock sold (sales) and the cost of producing those sales (which may be the production costs of manufactured goods for a manufacturing company or the cost of purchasing the supplies for a trading company) is known as the gross profit.

The trading account simply shows how gross profit is arrived at:

$$\text{Net sales} - \text{Cost of sales} = \text{Gross profit}$$

The trading account includes *only the items in which an organisation trades*. For example, if a small supermarket buys baked beans and sells them to its customers, then the cost of purchasing these and the amounts received from selling them will appear in the trading account. However, if the supermarket's owner decided to sell the business's van, this would not be included in the trading account as he or she is not in the second-hand vehicle business.

Sales

Sales are often described as turnover. As we have seen earlier, sometimes goods which have been sold are returned inwards as sales returns. We obviously do not want to include these in the sales figures because they have come back to us. Net sales, which is the final sales figure, is therefore:

$$\text{Sales} - \text{Returns inwards (sales returns)} = \text{Net sales}$$

Purchases

As with sales, some purchases may have been returned but, in this instance, the returns will have been outwards as purchases returns. Purchases may also include the cost of transporting the goods to the organisation, which must be added to the cost of buying goods, known, as we saw earlier, as carriage inwards. Net purchases, where there is carriage inwards and purchases returns, could therefore be:

$$\text{Purchases} + \text{Carriage inwards} - \text{Returns outward (purchases returns)}$$
$$= \text{Net purchases}$$

Stocks

The final sales figure must take into account the value of stocks. Opening stock is effectively a purchase as these will be sold in the current trading period. On the other hand, closing stock must be deducted from the purchases as these will be sold next year.

Cost of sales

The calculation for cost of sales, including a full set of adjustments to purchases and stocks, would therefore be:

$$\text{Opening stock} + \text{Purchases} + \text{Carriage inwards}$$
$$- \text{Returns outwards} - \text{Closing stock}$$
$$= \text{Cost of sales}$$

We can show all these with an example:

The trading account of D. Gough for the year ended 31 December 2004

	£	£	£
Sales			21,000
Less: Returns inwards			1,000
Net sales			20,000
Opening stock			
(1 January 2001)		4,500	
Purchases	12,100		
Carriage inwards	300		
	12,400		
Less: Returns outwards	500		
Net purchases		11,900	
		16,400	
Less: Closing stock		3,700	
(31 December 2001)			
Cost of sales		12,700	
Gross profit		£7,300	

So far, and with all the organisations we have looked at, we have assumed a gross profit is made. This may not always be the case! If the cost of sales is greater than the net sales figure, an organisation may make a gross loss.

The profit and loss account may be drawn up beneath the trading account and covers the same period of trading. The gross profit (or gross loss)

Prepare accounts for each of the following sets of figures:

1 M. Patel on 31 December 2004. His figures are as follows: closing stock 4,100, returns outwards 700, carriage inwards 400, purchases 15,300, returns inwards 500, opening stock 3,900 and sales 34,800.

2 J. Gallian on 31 December 2004. Her figures are as follows: closing stock 3,200, returns outwards 550, carriage inwards 324, purchases 10,125, returns inwards 650, opening stock 4,789 and sales 15,000.

figure becomes the starting point for the profit and loss account.

Some organisations receive income from sources other than sales. These may be rents received, commission received or profits on the sales of assets. As these are extra income, they are added to the gross profit.

In addition, every organisation incurs expenses and a range of overheads, and these are deducted to show the true net profit (or loss) of the business. These expenses might, for example, include:

* rent of premises

* discount allowed

* gas

* electricity

* stationery

* cleaning costs

* insurances

* business rates

* depreciation

* bad debts

* interest on loans

* sundry expenses

* motor expenses

* accountancy and legal fees.

$$\text{Net profit} = \text{Gross profit} + \text{Income from other sources} - \text{Expenses}$$

Net profit is the final profit in the business and will belong to the owner.

The trading and profit and loss account of D. Gough for the year ended 31 December 2004

	£	£	£
Sales			21,000
Less: Returns inwards			1,000
Net sales			20,000
Opening stock (1 January 2001)		4,500	
Purchases	12,100		
Less: Returns outwards	500		
Net purchases		11,600	
		16,100	
Less: Closing stock (31 December 2001)		3,700	
Cost of sales			12,400
Gross profit			7,600
Add other income:			
Discount received			2,000
			9,600
	£	£	£
Less expenses:			
Electricity		510	
Stationery		125	
Business rate		756	
Interest on loans		159	
Advertising		745	
Depreciation – motor vehicles	1,000		
Insurances		545	
Sundry expenses		124	
Total expenses			3,964
Net profit			£5,636

It is important to note that trading accounts will apply only to organisations who *trade* in goods or who are involved in the process of manufacturing. Service sector businesses (such as a dentist, estate agent or solicitor) will not require a trading account because they are not buying and selling goods. Instead, their final accounts will consist simply of a profit and loss account and a balance sheet. Instead of starting with gross profit, their profit and loss account will start by listing the various forms of income, such as fees received:

The balance sheet

Whereas the trading account provides an ongoing picture, a balance sheet is a snapshot of what an organisation owns and owes on a particular date.

A balance sheet is a clear statement of the assets, liabilities and capital of a business at a particular moment in time (normally at the end of an accounting period, e.g. quarter, year, etc.).

Looking at the balance sheet can thus provide valuable information because it summarises a business's financial position at that instant in time.

The balance sheet balances because the accounts record every transaction twice. For example, if you lend me £100 we can say that:

* I owe you £100 (a liability or debt)

* I now have £100 (an asset, something I own).

Look at the balance sheet of D. Bicknell. As you can see, a balance sheet is represented by a simple formula that underlies all accounting activity:

Assets = Liabilities + Capital

At the end of a trading period a business will have a number of assets and liabilities. Some of these will be for short periods of time while others will be for longer periods. Whatever the nature of the individual assets and liabilities, the balance sheet will balance.

As you work through this section, look at the balance sheet illustrated below:

The balance sheet of D. Bicknell as at 31 December 2004

	£	£	£
Fixed assets			
Land and buildings			80,000
Machinery			13,200
Motor vehicles			8,700
			101,900
Current assets			
Stocks		9,700	
Debtors		3,750	
Bank		2,100	
Cash		970	
		16,520	
Less: Current liabilities			
Creditors	8,000		
Value Added Tax owing	1,000	9,000	
Working capital/net current assets			7,520
			109,420
Less: Long-term liabilities			
Bank loan	9,000		
Mortgage	30,000		
			39,000
Net assets			£70,420
Financed by:			
Capital		70,000	
Add: Net profit		5,286	
		75,286	
Less: Drawings		4,866	
			£70,420

Every balance sheet will have a heading containing the name of the organisation as well as the date upon which the snapshot is taken.

Final accounts of a limited company

So far, our analysis of accounts has centred on those of a sole trader. Before looking further at how to interpret and analyse financial information, we are going to look at another type of business organisation, that of a company. Accounts of a company are prepared on a similar basis to those for a sole trader, but there are some important differences in the appropriation of profit and in the organisation's capital structure.

As we have seen, a limited company has:

* A legal identity separate from that of its owners.

* Owners who are known as shareholders and who have limited liability.

* A management that is delegated to a board of directors, who may or may not be shareholders.
* A commitment to pay Corporation Tax on any profits made.

Companies must comply with the Companies Acts, and the Companies Registration Office controls their formation. There are two types of limited companies:

* Public, which have their shares traded on the Stock Exchange
* Private, for which there are restrictions on the trading in their shares.

One clause of the Memorandum of Association states the share capital of the company and indicates how it is to be divided into separate shares. Authorised share capital is the amount the shareholders have authorised the directors to issue. Issued share capital is the amount that has actually been issued by the directors.

Using www.heinemann.co.uk/hotlinks (express code 1130P, then go to Unit 2), visit the London Stock Exchange website and you will see there are a number of types of securities. These may include:

* Ordinary shares – dividends/profits for these are normally expressed as a percentage of the nominal value of the shares or as a monetary value per share
* Preference shares – these carry a preferential right to receive a dividend
* Debentures – these are split into units in the same way as shares but are, in effect, loans to the company that may be secured on specific assets.

A company's capital is split into shares that are recorded at a nominal value. Nominal values might be at 5p, 10p, 25p, 50p or £1. For example, a company with 10,000 shares issued at a nominal value of £0.50 has a share capital of £5,000, and this would be disclosed in the capital section of the balance sheet. The difference between the issue price paid by the shareholder and the nominal value is called the share premium.

Limited companies rarely distribute all their profits. A proportion is usually retained in the form of reserves. There are two forms of reserves:

* Revenue reserves – These are usually left as the balance of the 'profit and loss account' or 'retained profits'. To give shareholders confidence in the funding of the business, directors may decide to transfer some of the profit and loss account balance into a general reserve.
* Capital reserves – They may include revaluation reserves that occur when property is revalued and also share premium, the value of the higher amount than the nominal value of shares.

The trading account of a limited company is similar to the trading account of any other type of organisation. However, in the profit and loss account:

* Directors' fees or salaries may be included, because these people are employed by the company and their fees and salaries are an expense.
* Debenture payments, being the same as loan interest, may also appear as an expense.

Beneath the profit and loss account of a company will appear the appropriation account. This is designed to show what happens to any profit and how it is divided. An appropriation account for a company with a net profit of £250,000 would look like this:

	£	£
Net profit		250,000
Less: Corporation Tax		100,000
Profit after taxation		150,000
Less: Proposed dividends		
Ordinary shares	70,000	
Preference shares	20,000	90,000
		60,000
Less: Transfer to general reserve		40,000
		20,000
Add: Retained profit from previous year		30,000
Balance of retained profit carried forward		50,000

Corporation tax is the first charge on profits and has to be paid to the Inland Revenue. Proposed dividends are the portion of the profits paid to the shareholders. After dividends have been paid, it is possible to allocate profits to reserves. Any profit left over at the end of the year, after taxes and shareholders of all kinds have been paid, is added to the balance of profit from the previous year to give the new retained profit:

Balance of profit at end of year =
Net profit from current year +
Retained profits from previous years
− Corporation Tax − Transfers to reserves − Dividends

In the balance sheet of a company, the fixed and current assets are presented in the same way as in any other balance sheet.

The current liabilities are the liabilities due to be paid within 12 months of the date of the balance sheet. In addition to those which normally appear in this section, limited companies also have to show Corporation Tax that is due to be paid during the next 12 months, as well as ordinary and preference share dividends to be paid. Long-term liabilities may include debentures.

Learning activity

Chris Read Ltd has just announced a net profit of £300,000. Prepare the appropriation account for the end of December 2005 from the following details:

✱ The taxation rate is 25%.

✱ There are 500,000 ordinary shares of £1 each.

✱ A dividend of 10% is proposed.

✱ There are 300,000 10% preference shares of £1 each, fully paid. The 10% dividend is to be paid.

✱ £50,000 is to be transferred to the general reserve.

✱ Retained profit from the previous year was £125,000.

At the beginning of the 'Financed by' section of the balance sheet, details will appear of the authorised capital, specifying the type, value and number of shares the company is authorised to issue. These are in the balance sheet for interest only and their value is excluded from the totals. 'Issued capital' contains details of the classes and numbers of shares that have been issued (obviously, the issued share capital cannot exceed the authorised).

Reserves are shown beneath the capital. Reserves and retained profits are the amounts the

The balance sheet of Wargrave Ltd as at 31 December 2004

	£	£	£
Fixed assets			
Land and buildings			320,000
Machinery			24,000
Motor vehicles			12,000
			356,000
Current assets			
Stocks		12,250	
Debtors		7,100	
Bank		23,200	
Cash		500	
		43,050	
Less: Current liabilities			
Creditors		500	
Proposed dividends:			
Ordinary shares	12,000		
Preference shares	10,000		
Corporation Tax	10,350	32,850	
Working capital/			
net current assets			10,200
			366,200
Less: Long-term liabilities			
Bank loan		10,000	
10% debentures		8,000	
			18,000
Net assets			348,200
Financed by			
Authorised share capital			
400,000 ordinary shares of £1			400,000
100,000 10% preference			
shares of £1			100,000
			500,000
Issued share capital			
200,000 ordinary shares			
of £1 fully paid			200,000
100,000 10% preference			
shares of £1 fully paid			100,000
			300,000
Reserves			
General reserve		6,000	
Balance of retained profit		42,200	
		48,200	
Shareholders' funds			348,200

directors and shareholders decide to keep within the company. Shareholders' funds comprise the total of share capital plus reserves.

Cash flow forecasting

Whereas profit is a surplus from trading activities, cash is a liquid asset that enables an organisation to buy the goods and services it requires in order to add value to them, trade and make profits. It is therefore possible for an organisation to be profitable while, at the same time, creditors have not been paid and liquid resources have not been properly accounted for.

On the other hand, an organisation must look carefully to see that its use of cash is to its best advantage. For example, if it holds too much cash in the bank, it might be sacrificing the potential to earn greater income.

An organisation must therefore ensure it has sufficient cash to carry out its plans and that the cash coming in is sufficient to cover the cash going out. At the same time it must take into account any cash surpluses it might have in the bank.

Looking carefully at the availability of liquid funds is essential to the smooth running of any organisation. With cash planning or budgeting it is possible to forecast the flows into and out of an organisation's bank account so that any surpluses or deficits can be highlighted and any necessary action can be taken promptly. For example, overdraft facilities may be arranged in good time so funds are available when required.

The cash flow forecast is an extremely important tool within an organisation and has a number of clear purposes. For example:

✱ The forecast can be used to highlight the timing consequences of different expenditures, ensuring that facilities, such as an overdraft, can be set up to pay bills.

✱ The cash flow forecast (see example in Figure 2.34) is an essential document for the compilation of the business plan. It will help to show whether the organisation is capable of achieving the objectives it sets. This is very important if the business applies for finance, where the lender will almost certainly want to know about the ability of the applicant to keep on top of the cash flow and meet the proposed payment schedules.

✱ The cash flow forecast will help to boost the lender's confidence and the owner's confidence. By looking into the future it will provide them with the reassurance they

	JULY	AUG	SEPT	OCT	NOV	DEC
Receipts						
Sales	900	1,125	1,350	825	2,100	1,950
Total receipts	900	1,125	1,350	825	2,100	1,950
Payments						
Raw materials	520	600	580	640	680	640
Direct labour	400	650	650	750	725	800
Variable expenses	300	420	520	560	590	610
Fixed expenses	50	50	50	50	50	50
Total payments	1,270	1,720	1,800	2,000	2,045	2,100
Receipts – payments	(370)	(595)	(450)	(1,175)	55	(150)
Balance b/f	4,500	4,130	3,535	3,085	1,910	1,965
Balance c/f	4,130	3,535	3,085	1,910	1,965	1,815

FIGURE 2.34 *Example of a cash flow forecast*

require that their plans are going according to schedule.

* It will also help with the monitoring of performance. The cash flow forecast sets benchmarks against which the business is expected to perform. If the organisation actually performs differently from these benchmarks, the cash flow forecast may have highlighted an area for investigation. As we have seen, investigating differences between forecast figures and actual figures is known as variance analysis.

To prepare a cash flow forecast you need to know what receipts and payments are likely to take place in the future and exactly when they will occur. It is important to know the length of the lead-time between incurring an expense and paying for it, as well as the time lag between making a sale and collecting the money from debtors. The art of successful forecasting is being able to calculate receipts and expenditures accurately.

When working though a cash flow forecast, it is important to look carefully at the timing of every entry.

For example, C. Moon Ltd has £500 in the bank on 1 January. The owner, Christine Moon, anticipates that her receipts over the next six months are likely to be:

JAN	FEB	MARCH	APRIL	MAY	JUNE
£2,300	£1,400	£5,300	£6,100	£4,700	£1,400

She has also worked out what her payments are likely to be over the next six months:

JAN	FEB	MARCH	APRIL	MAY	JUNE
£1,400	£4,100	£5,600	£5,000	£3,100	£900

Christine Moon is concerned about whether she needs an overdraft facility and, if so, when she is likely to use it. Construct a cash flow forecast and advise her on her financial requirements.

The forecast shows that C. Moon Ltd needs to set up an overdraft facility between the months of February and April.

	JAN £	FEB £	MAR £	APR £	JUNE £	JULY £
Balance	500	1,400	(1,300)	(1,600)	(500)	1,100
Receipts	2,300	1,400	5,300	6,100	4,700	1,400
	2,800	2,800	4,000	4,500	4,200	2,500
Payments	1,400	4,100	5,600	5,000	3,100	900
	1,400	(1,300)	(1,600)	(500)	1,100	1,600

Budgeting

As well as recording financial information and making judgements about the effectiveness of the information, businesses need to manage their finances. The two main elements of financial management are budgeting and cash flow.

Budgets help businesses to plan, set targets and control expenditure. To understand how budgets are used you need to know what they are, how they work and their particular purposes. You will need to be able to identify and interpret variance and explain the benefits of budgeting to businesses.

Businesses need to control their working capital. To understand how they can do this you need to know what working capital is and how businesses manage their cash. You also need to know that businesses may have cash flow problems and that they need to be solved. This

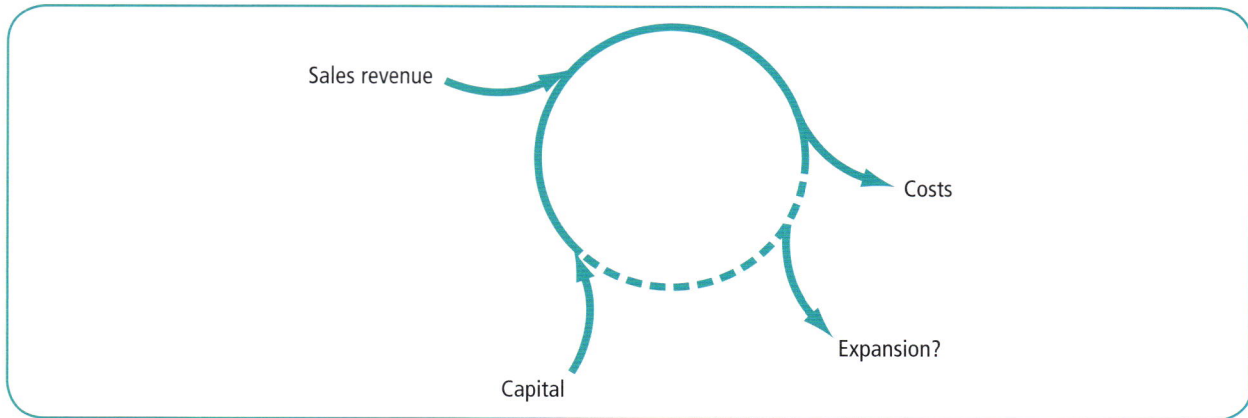

FIGURE 2.35 *The 'money-go-round'*

involves examining credit control and other methods businesses use to maintain their working capital.

Financial planning involves defining objectives and then developing ways to achieve them. To be able to do this, a financial manager must have a realistic understanding of what is happening and what is likely to happen within the organisation – for example, when is money going to come in, what is it needed for and would it be possible to use some of it for expansion and development? In the 'money-go-round' (see Figure 2.35), capital and sales revenue come into a business, but is there enough left over, after paying all the costs, for expansion and development?

Looking into their future helps all organisations to plan their activities so that what they anticipate and want to happen can actually happen. This process of financial planning is known as budgeting. It is considered to be a system of responsibility accounting because it puts an onus on budgeted areas to perform in a way that has been outlined for them, and its success will depend upon the quality of information provided. Businesses that do not budget may not be pleased when they view their final accounts. Budgeting helps the financial manager to develop an understanding of how the business is likely to perform in the future.

We all budget to a greater or lesser extent. Our short-term budget may relate to how we are going to get through the coming week and do all the things we want to do. Our slightly longer-term budget may involve being able to afford

CASE STUDY

Managing Student Finances

One of the big problems for most students today is how to manage their finances effectively. In order to be able to spread their income and student loan across all of their financial responsibilities students need to be both sensible and resourceful. Students have many different financial commitments and yet for many of them, it is the first time away from home in a different environment and a situation where they have to manage money for the first time. Some of the consequences of not managing their money can be quite serious.

1 Why is it important for students to budget?
2 What practical steps could they take to budget?

Christmas presents in two months' time. Our longest-term budget could involve the planning necessary to afford the car tax, MOT and motor insurance, which are all due ten months from now. Also, when can we afford in the longer term to replace the car?

In exactly the same way, businesses try to see far into the future. The problem is that, the further one looks into the future, the more difficult it is to see it accurately.

A budget is a financial plan developed for the future. Many businesses appoint a budget controller whose sole task is to co-ordinate budgetary activities. A short-term budget would be for up to one year, a medium-term budget would be for anything from one year to five years and a budget for a longer period than this would be a long-term budget.

Wherever budgeting takes place, it is important to draw upon the collective experience of people throughout the business. A budgeting team might consist of representatives from various areas of activity. The team will consider the objectives of the budgeting process, obtain and provide relevant information, make decisions, prepare budgets and then use these budgets to help to control the business.

Budgeting provides a valuable benchmark against which to measure and judge the actual performance of key areas of business activity. There are therefore many benefits of budgeting:

* It helps to predict what the organisation thinks will happen. Given the experience within the organisation, budgets help to show what is likely to take place in the future.

* Budgets create opportunities to appraise alternative courses of action. Information created for budgeting purposes forms the basis of decisions that have to be taken. The research necessary for budgeting will look at alternative ways of achieving the organisation's objectives.

* Budgets set targets. If communicated to people throughout the organisation, the budgets will help them to work towards the targets that have been set.

* They help to monitor and control performance. This can be done by studying actual results,

comparing these to budgeted results and then finding out why differences (known as variances) may have occurred. Sometimes variances are bad, while at other times they may be good. Whatever the causes of the variances, they are a useful starting point for dealing with issues within the business.

* Budgets are fundamental to the process of business planning. They provide a series of quantitative guidelines that can be used for co-ordination and then followed in order to achieve the organisation's business objectives.

* They can be used as a source of motivation. As part of the consultation process, budgets help to keep people involved. They also help to create goal congruence, so that the aims and objectives of the individual are the same as those for the organisation.

* Budgets are a form of communication. They enable employees from across the organisation to be aware of performance expectations with regard to their individual work area.

Budgeting may also have some useful spin-offs. Every year the business is reviewed and this gives members of the various departments a better understanding of the working of the organisation as a whole. In fact, by participating in the budgetary process they feel their experience is contributing to policy decisions.

It also increases co-operation between departments and lowers departmental barriers. In this way members of one department can become aware of the difficulties facing another department. By being involved in the budgetary process, non-accountants also appreciate the importance of costs.

In reality, budgeting may take place in almost all parts of an organisation. Budgeting should also be viewed as something that is going on all the time and as a source of useful information and guidance for managers.

The process of budget setting

The process of setting budgets has to be seen within the context of the longer-term objectives and strategies at the highest level of management of any organisation. The administration of the budgeting process will usually be the responsibility of the accounts department. Many organisations set up a budget committee to oversee the process.

The budgetary process is usually governed by a formal budget timetable. This helps to link the budget in with all other aspects of business planning (see Figure 2.36).

The accounts department is involved at all stages of the budgeting process, and an effective accounts team will provide a range of advice to managers as the exercise develops. Spreadsheets are an effective 'what-if' tool that are often used to help within the budgeting process.

Setting up a system of 'responsibility accounting' such as budgeting involves breaking down an organisation into a series of 'control centres'. Each individual manager then has the responsibility for managing the budget relating to his or her particular control centre.

Budgetary reports, therefore, reflect the assigned responsibility at each level of the organisation. As all organisations have a structure of control, it is important the budgetary system fits around this. The reports should be designed to reflect the different levels within the organisation and the responsibilities of each of the managers concerned.

If the budgeting process reflects the different levels of control, managers will be kept informed not just of their own performance but also of that of other budget holders for whom they are responsible. They will also know that managers above them will be assessing their performance. This system can be reviewed regularly at meetings attended by all the individual managers concerned (see Figure 2.37).

Although it could be claimed that they are mechanistic, budget models formalise the inter-relationships between departments and provide

Learning activity

Find out more about the budgeting process within your school or college. For example, how are budgets set, what processes take place and who are the budget holders? What happens if budget holders overspend?

BUDGET TIMETABLE FOR YEAR 1 APRIL 2005 TO 31 MARCH 2006		
Date	Narrative	Responsibility
1 Sept	Board of directors to review long-term objectives and strategies and specify short term goals for the year	Directors
22 Sept	Budget guidelines and standard forms issued to line managers	Accounts
6 Oct	Actual results for year are issued to line management, so that comparisons can be made with current budget and last year's actual results	Accounts
20 Oct	Budget submissions are made to the management accountant	Line management
27 Oct	First draft of the master budget is issued	Accounts
3 Nov	First draft of the budget is reviewed for results and consistency – line managers to justify their submissions	MD and individual directors
7 Nov	New assumptions and guidelines issued to line management	Accounts
10 Nov	Budgets revised and resubmitted	Line management
21 Nov	Second draft of master budget issued	Accounts
28 Nov	Final review of the draft budget	Managing Director and financial director
1 Dec	Final amendments	Accounts
12 Dec	Submission to the board for their approval	Financial director

FIGURE 2.36 *A budget timetable*

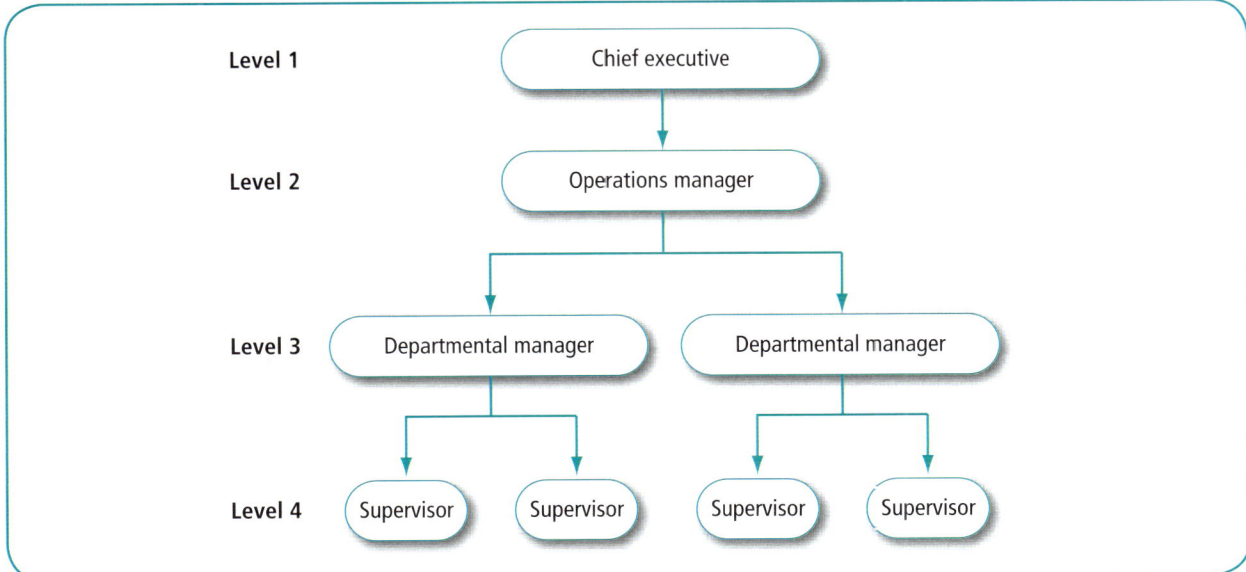

FIGURE 2.37 *A reporting hierarchy*

a basic understanding of work flows within business organisations.

The overall budget as a plan will have real value only if the performance levels set through the budget are realistic. Budgets based upon ideal conditions are unlikely to be met and will result in departments failing to meet their targets. For example, the sales department may fail to achieve their sales budget, which may result in goods remaining unsold. Budgets can be motivating only if they are pitched at a realistic level.

There are two approaches to budget setting. The top-down approach involves senior managers specifying what the best performance indicators are for the business across all departments and budgeted areas. The bottom-up approach builds up the organisational master budget on the basis of the submissions of individual line managers and supervisors, based upon their own views of their requirements. In practice most organisations use a mixture of both methods (see Figure 2.38).

Budget setting should be based upon realistic predictions of future sales and costs. Many organisations base future predictions solely on past figures, with adjustments for forecast growth and inflation rates. Although the main advantage of this approach is that budgets are based upon actual data, future conditions may not mirror past ones.

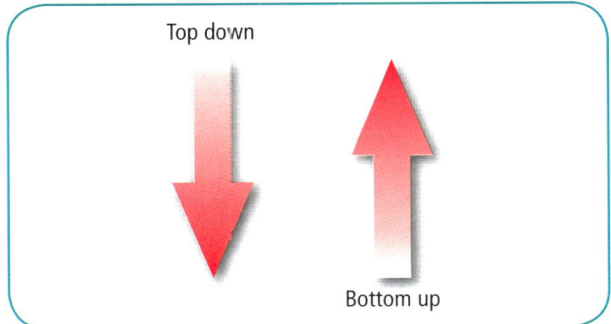

FIGURE 2.38 *Approaches to budget setting*

One of the dangers of budgeting is that, if actual results are dramatically different from the budgeting ones, the process could lose its credibility as a means of control. Following a budget too rigidly may also restrict a business's activities. For example, if the budget for entertainment has been exceeded and subsequent visiting customers are not treated with the usual hospitality, orders may be lost. On the other hand, if managers realise that towards the end of the year a department has underspent, they may decide to go on a spending spree.

Budgeting is a routine annual event for many different types of organisations. The process may start in the middle of the financial year, with a revision of the current year's budget and with first drafts of the budget for the coming year. Some organisations plan further ahead with an outline plan for 3–5 years.

Using budgetary control variances

Budgets provide an opportunity for everyone to play a part in either the strategic or tactical development of the organisation. As the activities following the budgetary process unfold, they provide a benchmark against which actual performance can be measured and judged.

As a result, an essential feature of the budgetary control system is the feedback of actual results. The process of measuring the difference between budgeted (intended) and actual outcomes is known as variance analysis. Variance analysis makes it possible to detect problems. Reasons can be sought for variances and speedy action can be taken to improve performance.

Budgeting should be viewed as something that is going on all the time and as a source of useful information and guidance for managers.

Creating budgets

In practice, budgeting may take place in almost all parts of an organisation. The money values attached to budgets are often linked to quantities, such as units, weights and other forms of measurement. This also helps to tie the budgeting process in with operational activities so that the budget can be used as a management tool. We shall discuss three key areas of budgetary forecasts:

* *The capital budget* The word 'capital' refers to the buying of fixed assets. Do we plan now for the money we will need in the future to buy another machine? The capital budget is a simple statement of intent or forecast, which specifies the planned purchase of assets, the date of intended purchase and the expected cost of purchase.

* *The cash budget or cash flow forecast* This forecast looks at the cash coming in to the organisation as well as the cash going out. It is a prediction by a business of how much money it thinks it will receive and how much it thinks it will pay out over a specified time. By forecasting cash flow, managers will know what their future

financial requirements will be and will be able to take action beforehand if they need an overdraft or some form of loan.

* *Subsidiary budgets and the master budget* Functional budgets for different business activities and budgets for individual balance sheet items are called subsidiary budgets. The exact nature of subsidiary budgets will depend on the organisational structure and the operational processes of an organisation. The term 'master budget' includes the budgeted profit and loss account, balance sheet and cash budget.

The capital budget

Capital expenditure refers to the acquisition of fixed assets. Capital budgets are prepared to plan for the purchase of fixed assets.

The capital budget is prepared after reviewing fixed asset needs for the budget period. This will be done in the light of business objectives and planned strategy for the next budget period. The next step is to consider the condition and capacity of existing fixed assets. For example, a planned expansion into new markets will require a review of existing assets to ensure sufficient business capacity is available. Capital expenditure may also be required to renew existing assets, such as worn-out equipment. In recognising that more fixed assets are required, it is necessary to plan their purchase, including the time and cost of acquisition.

It follows from the nature of this type of expenditure that some years will require more capital expenditure than others. Together with the fact that, for many businesses, the value of fixed assets used is significant, it is important capital budgets are prepared to ensure adequate finance is planned.

Classifications of capital expenditure will follow those you are already familiar with from constructing the fixed assets section of the balance sheet. Typically they include:

* land and buildings
* factory plant and machinery
* office fixtures and fittings

* computer equipment
* motor vehicles.

Expenditure may be further analysed into assets required for:

* expansion of existing product ranges
* expansion into new products
* replacement of existing assets
* satisfying health and safety requirements.

In this way information is provided as to whether the business is expanding or just maintaining its productive capacity. It may also indicate whether items of capital expenditure are essential or merely desirable.

Look at the capital budget of Jason Robards (see Figure 2.39). The forecast shows that, over the year, £50,000 is needed for a CNC machine, £20,000 for two motor vans, £5,500 for a new computer, £50,000 for a new building extension, £40,000 for improving the production line and £9,500 for installing a new air conditioning system. The capital budget quickly provides an indication that £175,000 is needed for capital purchases for the year and then itemises amounts required month by month.

When evaluating expenditure on capital items, the business managers will consider the likely returns on making the investment and the associated risk of not reaping the hoped-for benefits. The cost of purchasing assets should be evaluated against a range of benefits such as increased sales or reduced costs. In many cases it is necessary to perform a cost–benefit analysis to recognise the more qualitative aspects of the proposal. For example, expenditure on welfare facilities (such as employee social clubs and catering facilities) will be evaluated for the

Learning activity

Whitehills Leisure Centre provides customers with a gym, swimming pool and team sports hall. The centre's management is reviewing capital expenditure needs for 2006. They intend to expand facilities during the year with four squash courts and more equipment for the gym. The squash courts will be built in May at a cost of £75,000. The additional gym equipment will comprise three exercise bikes costing £1,000 in March, a rowing machine costing £1,200 in July and weight-lifting equipment costing £2,000 in November.

The receptionist has been complaining about the number of repair visits required recently for the computerised cash till, and so it has been decided to replace this in January at a cost of £1,600.

The floor surface around the swimming pool is too slippery when wet and so the management have decided this should be replaced in January at a cost of £5,000 to minimise the risk of accidents. It has also been decided to refurbish the changing rooms. New lockers and benches will cost £5,000 in June.

Prepare a capital budget for Whitehills Leisure Centre for the year ended 31 December 2006, with separate sections for expansion, replacement and health and safety.

	Jan £	Feb £	March £	April £	May £	June £	July £	Aug £	Sept £	Oct £	Nov £	Dec £	Total £
Replacement													
CNC machine						50,000							50,000
2 motor vans								20,000					20,000
Computer			5,500										5,500
Expansion													
Building extension									50,000				50,000
Production line										40,000			40,000
Health and safety													
Air conditioning		9,500											9,500
Total	0	9,500	5,500	0	0	50,000	0	20,000	50,000	40,000	0	0	175,000

FIGURE 2.39 *A budget timetable for Jason Robards*

goodwill and lower staff turnover such facilities may encourage.

Remember that, even though we are looking at the capital budget and the cash budget individually, all budgets are linked to the master budget. Once prepared, the details from the capital budget are incorporated into the cash budget.

Subsidiary budgets and the master budget

Subsidiary budgets include all parts of a business organisation. When put together they are used to produce the master budget, which includes the profit and loss account, balance sheet and cash budget, all of which help to map the future of a business organisation for the next accounting period.

A key feature of the budgeting process is the feedback it provides for individuals and groups throughout an organisation. Feedback should reflect the information needs of each level of the organisation, with each level of reporting being inter-related with levels above and below. For example, a budget holder will wish to be

Learning activity

The Premier Christmas Pudding Co. require you to prepare their budget statements for the seven months to January 2006. You have been given the following information:

✱ The sales forecast for 1 kg puddings is as follows:

July	Aug	Sept	Oct	Nov	Dec	Total
100	100	500	1,300	10,000	20,000	32,000

✱ No sales of puddings have been made in the previous six months.

✱ Each 1 kg pudding sells for £2.50.

✱ Customers are mainly retailers and wholesalers who take one month to pay for puddings received.

✱ It is company policy to hold a minimum stock of puddings each month that is equivalent to the next month's forecast sales. After December, sales are not forecast until July of the next year. The requisite minimum stock would be held at the end of June, valued at £1.20 per pudding.

✱ Sufficient dry fruits are held in stock to cover the next month's forecast production. Other ingredients are purchased in the month of use.

✱ All suppliers are paid on delivery.

✱ Production capacity is limited to 10,000 kg per month.

✱ Direct labour is employed on a piece-work rate of £0.20 per kg of pudding.

✱ Costs for a 100 kg batch are as follows:

	kg	£
Dried fruit	50	60
Other	50	30
Packaging		10
Distribution		20

✱ The whole period's packaging materials will be received from the printers at the beginning of July. The packaging is of a special design to celebrate the firm's 50th anniversary. In case sales exceed forecast, sufficient packaging for 35,000 puddings has been ordered. Excess packaging is to be disposed of in December.

✱ Administration overhead is fixed at £3,000 per month and is payable up to the end of January 2006.

✱ The bank balance at the end of June 2005 is forecast to be £15,930.

✱ No losses are assumed in the production process.

For each of the seven months up to 31 January 2006, prepare:

1 The sales budget

2 The finished stock and production budget

3 The raw materials stock and purchases budget (separate for mixed fruit, packaging and other)

4 The direct labour budget

5 The cash budget

6 The forecast trading and profit and loss account.

informed of his or her own performance as well as that of the budget holders for whom he or she is responsible.

Variance analysis

Earlier in this chapter we looked at the construction of budgets related to functional aspects of an organisation for the control and monitoring of performance. The key benefit of the budgeting process is to analyse how closely actual performance relates to budgeted performance. Wherever actual differs from budgeted performance a variance takes place. The process of analysing the difference between actual performance and budgeted performance is called variance analysis.

Variances are recorded as being either adverse (A) or favourable (F), depending upon whether actual expenditure is more or less than budget. For example, if actual expenditure is less than

> ✱ **DID YOU KNOW?**
>
> According to George Spafford, 'We want to do variance analysis in order to learn. One of the easiest and most objective ways to see that things need to change is to watch the financials and ask questions. Don't get me wrong: You cannot and should not base important decisions solely on financial data.'

budgeted expenditure, the variance would be favourable. On the other hand, if actual expenditure is more than budgeted expenditure, the variance is adverse.

Figure 2.40 shows that managers cannot be answerable for cost over-runs if they occur in areas where they have no control. For example, whereas expenditure on machine maintenance may be controlled, this is not true of depreciation, which is outside the manager's control.

Understanding variances

Variances may arise for a number of reasons. These include:

✱ *Random deviations which are uncontrollable* As we saw above, these are outside the control of individual managers.

✱ *An incorrectly set budget* This may require further research and management action.

✱ *Failure to meet an agreed budget* This would be because a manager has failed to meet the appropriate figures and deadlines.

Problems of the budgetary process

Budgetary and control systems vary from one organisation to another. They are found both in the private sector and the public sector, and in all sorts of organisations from the very small

MACHINE SHOP OVERHEAD REPORT FOR OCTOBER 2004	Budget £	Actual £	Variance £	
Controllable				
Indirect wages	8,000	8,200	200	A
Machine maintenance	2,250	1,900	350	F
Consumable materials	500	550	50	A
Total controllable costs	10,750	10,650	100	F
Uncontrollable				
Depreciation	5,700	6,000	300	A
Property cost apportionment	8,500	9,000	500	A
Total uncontrollable costs	14,200	15,000	800	A
Total cost centre overhead	24,950	25,650	700	A
A = Adverse				
F = Favourable				

FIGURE 2.40 *Controllable and uncontrollable costs*

to the very large. Given the different aims of organisations, budgetary systems reflect the context in which they are put to use. There are, however, certain problems associated with budgeting processes that have to be recognised.

First, reliance upon budgeting and its processes is no substitute for good management. Budgeting should simply be viewed as one tool among many for managers to use. If forecasting is poor or inadequate allowances are made, the process may create unnecessary pressure upon managers to perform in a particular way. This may be stressful and cause antagonism and resentment within the organisation.

The creation of rigid financial plans that are 'cast in stone' may cause inertia in certain parts of a business and reduce its ability to adapt to change. Budgets may also not reflect the realities of the business environment and act simply as a straitjacket upon the performance of managers and decision-makers. It has also been argued that delays and time lags can make it difficult to compare budgeted and actual results.

Break-even analysis

Before looking at break-even analysis we need a basic understanding of costs. One method of classifying costs is according to changes in output. This identifies costs as either fixed or variable.

Fixed costs are costs that do not increase as total output increases. For example, if an organisation has the capacity needed it might increase its production from 25,000 units to 30,000 units. However its fixed costs such as rent, rates, heating and lighting will be the same, since they also had to be paid when the organisation was producing 25,000 units.

In contrast variable costs are those costs that increase as total output increases because more of these factors need to be employed as inputs in order to increase outputs. For example, if you produce more items you need more raw materials.

The **break-even point** is the point at which sales levels are high enough not to make a loss, but not high enough to make a profit.

The concept of break-even is a development from the principles of *marginal costing*. Marginal costing is a commonly employed technique that uses costs to forecast profits from the production and sales levels expected in future periods. The benefit of marginal costing over other costing methods is that it overcomes the problem of allocating fixed costs – only variable costs are allocated as we shall see.

The difference between an item's selling price and the variable costs needed to produce that item is know as *contribution*.

Contribution = Selling price per unit *less* variable costs per unit

By producing and selling enough units to produce a total contribution that is in excess of *fixed costs*, an organisation will make a profit.

For example, Penzance Toys Ltd manufactures plastic train sets for young children. They anticipate that next year they will sell 8,000 units at £12 per unit. Their variable costs are £5 per unit and their fixed costs are £9,000. From the above formula we can deduce that the contribution is £12 minus £5, which is £7 per unit. Therefore, for each unit made, £7 will go towards paying the fixed costs. We can also see this using totals to show how much profit will be made if the company sells 8,000 units. The problem can also be looked at by constructing a table, as follows:

Units of production	Fixed costs (£)	Variable costs (£)	Total costs (£)	Revenue (£)	Profit (loss) (£)
1,000	9,000	5,000	14,000	12,000	(2,000)
2,000	9,000	10,000	19,000	24,000	5,000
3,000	9,000	15,000	24,000	36,000	12,000
4,000	9,000	20,000	29,000	48,000	19,000
5,000	9,000	25,000	34,000	60,000	26,000
6,000	9,000	30,000	39,000	72,000	33,000
7,000	9,000	35,000	44,000	84,000	40,000
8,000	9,000	40,000	49,000	96,000	47,000
9,000	9,000	45,000	54,000	108,000	54,000
10,000	9,000	50,000	59,000	120,000	61,000

FIGURE 2.41 *Profit increases as the units of production increase*

	£
Sales revenue (8000 x £12)	96,000
Less: Marginal costs (8000 x £5)	40,000
Total contribution	56,000
Less: Fixed costs	9,000
Net profit	47,000

How break-even analysis helps monitor business performance

Marginal costing is particularly useful for making short-term decisions – for example, helping to set the selling price of a product, or deciding whether or not to accept an order. It might also help an organisation to decide whether to buy in a component or whether to produce it themselves.

Break-even analysis is a concept that is central to the process of marginal costing. Breaking even is the unique point at which an organisation neither makes profit or loss. If sales go beyond the break-even point, profits are made, and if they are below the break-even point, losses are made. In marginal costing terms, it is the *point at which the contribution equals the fixed costs*.

Calculating and interpreting break-even charts

To calculate the break-even point there are two stages:

Calculate the unit contribution (selling price less variable cost per unit)

Divide the fixed costs by the unit contribution:

$$\text{Break-even point} = \frac{\text{Fixed costs}}{\text{Unit contribution}}$$

For example, in Penzance Toys Ltd the contribution per unit is £7 and the fixed costs are £9,000. The break-even point would therefore be:

$$\frac{9,000}{7} = 1,286 \text{ units (to nearest unit)}$$

The *sales value* at the break-even point can be calculated by multiplying the number of units by the selling price per unit. For Penzance Toys this would be:

$$1,286 \times £12 = £15,432$$

Hussey and family Ltd is a small business selling hives to local beekeepers. Each hive is sold for £25. Fixed costs are £18,000 and variable costs are £13 per unit. The company wishes to achieve a profit of £18,000. Calculate the break-even point in both units and sales value. Calculate both the units and sales value necessary to achieve the selected operating profit.

Penzance Toys have covered their costs (fixed and variable) and broken even with a sales value of £15,432. Anything sold in excess of this will provide them with profits.

If an organisation has a *profit target* or selecting operating point to aim at, break-even analysis can be used to calculate the number of units that need to be sold and the value of sales required to achieve that target.

For example, we can image that Penzance Toys wish to achieve a target of £15,000 profit. By adding this £15,000 to the fixed costs and dividing by the contribution, the number of units can be found that need to be sold to meet this target. Thus:

£9,000 + £15,000 = 3,429 units (to nearest unit)

The difference between the break-even point and the selected level of activity designed to achieve the profit target is known as the *margin of safety*.

A break-even chart can be used to show changes in the relationship between costs, production volumes and various levels of sales activity. The following is the procedure to construct a break-even chart:

* Label the horizontal axis for units of production and sales

* Label the vertical axis to represent the values of sales and costs

* Plot fixed costs. Fixed costs will remain the same over all levels of production, so plot this as a straight line parallel to the horizontal axis

* Plot the total costs (variable and fixed costs). This will be a line rising from where the fixed cost line touches the vertical axis. It is plotted by calculating the total costs at two or three random levels of production

* Sales are then plotted by taking two or three random levels of turnover. The line will rise from the intersection of the two axes.

The break-even point will be where the total cost line and the sales line intersect. The area to the *left* of the break-even point between the sales and total cost lines will represent *losses*, and the area to the *right* of the break-even point between these lines will represent *profit*.

For example, Eddie Bowen plans to set up a small restaurant. In doing so he knows he will immediately incur annual fixed costs of £10,000. He is concerned about how many meals he will have to sell to break even. Extensive market research indicates a typical customer will pay £8 for a meal, and Eddie knows that variable costs (such as cooking ingredients and the costs of serving customers) will amount to about £3. Eddie has set himself a profit target of £14,000 for the first year of operation. Our task is to advise Eddie on the number of meals he has to sell and to indicate to him his margin of safety.

Eddie's *unit contribution* is:

£8 − £3 (Selling price − Variable cost) = £5 per meal

His *break-even point* in units will be:

£10,000 (Fixed costs) divided by £5 unit contribution = 2,000 meals

The *sales value* of the meals will be:

2,000 meals x £8 (Selling price) = £16,000

His *profit target* will be achieved by:

$$\frac{£10,000 \text{ (Fixed costs)} + £14,000 \text{ (Profit Target)}}{£5 \text{ (Unit contribution)}} = 4,800 \text{ meals}$$

The *margin of safety* will be the difference between the selected level of activity and the break-even point. It will be between 4,800 meals with a turnover of £38,400 and 2,000 meals with a turnover of £16,000.

The three random levels of variable costs and sales chosen for the purpose of plotting the break-even chart are at 1,000 meals, 3,000 meals and 5,000 meals. They are:

	1,000 MEALS £	3,000 MEALS £	5,000 MEALS £
Variable costs (£3 per meal)	3,000	9,000	15,000
Fixed costs	10,000	10,000	10,000
Total costs	13,000	19,000	25,000
Sales	8,000	24,000	40,000

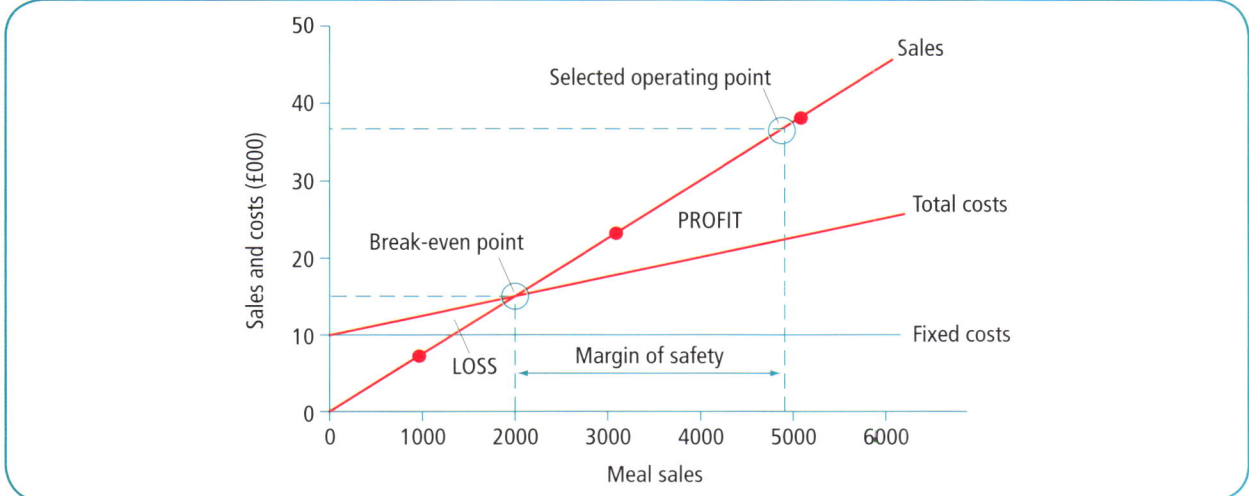

FIGURE 2.42 *Eddie Bowen's break-even chart*

We can now plot the break-even chart (Figure 2.42) which shows graphically the break-even point of 2,000 meals with a sales revenue of £16,000. The margin of safety can be seen on the chart if we identify the selected level of profit (at 4,800 meals) and the targeted turnover (of £38,400), and compare this point with the break-even point.

The break-even chart is a simple visual tool enabling managers to anticipate the effects of changes in production and sales upon the profitability of an organisation's activities. It emphasises the importance of earning revenue and is particularly helpful for those who are unused to interpreting accounting information.

How changes in variables such as fixed costs affect break-even

The break-even chart can be used to explore changes in a number of key variables. These may include:

* *Sales volume and value* By looking at the chart it is possible to predict the effects of changes in

sales trends. For example, a sudden fall in sales may lead to a loss and a sudden increase may improve profitability.

* *Profits or losses at a given level of production* The break-even chart enables a business to monitor levels of production. By doing this, important decisions can be made if changes take place.

* *Prices* It is possible to use the break-even chart to analyse different business scenarios. For example, given market research information, what would happen if we reduced the price by £2.

* *Costs* The effects of any sudden change in costs can be plotted on the break-even chart.

Any of the above may affect an organisation's ability to achieve its selected operating point and margin of safety. The break-even chart is thus a useful management tool upon which to base action that enables an organisation to achieve its plans.

John Smith had a visit from an aged relative who wanted advice. For many years she had run a small hotel in a market town in the Thames Valley. After careful consideration she had decided to 'call it a day' and retire, but she was keen to see the business continue and wished to retain her ownership in it.

John is interested in a proposition she has put forward, which involves running the hotel on her behalf. The hotel has been allowed to deteriorate over the years and, in John's opinion, it is obvious that extensive refurbishment is necessary before he could realistically consider her proposal. The hotel is, however, in a prime spot, was extensively used little more than ten years ago, and John feels that, with hard work, it has the potential to become successful again.

He has arranged a number of quotations to be made for the building work. The most favourable received was for £180,000, which involved extensive interior redecoration and refurbishment as well as completely reorganising the reception and kitchen areas.

John's intention is that the finance for the building work should come from a five-year bank loan with a fixed annual interest rate of 10%, payable each calendar month, and based upon the original sum. The loan principal would be paid back in five equal annual instalments. He has estimated the following fixed and variable costs:

Fixed

* Annual loan repayment £36,000
* Annual interest on loan £18,000
* Business rate and water rates £7,000 per annum
* Insurance £4,500 per annum
* Electricity £1,300 per quarter
* Staff salaries £37,000 per annum.

Variable

These include direct labour (such as cleaners and bar staff), as well as the cost of food, bar stocks, etc. After careful research John has estimated these to be £2,000 for each 100 customers who visit the hotel.

John has had a local agency conduct an extensive market research survey and feels confident that the hotel will attract about 100 customers per week, who will each spend on average (including accommodation, food and drinks) about £70 in the hotel.

Work out the break-even point for the hotel in both numbers of customers and value.

Work out the numbers of customers required to make a gross profit of £35,000.

Draw a break-even chart showing the break-even point, the profit target and the margin of safety.

What other information might John Smith require before deciding to go ahead with the project?

The limitations of break-even analysis

Break-even analysis is often considered by some to oversimplify organisational behaviour by reducing it to an equation: how to generate sufficient contribution to cover fixed costs and provide a surplus (profits).

The limitations are as follows:

* It can be argued that, in real situations, fixed costs actually vary with different levels of activity, and so a stepped fixed cost line would provide a more accurate guide.

* Many organisations fail to break even because of a limiting factor restricting their ability to do so (e.g. a shortage of space, labour or orders).

* The variable cost and sales lines are unlikely to be linear (i.e. straight). Discounts, special contracts and overtime payments mean the cost line is more likely to be curved.

* Break-even charts depict short-term relationships, and forecasts are therefore unrealistic when the proposals cover a number of years.

Theme Holidays Ltd is a private company that specialises in providing holidays for adults and children who require a unique form of entertainment. All their holidays involve overseas packages based upon a theme. Half the packages are based upon Disneyland Parks, while the other half are based upon theme destinations in the USA.

Theme Holidays are currently reviewing their profitability for 2006. They anticipate fixed overheads will be £450,000 for the year. With the Disneyland Paris packages, a quarter of the variable costs will go in travel costs, at an average of £30 per package. They anticipate selling packages at an average of £160 per holiday in 2006.

The American holidays are sold at an average price of £650 per holiday. Travel costs of £200 for the American holidays comprise half the variable costs of the holiday.

Market research has revealed that, during 2006, Theme Holidays expect to sell 400 holidays.

Work out the contribution for both the European and American holidays.

Calculate the company's profit for the year before tax and interest.

Market research also revealed that, if Theme Holidays reduced their prices by 10%, they could sell 300 more holidays per year. Calculate how this would affect profitability and advise accordingly.

Theme Holidays are aware of the size of their fixed overheads. How would a 10% reduction in fixed overheads through cost-cutting measures affect both of the above?

* Break-even analysis is (like all other methods) dependent upon the accuracy of forecasts made about costs and revenues. Changes in the market and in the cost of raw materials could affect the success of this technique.

2.4 The use of software to aid decision-making

The success of business organisations depends in large measure on the efficient and accurate production of goods or services. But its survival also depends on the rapid and accurate processing and distribution of information.

In today's business environment this process is almost totally dependent upon new technology. This is because:

* The scale of many large organisations makes it impossible for every meeting to be conducted face-to-face

* Many organisations are geographically spread out, and require communication links between interrelated plants and offices

* Modern business decision-making frequently requires up-to-date information from a variety of sources

* Competition between business organisations is more fierce

* The pace of industrial development has increased. Organisations must therefore be quicker in responding to factors such as technological change, market forces and competition from rivals.

List the different ways you communicate with friends in a typical day. How many of these different forms of communication such as MSN Messenger and the telephone are dependent upon technologies. Describe how such technologies are transforming the ways in which individuals communicate.

Over the last ten years the modern office workplace has changed dramatically. Paper may still be around in many of these offices, but it is usual for almost every employee to have access to a computer terminal and the expectation is that, where employees use computers, they have the capability to use the many different software applications relevant for their particular jobs. For example, when using computers individuals may be required to use a range of applications such as databases, spreadsheets, word processing packages, the Internet, e-mail, and so on.

In nearly all cases, these computers will be networked. Networking involves linking together two or more computers to allow facilities and information to be shared. This has the effect of decentralising information and communications so that managers and employees have more information upon which to base their decisions. A computer network may be specially developed for almost any type of organisation or application. Terminals may be just a few metres apart or they may exist in completely different parts of the world.

A local area network (LAN) may be used to connect computers within a single room, building or group of buildings on the same site, without the use of telecommunications links. LANs may be linked to a file server, which is a permanent data store that provides files and software for other PCs and also acts as a storage base (see Figure 2.43). Using a form of device such as a hub that links computers, it is relatively easy to connect computers to provide some form of network. Computer gamers often connect their machines together using a hub, so that they can compete with each other in the same room or the same house.

A wide area network (WAN) may be used to connect computers on different sites by making use of telecommunications. The great benefit is that WAN networks extend the use of the computer beyond the office by using a modem (modulator/demodulator), which converts computer signals for transmission over the telephone lines before reconverting them again.

Modems are used because telephone lines are primarily used for speech transmissions and not for use by computers. Waves travelling along lines are analogue waves, where sounds and images are converted into corresponding variations in electrical voltages or currents. However, the digital revolution has seen the creation of new formats that enable the transmission of video and voice signals.

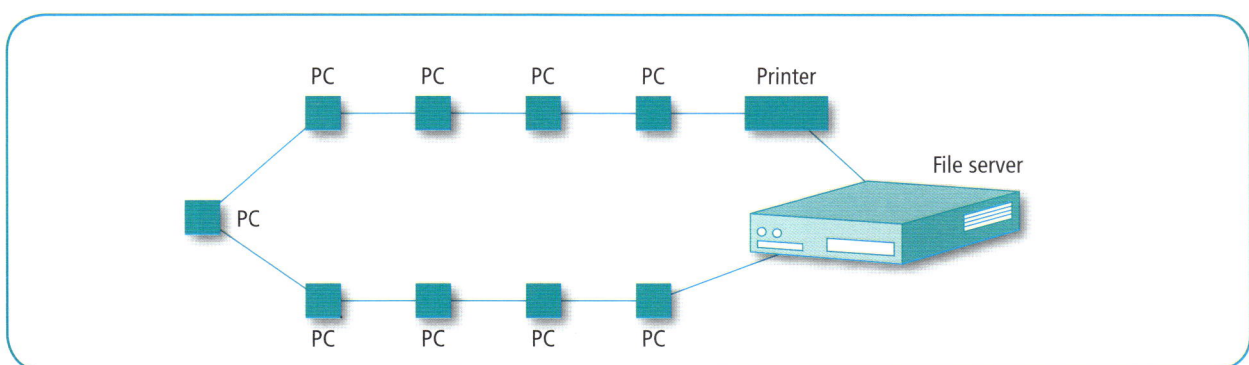

FIGURE 2.43 *Examples of a local area network (LAN)*

Spreadsheets

A spreadsheet is a table of numbers which can be organised and altered on a computer according to preset formulae. Spreadsheets, as we will see, are particularly useful for forecasting and financial modelling, as they show the effects of financial decisions without the need to repeat the calculations manually.

For example, a firm will make a forecast of all the money coming in and going out over a twelve-month period. The spreadsheet can alter the inputs to calculate the effect, for example, of lowering a heating bill by a certain amount each month. The computer will automatically recalculate the columns to change the heating figures, total cost figures and cash flows for each month. In this way a manager, accountant or other user of a spreadsheet can quickly carry out business calculations such as introducing and finding out the effect of minor changes of variables.

As we can see in Figure 2.44 a spreadsheet presents the user with a series of rows and columns. Above each column are letters of the alphabet and the rows are each numbered. The box created where a column meets a row is called a cell and the cell reference is made up from its column letter and row number. So, B3 would be in the second column on the third row down.

	A	B	C
1	A1	B1	C1
2	A2	B2	C2

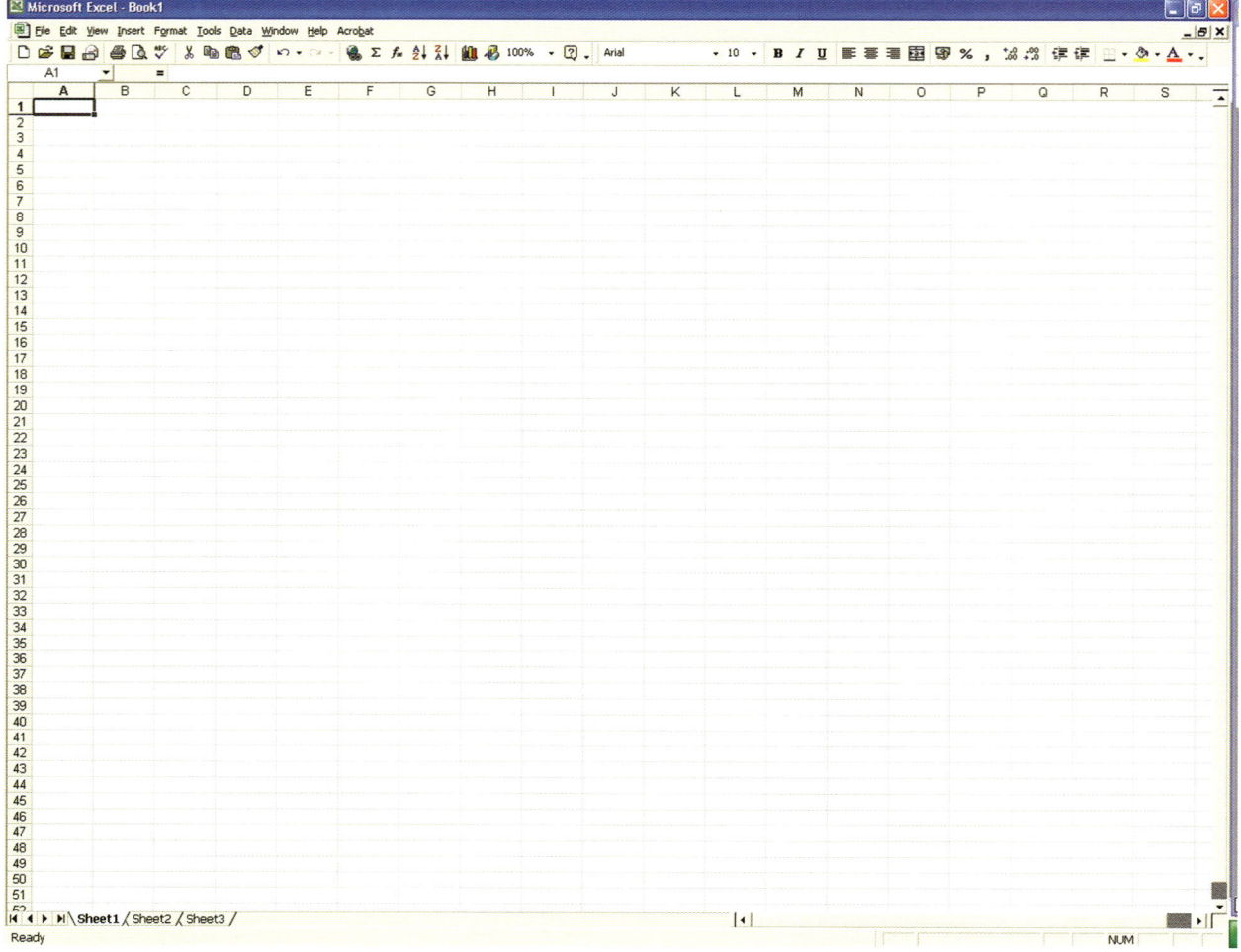

FIGURE 2.44 *Example of a spreadsheet screen*

Cells in a spreadsheet may contain:

* *Text* This may be used to provide column titles or labels that help the spreadsheet user to understand the significance of other data.

* *Numbers* These are at the very heart of spreadsheet use, and numbers are sometimes called values. For example, they could appear as a currency or be a percentage.

* *Formulas* The way in which spreadsheets work depends upon formulas. It is the formulas that enable spreadsheets to make calculations. For example A1 + B2 will add together the values found in these two cells. A formula expressed as A2+B3*C3/D1 will tell the spreadsheet to add the values of A2 and B3, having multipled cell B3 by C3 and then having divided cell C3 by D1.

One term used within the spreadsheet is one called a *function*. The SUM function adds up all of the values between two cells. By putting three values into a box and then by highlighting the three cells as well as pressing the SUM function represented by Σ it is possible to add the three

Learning activity

Put 3 values into separate boxes within a spreadsheet C3, C4 and C5. Add the contents of the three cells. What formula was put into cell C6?

The way in which the cell addresses change when the formula is developed is called relative referencing, as the address changes according to whether it is copied. When rows are highlighted and copied the row number will change rather than the column letter.

Simple cash budget

Date	Jan	Feb	March	April	May	June	July	Aug	Sept	Oct	Nov	Dec
Opening balance	100	105	115	115	115	127	136	141	146	151	151	146
Receipts												
cash sales	20	30	30	30	30	30	30	25	25	25	20	25
credit sales	40	45	40	40	45	40	40	40	40	30	30	35
Total	60	75	70	70	75	70	70	65	65	55	50	60
Payments												
materials	25	35	35	35	33	30	35	30	25	25	25	25
overheads	20	20	25	25	20	21	20	20	25	20	20	21
wages	10	10	10	10	10	10	10	10	10	10	10	10
Total	55	65	70	70	63	61	65	60	60	55	55	56
overall +/-	5	10	0	0	12	9	5	5	5	0	-5	4
Closing balance	105	115	115	115	127	136	141	146	151	151	146	150

FIGURE 2.45 *A simple cash budget, prepared manually*

cells together. If the columns are C1, C2 and C3 you can see that the spreadsheet has added them together and this is represented by the SUM(C1: C3).

Cash flow, budgeting and profit forecasting

One of the benefits of using a spreadsheet is that, having developed and entered the formulas, it is possible to change figures and predict different outcomes.

Simple cash budget

The example shown in Figure 2.46 was prepared in a spreadsheet.

The receipts simply involved totalling two boxes to produce total receipts which in this instance involved the sum of B7+B8.

The total for payments involved totalling materials, overheads and wages which came out at B12+B13+B14.

Overall +/- was B9−B16 and the closing balance was B4+B9−B16. The closing balance has to become the opening balance for the next period and so C4, the opening balance on the second column, is now shown to =B18. By highlighting, these decisions can be extended across the page.

Spreadsheets like this that forecast either cash or profits are relatively simple to construct and easy to change. By simply changing the opening balance at the beginning of the spreadsheet all of the other calculations instantly change.

Break-even analysis

Entering figures into a spreadsheet can also be used for break-even analysis. The great benefit of doing this is that spreadsheets such as Excel are linked to charting tools and the spreadsheet can be used as a basis for producing a break-even chart shown in Figure 2.47. In the example the Fixed costs are £40,000, Variable cost per unit £10 and Sales price per unit £20. Output is then calculated at various levels from 1,000 units to 8,000 units. These are then highlighted and an appropriate line chart is chosen.

Word processing

At its most basic the function of a word processor is to manipulate text. Its great advantage is that it allows the user to make unlimited changes to text on screen before the final document is printed out.

Word processors make life easier for the writer in a number of ways:

Learning activity

If fixed costs are £30,000, variable costs per unit are £5 and sales price per unit is £40, construct a spreadsheet at each 2,000 sales of units and then use the spreadsheet to draw a break-even chart.

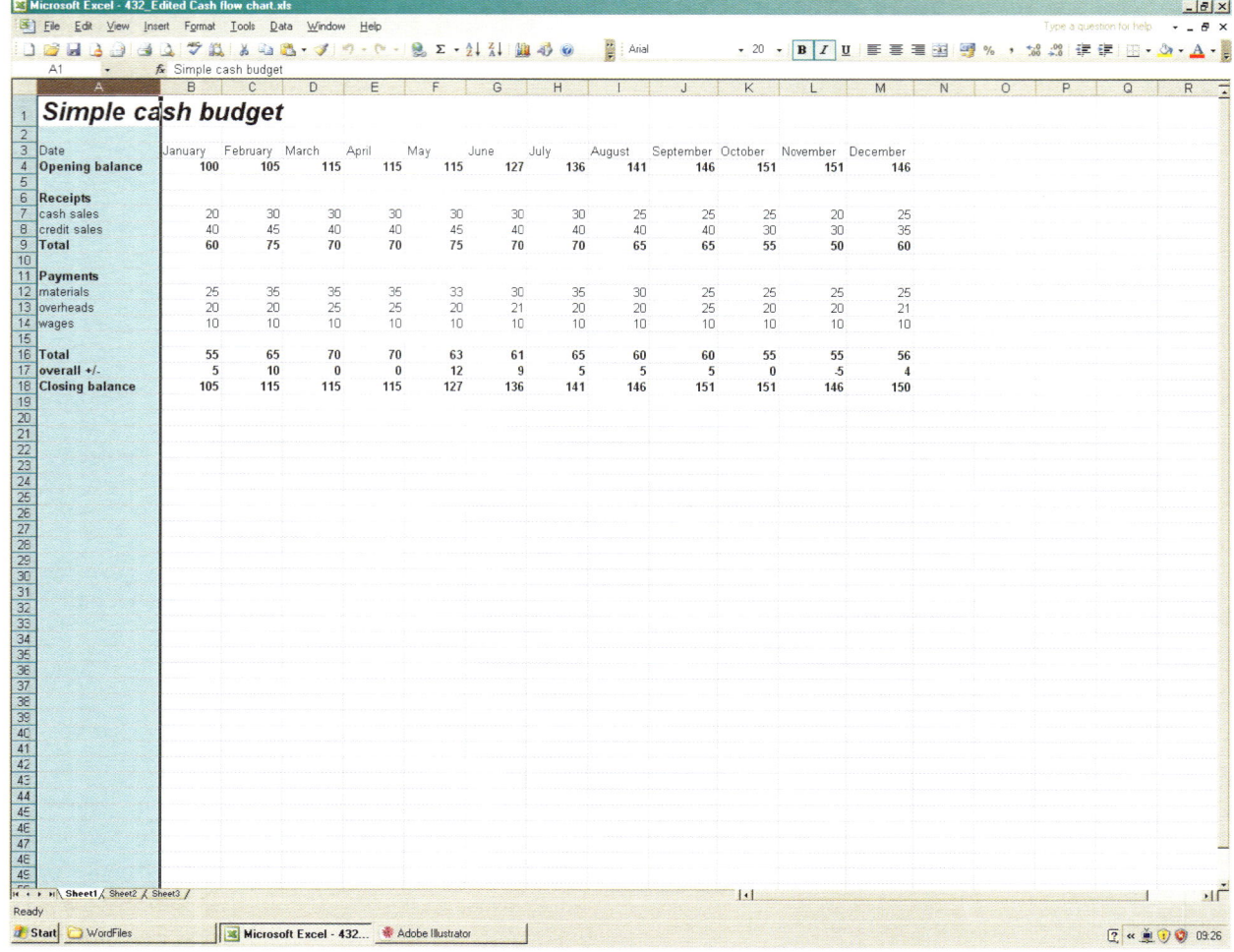

FIGURE 2.46 *A simple cash budget can be easily prepared as a spreadsheet*

* New text can be put on screen while existing text moves to create space for it

* Blocks of text can be moved around on the document that is being created

* The text can be spaced out to fill the whole line

* A word or phrase can be searched for, and can be removed or replaced by another word or phrase. A spelling mistake which is repeated throughout the document can be corrected in a single operation

* A header or footer can be added to the top or bottom of the document.

There are, of course many other functions, many of which you will be familiar with. For example, you can use different styles and fonts, insert graphics into text, use a spell-checker, thesaurus,

bullets, borders, tables, numbers, word count and even auto summarise.

Databases

A database is a store of information held on a computer. Examples might include anything from a list of customer accounts held by a bank or building society to a record of members of a church congregation and their addresses held by a parish priest. Another use might be to record tickets sold by a football club for various matches.

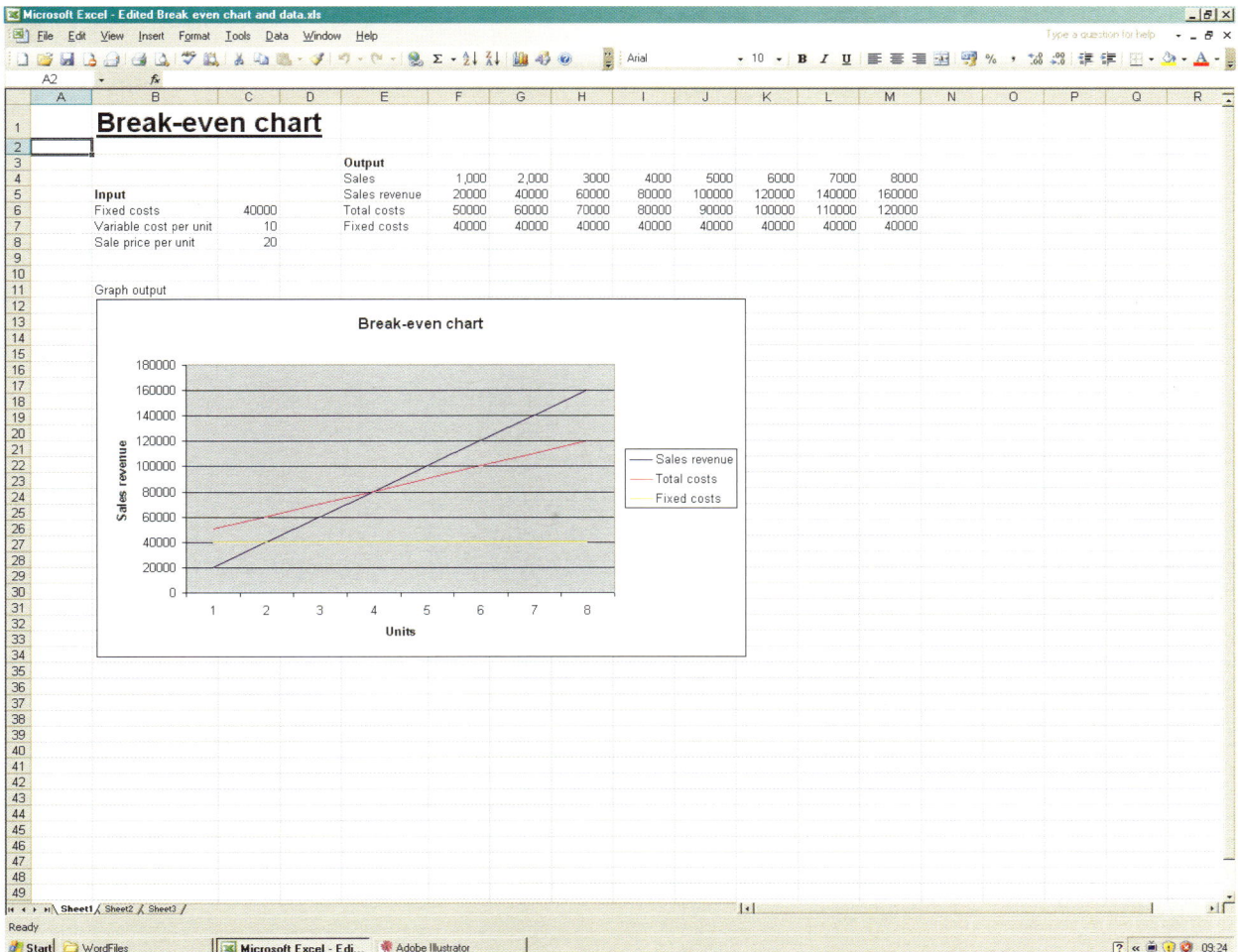

The spreadsheet shows:

Break-even chart

	Output								
	Sales	1,000	2,000	3000	4000	5000	6000	7000	8000
Input	Sales revenue	20000	40000	60000	80000	100000	120000	140000	160000
Fixed costs 40000	Total costs	50000	60000	70000	80000	90000	100000	110000	120000
Variable cost per unit 10	Fixed costs	40000	40000	40000	40000	40000	40000	40000	40000
Sale price per unit 20									

FIGURE 2.47 *A break-even analysis and chart, prepared as a spreadsheet*

In the university in which this author works, the database is the fundamental way in which the institution tracks the activities of students and the courses they register for.

The essence of a database is that data can be accessed and analysed in a number of different ways, depending upon the needs of the user. For example, suppose that Amin Stores wishes to record the account details of all of its customers. It would store the information in a number of fields – addressee, value of goods supplied, payments received and balance of account. If a customer rings up asking for the state of their account, Amin can simply order the computer to produce the appropriate information and display it on screen.

Accounting software

The widespread use of computers by all types of organisations has seen many organisations opt to computerise their book-keeping systems.

Computerised accounting systems simply incorporate manual-based theories using customised packages.

There are a number of advantages of using computerised accounting packages:

* Computers help to improve the control of funds coming into and going out of an organisation and make this control more effective.

* They improve accuracy, particularly where large amounts of data are entering into accounts (i.e. they take away much of the tedium of data entry into double-entry accounts).

CASE STUDY

Sage Line 50

You can reach the Sage Line 50 website through www.heinemann.co.uk/hotlinks (express code 1130P, then go to Unit 2).

Sage Line 50 is the UK's best-selling accounting software. It is an integrated package designed to provide users with the opportunity to make best use of their accounting data. The package makes all facts and figures readily available so that managers can quickly analyse their trading situation and solve problems or seize new opportunities. The package handles sales and purchases, stock control and order processing. It also generates invoices, produces statements, creates reports and can be used to create sales letters.

There are a number of elements to the system, including the following:

- *Sales Ledger* This shows who the customers are, what and when they buy and how much they owe and for how long.
- *Purchases Ledger* This enables the users to get the best value from their suppliers, enabling them to be in a strong position to get better discounts and higher credit levels.
- *Nominal Ledger* This brings together all the transactions and balances from other ledgers to create a chart of accounts to suit specific user requirements.
- *Financials* This enables Sage Line 50 to deal with management accounts, VAT returns and budget analysis.
- *Bank* The system manages accounts as well as transfers between accounts.
- *Fixed Assets Register* This enables the system to maintain records of all fixed assets and set up depreciation rates.
- *Stock* Sage Line 50 helps the user to achieve the right balance with reliable and up-to-date information on each stock item.

- *Invoicing* Prices, discounts and VAT are automatically calculated, with every invoice cross-referenced to ledgers.
- *Order processing* This provides a window into orders received and placed.
- *Report generator* This sets templates to allow the users to retrieve, sort and print out all of the information they require.

Sage Line 50 is easy to set up and use. Various forms, such as cheques, bank statements and invoices, are all created on screen and 'Wizards' take the user through various procedures. The real benefit of using this sort of package is speed and efficiency. Sage Line 50 has an automatic backup system, making it easy to spot and amend mistakes, and there is also password security access.

A key benefit of using Sage Line 50 is that it integrates with all other office software. For example, data from the system can be transferred into spreadsheets. Information can also be integrated into mail-merge and marketing databases.

There are single user or network versions of Sage Line 50. The networking option allows more than one user on to the system at any one time.

Although there are a variety of computerised accounting systems available, there are not many major differences between the packages. This is because all computerised accounting systems adhere to basic accounting concepts and practices.

1 Why does a package such as Sage Line 50 mirror the workings of a book-keeping system?
2 What are the advantages of using such a package?

* Accounting data is, by its very nature, arithmetical, which is well suited to being recorded and maintained by computer.

* Computerised book-keeping systems can supply reports and account balances much more quickly (such as trial balance, stock valuation, payroll analysis, VAT return, etc.).

* Many reports can be produced quickly and easily in a way that would not be possible in a manual system because of time and cost. For example, it would be easy to go through the sales ledger to find out all the customers (aged debtors) who have not paid their debts and send them reminders to do so.

* They help to provide managers with a readily accessible view of how the business organisation is functioning.

Computer programs for financial accounts usually follow the same system of ledger division into general and personal. In doing so the system provides an element of continuity with past practices. Commercially available accounting software is usually described as an 'integrated package', covering a range of accounting activities. For example, an accounting package would:

* update customer accounts in the sales ledger

* update supplier accounts in the purchases ledger

* record bank receipts and payments

* print out invoices

* make payments to suppliers and for expenses

* adjust records automatically.

Many packages offer more than just the control of each of the ledgers. Some may also provide for payroll, stock control production planning, electronic data interchange (EDI) and financial planning. These can be integrated with the rest of the accounting system.

An integrated accounting system means that, when a business transaction takes place and is input into the computer, it is recorded into a range of accounting records at the same time. For example, if a sales invoice is generated for a customer:

* The customer's account will be adjusted with the invoice total.

* The sales account will increase and VAT will be applied.

* Stock records will change.

Project planning

At a time when increasingly people work in one or more project teams, an evolving application for computer software is in project planning. Computer programs allow projects to be broken down into a number of interrelated stages called activities. First the activities are defined and the time taken by each is estimated. Then the way in which the activities depend upon each other is defined. The computer calculates the total time for the project and shows the activities that must be completed on time in order for the project not to be delayed.

For example, in the case of a project to build a new office the activities and times might be as follows:

1	Prepare land and build foundations	30 days
2	Build walls	30 days
3	Build roof	15 days
4	Install equipment	30 days
5	Equip office	20 days

Activity 1 must be done first, then Activity 2, then Activity 3. However, Activities 4 and 5 – although they come after Activity 3 has finished – can be done at the same time. Therefore the total time for the project is only 105 days (30 + 30 + 15 + 30), not 125 days. The computer output will also show that Activity 5 is not critical: that is, it can start late or take longer than planned without delaying the project.

Many organisations use packages such as Microsoft Project that not only help to calculate the path (critical path) that should be used to finish the project on time, but also have charting tools that show how the project is progressing.

The Internet

The Internet came into being in the last quarter of the twentieth century. It was born in 1969, the year of the Apollo moon landings. For a number of years it was used mainly by computer buffs or 'Netties' who wallowed in their own brand of computer jargon but it has become widely accessible to a broader group of users.

Today, the Internet is providing a magnet for most of the world's major businesses, many of whom have spotted opportunities for advertising and communications to open up a whole new world of e-commerce. Net shopping is becoming increasingly important across a wide range of areas of buying and selling.

The Internet is also an excellent medium for sources of information.

Search engines such as Google can be used to search for a whole variety of topics simply by inserting helpful words or research terms. Try Google at www.heinemann.co.uk/hotlinks (express code 1130P, then go to Unit 2).

There are specialist engines for academics such as Google scholar that can be used to search for articles related to specialist education-related topics. Try Google scholar at www.heinemann.co.uk/hotlinks (express code 1130P, then go to Unit 2).

Organisations can use the Internet to search for information about competitors.

There are many specialist search engines, such as Emerald Fulltext, that provide business journals in fulltext format which saves having to deal with paper copies.

The Internet can be used as a form of market research in itself, so that those browsing a site can be asked to fill in and submit a questionnaire.

E-mail

As an alternative to written communications, the workplace is now characterised through electronic communications such as through e-mail. The sender simply forwards a document to a sender's e-mail address on their computer. When the receiver logs onto the system, he or she can see on screen that there is a message waiting which he or she can either read at the time or later. Anyone who is connected to the Internet has the capability to use e-mail. The advantages of using e-mail is that it is:

* Faster than ordinary mail
* The message does not have to be printed
* It is more environmentally friendly as less paper and energy are used.

One problem is that some people do not read their e-mails frequently enough. Another problem is that sometimes individuals get saturated by the sheer number of e-mails that they receive and the danger is that they may miss important ones.

E-commerce

Whereas e-business as a term refers to how organisations use information and communications technology (ICT) within their businesses to improve their operations, e-commerce refers more to how organisations use ICT for trading purposes.

According to many surveys, and despite what is happening to many economies around the world, the statistics tend to show that e-commerce is booming. For example, in the USA it was reported that e-commerce sales grew by 21.2 per cent over the same quarter in the previous year. In the same period, total retail sales increased by only 6.5 per cent.

You only have to look at a range of websites to see how organisations trade. There are now electronic banking facilities and a whole range of products and services can be purchased over the web, from a variety of different types of businesses, both large and small. e-Bay has been successful in allowing individuals to trade their own products and one of the most popular ways of buying books today is from Amazon.

Legal and corporate issues

Using IT in the business environment represents a whole new way of working. There have been a variety of issues associated with this. For example, some individuals find it difficult to spend all day

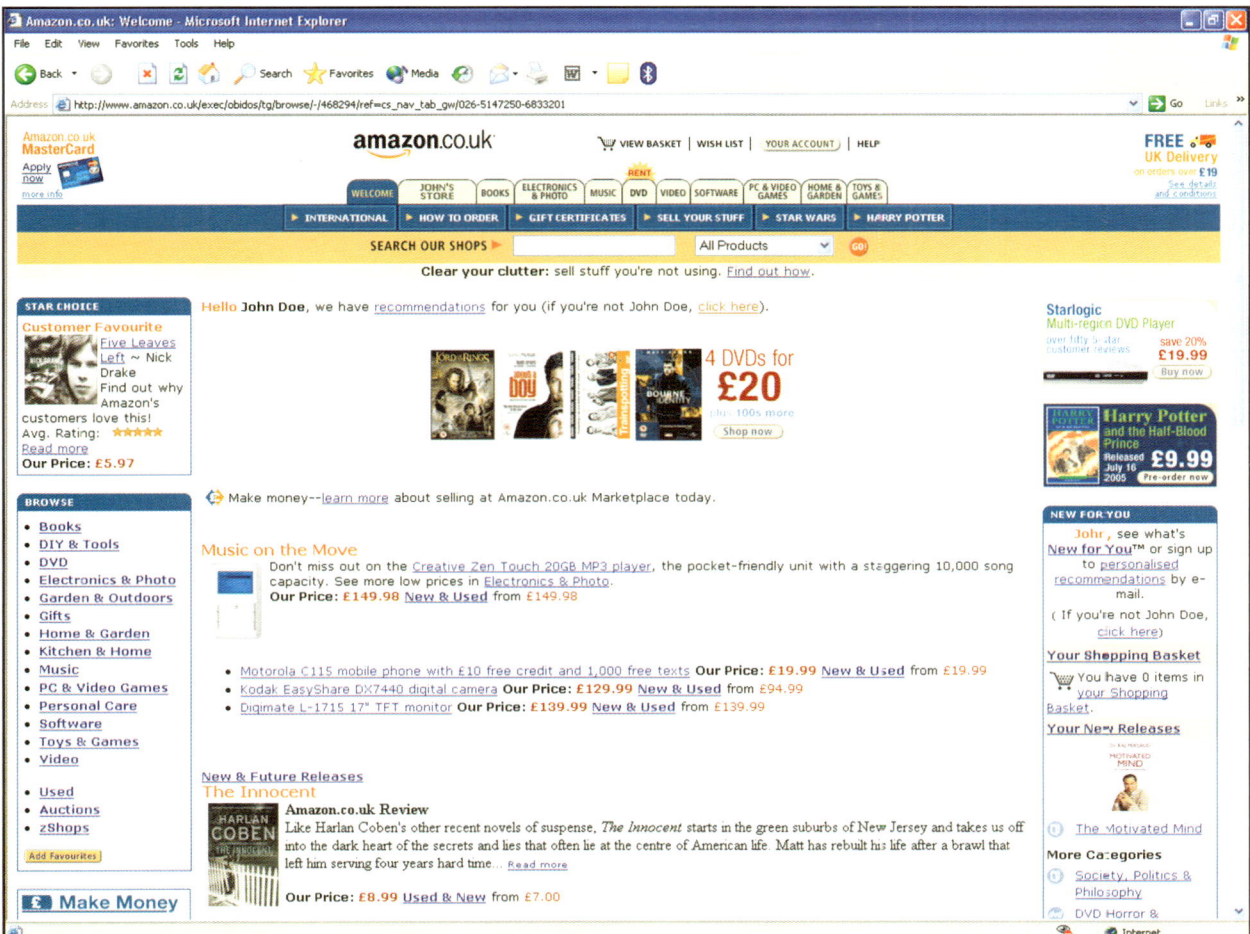

FIGURE 2.48 *The Amazon website is a popular example of e-commerce*

looking at a screen without getting a headache. Others have developed repetitive strain injuries (RSI). Clearly, organisations are finding that they have to develop different responsibilities to their employees based upon the use of technologies in the business environment.

With so much data around, an important element of dealing with it all is data protection. The Data Protection Act regulates the use of computerised information which relates to 'individuals' and the provision of services in respect of such 'information'.

The Act covers the holding of computer records only, and not manual records. The Act requires those using personal data to register with the Data Protection Registrar. Registered data users must then follow the eight principles of the Act:

* Data must be obtained and processed fairly and lawfully

* Data must be held only for specific lawful purposes which are described in the entry in the register

* Data should not be used in any other way than those related to such purposes

* Data should be adequate, relevant and not excessive for those purposes

* Personal data should be accurate and kept up-to-date

* Data should be held no longer than is required

* Individuals should be entitled to access their data and, if necessary, have it corrected or erased

* Data must be protected with appropriate security against unauthorised access or alteration.

There are a variety of exemptions from the Act, including information kept by government departments for reasons of national security. To ensure that data is held only for legitimate purposes many organisations appoint a data protection officer whose job it is to monitor the use of computerised information.

UNIT ASSESSMENT

You will investigate the setting up of a small business, which provides a service only in your local area.

Possible examples to choose include businesses:

* providing Desk Top Publishing (DTP)

* providing web design support for local business

* printing logos on to T shirts and other clothing

* running a school shop

* offering health food

* supplying sandwiches or food for special occasions

* providing health or gym facilities.

Each individual student's assessment evidence should consist of a presentation using ICT, to include:

1   A plan for the business covering the proposed legal form, main objectives and stakeholders of the business. Research and analysis of the market in which it will operate will also be provided.

2   An explanation of how the business will manage its activities, including the human, physical and financial resources needed and an analysis of how the business will manage these to provide a quality output.

3   Financial management information to include identification of and explanation of the main start-up and running costs for the business and consideration of how the business will monitor its performance, with particular reference to cash flow forecasts and break-even analysis using software where appropriate.

4   An explanation of how software can support the business including evidence of how it will help the business to operate efficiently.

Here is an outline of what you need to do to score high marks for this assignment.

* Show that you have detailed knowledge and understanding of key planning factors associated with starting a business. To be able to show this you need to provide evidence – by giving detailed explanations of each area that you research. These areas are the proposed legal form, the objectives of the business, the stakeholders and their stake in the business. In addition you will need to provide a good analysis of the market situation including consideration of areas such as pricing, the appropriateness of the product for the market, the suitability of advertising and other means of promotion, and the effectiveness of the distribution channels.

* Show that you have detailed knowledge and understanding of approaches to managing business activities. You can provide evidence of this by analysing practical issues such as the relevance and cost of the resources, and the approach that the business uses to managing quality.

* Show that you have detailed knowledge and understanding of financial management. You can provide evidence of this by providing an appropriate selection of start-up and running costs, and a well-structured and integrated assessment of monitoring performance by producing and evaluating cash flow forecasts and break-even calculations.

* Show that you have detailed knowledge and understanding of business software. You can show evidence of this by providing a clear analysis of how spreadsheets, word processing, and various pieces of software might help to improve the efficiency of the business that you have chosen to study.

UNIT 3

Investigating marketing

This unit contains four parts:

3.1   Identifying marketing aims and objectives

3.2   Using appropriate methods of market research

3.3   Choosing an appropriate marketing mix

3.4   Other factors influencing the marketing mix

Introduction

If you have been stopped in the shopping mall 'just to answer a few questions' or heard a TV advertisement which says 'nine out of ten customers preferred', you have seen some aspects of marketing. You may have wondered how a supermarket decides which products to promote or place on the top or bottom shelf. These are all very visible parts of a highly skilled and sophisticated marketing process which interacts with all the other functions of a business.

It is very easy to take our lifestyle and the sheer range of products and choices that we see or think about every day for granted. All around us we are blitzed by messages targeted at our needs. When we go into shops there are a huge variety of goods on view and we have to make a range of critical decisions that relate not just to our needs but also our income. At the same time, we are constantly offered a range of service opportunities to match our lifestyle. It is clear that all of the people and organisations offering so many different opportunities not only show a good understanding

FIGURE 3.1 *Marketing is important for any organisation*

of us as consumers and how our thoughts, perceptions and minds work, but they must also have carried out widespread and precise market research to find out about our needs.

> ## What you will learn in this unit

* The importance of marketing as a strategic activity
* How marketing objectives direct an organisation
* The need for market segmentation
* How market research can inform business strategies
* An appreciation of each of the elements of the marketing mix.

3.1 Identifying marketing aims and objectives

Marketing is about understanding the customer and ensuring that products and services match existing and potential customer needs. Marketing is also about looking at ways of influencing the behaviour of customers. Perhaps the most useful way to think about marketing is to think about it as two main phases.

As we will see the passive phase involves finding out about customer needs though market research as well as understanding the behaviour of customers. Having done all of this 'finding out' organisations will then have to *decide who to focus upon and who to sell or deliver goods or services to*. Then comes the active phase. This

Learning activity

Think of a simple product concept such as a new shoe horn, a different type of baked bean, a new vegetarian concept or a form of men's grooming. Also consider the introduction and development of a new type of sport – possibly one from overseas such as Australian Rules Football, a more interesting nightclub concept or some type of service focused upon making household chores easier to undertake.

List the sort of questions that would have to be answered by using marketing research to find out more about the behaviour of consumers. Then, discuss the processes that could be used to satisfy customer needs.

phase involves putting together lots of plans and actions that meet customer needs. This is not just about advertising. It starts from the product itself, includes the price that is charged and then focuses upon the organisation doing everything it can to successfully meet and satisfy customer needs better than its competitors.

Understanding customer wants and needs

Marketing is essential to the success of any business. Its primary aim is to enable businesses to meet the needs of their actual and potential customers, whether for profit or not. You need to understand that, if a business's marketing is to be successful, it must:

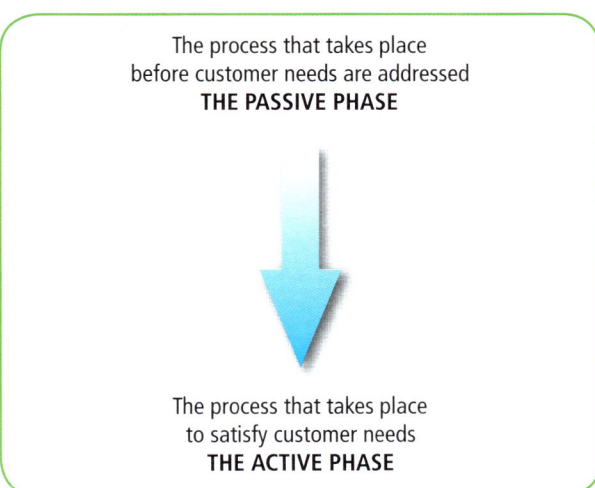

The process that takes place before customer needs are addressed
THE PASSIVE PHASE

The process that takes place to satisfy customer needs
THE ACTIVE PHASE

FIGURE 3.2 *The two phases of marketing*

Think about your own needs as a student for learning. What products and services are associated with such needs? For example, what services does your school or college provide for your needs and how could they be improved?

* understand customer needs

* understand and keep ahead of the competition

* communicate effectively with its customers to satisfy customer expectations

* co-ordinate its functions to achieve marketing aims

* be aware of constraints on marketing activities.

You need to understand how these criteria for successful marketing are related to the central aim of marketing – meeting actual and potential customer needs. You should also understand the importance to many businesses of developing and maintaining a relationship with the actual and potential customers and other stakeholders.

How easy it is to take all we have for granted! Wherever we look there are advertising messages bombarding us with images of goods or services designed to provide us with more choices and a better lifestyle. Shops, mail-order services and the Internet provide us with the opportunity to buy almost anything we want, as long as we have the 'filthy lucre'.

It was only in 1942 that Joseph Schumpeter, the great Austrian economist, wrote:

'Queen Elizabeth I owned silk stockings. The capitalist achievement does not typically consist of providing more silk stockings for queens, but in bringing them within the reach of factory girls in return for steadily decreasing amounts of effort.'

CASE STUDY
Using interactive TV to communicate with clients

A few years ago the first truly interactive TV advertisement appeared on the screens of the UK's homes. Chicken Tonight offered viewers willing to 'push the red button' money-off coupons for the tasty chicken treat in exchange for a couple of precious minutes of their time. The event was significant as it reminded everybody of the possibilities within a digital and interactive market.

Since then the digital media market has, to say the least, gone through turbulent times, with ITV Digital becoming Freeview, selling half a million set-top boxes in the first six months. With more viewers claiming to be interacting with their television, broadcasters are looking to interactive TV to reinvigorate their revenue streams.

By early 2005, 52.4% of income for digital channels came from channel subscription. Advertising accounted for 22.2%, and with sponsorship 1.3% the digital companies were looking to expand other income which stood at 24.1%.

ITV has already experimented with interactive versions of *Who Wants to be a Millionaire?* and the Brit Awards where viewers were invited to play along at home and vote for their favourite record or artist respectively for the chance to win cash or prizes. Plans are now being developed for more interactive advertising and promotions, particularly alongside Freeview where viewers are interacting all of the time, such as in programmes like *Big Brother* and *I'm a Celebrity, Get Me Out of Here*.

The potential for advertisers is there; 62% agreed that interactive advertising is a convenient way to get information about a product or service. Half of all digital viewers think that companies that use interactive are more innovative than their competitors and 58% think it stands out more than traditional TV ads.

1 **What is interactive advertising?**
2 **Why might companies wish to use it?**
3 **How might interactive advertising relate to your needs as a customer?**

Today we live in a *market economy*, in which many consumers have been able to enjoy the range of goods and services that were previously afforded by kings and queens only. The existence of a market makes it possible for consumers to express their preferences for the goods and services they would like, and prices act as signals to suppliers informing them which goods are in most demand.

In this marketplace, today's consumers indicate to suppliers through their purchases what should or should not be produced for the market. In effect they have become king or queen.

The Chartered Institute of Marketing defines marketing as:

'The management process responsible for identifying, anticipating and satisfying customer requirements profitably.'

This definition provides an important starting point to help you gain a clear picture of the major issues facing a market-focused organisation.

There are a number of key words in the above definition:

✱ *Management process* – the use of this term indicates the level of importance of marketing decisions. Successful marketing needs managerial input because it requires constant information gathering, as well as data analysis, in order for decisions to be made.

✱ *Identifying* involves answering questions such as 'how do we find out what the consumers' requirements are?' and 'how do we keep in touch with their thoughts and perceptions about our goods or service?'

✱ *Anticipating* takes into account that consumer requirements change all the time. For example, as people become richer they may seek a greater variety of goods and services. Anticipation involves looking at the future as well as at the present. What will be the Next Best Thing people will require tomorrow?

✱ *Satisfying* involves meeting consumer requirements. Customers seek particular benefits. They want the right goods, at the right price, at the right time and in the right place.

✱ *Profitability* is the margin of profit that *motivates* organisations to supply goods to consumers in a market. Of course, profit may be simply one motive for supplying goods to a market. Others may include market share or market leadership.

A recent major study of some 1,700 companies showed that marketing-orientated firms have enhanced profitability. In other words, good marketing helps managers to improve the performance of their part of the business and to meet the most basic of business objectives – profit.

Clearly, one of the key components of marketing is understanding customer wants and needs. Marketing is, therefore, the process through which Jaguar is able to identify the kinds of cars people will want to buy in the near future and the features that should be built into those cars. It helps Reebok anticipate changes in consumers' preferences for trainers, and digital television formats such as Freeview and Sky Television to identify the types of channels viewers will want to watch in the future.

In a relatively short period of time organisations have moved forward from *production orientation* to *sales orientation,* and, more recently, to *marketing orientation* (see Figure 3.3).

In a market dominated by production orientation, manufacturers feel they know what is best for customers. When there is little competition (for example, where there is only one supplier of telecommunications services in a particular geographical area or where there is only one producer of motor vehicles), organisations may not have to pay close attention to customer needs.

As consumer incomes began to rise after the Second World War, standards of living began to improve. During the 1950s and 1960s, emphasis was upon sales orientation. Prime Minister Harold Macmillan claimed that 'You've never had it so good!', and the focus was upon trying to persuade customers they needed the goods rather than attempting to find out about buyers' needs.

Marketing orientation is all about focusing the activities or organisations on meeting the needs of consumers. It means the consumer is the driving

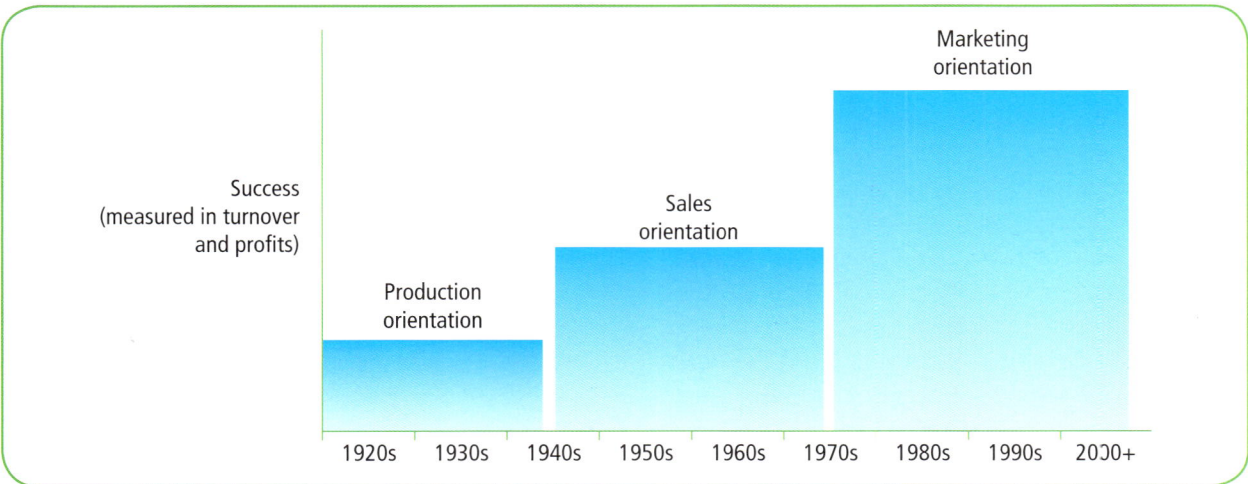

FIGURE 3.3 *Business orientation*

force behind everything an organisation does. No longer is marketing something that is simply added on to a number of company functions. Today, the customer drives all the activities of a market-focused organisation.

Learning activity

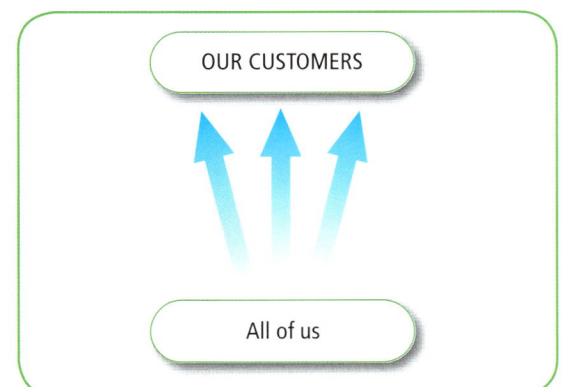

FIGURE 3.4 *Starbucks organisation chart*

Starbucks have 8,337 coffee bars throughout the world and yet the organisation has only been around since 1971 when the first coffee bar was opened in Seattle's Pike Place Market.

Look at the chart in Figure 3.4. What does it tell you about their orientation?

You can find the Starbucks website through www.heinemann.co.uk/hotlinks (express code 1130P, then go to Unit 3).

Learning activity

Use an example of an organisation known to you to describe how it anticipates market needs and opportunities.

Amazon, the world's biggest online bookseller (and CD supplier), provides a good example of marketing orientation. Amazon claim to provide 'the Earth's biggest selection'. The aim is to give consumers as much choice as possible using a consumer-focused, easy-to-use website. Amazon's approach represents the marketing-oriented view of e-commerce, i.e. that with a customer-focused website they are able to find new ways of delighting customers. This contrasts with the production appproaches of some other web users who have the view that if they have a website then customers will flock to them. They forget to find out how customers want the site to be structured and what they want from it.

It is, therefore, the ability to satisfy customers that marks the difference between a successful and unsuccessful organisation. This is why some schools are oversubscribed and have a huge demand for places while others have falling numbers. It is the reason why some supermarkets have people crowding the aisles whereas others are practically empty.

Learning activity

Discuss the following statement and relate the quote to two business organisations:

'Marketing, therefore, is concerned with attempting to reduce risk by applying formal techniques systematically to assess the situation and develop the company's response to it.'

At this stage it is important to emphasise that marketing is linked to planning, and that successfully meeting the objectives identified within these plans is crucial for business organisations. An organisation with a strategy knows where it is going because it is planning ahead. Marketing strategy is concerned with identifying and meeting the requirements of customers successfully so that the organisation can meet a range of objectives.

Marketing strategies are the means by which organisations attempt to find out exactly what their customers want, and then to influence customers in a way that is favourable to the organisation.

Marketing strategies require detailed research to find out:

* about the requirements of customers
* the right products to develop to meet customer needs
* how to position the product or service in relation to other products and services
* the right marketing mix.

It is important to be able to differentiate between marketing strategy and marketing tactics.

Learning activity

You have recently developed a revolutionary new type of seat that can be used in offices and would overcome any form of back pain. Working in groups, comment upon the sort of research you need to undertake before making a major investment in this product.

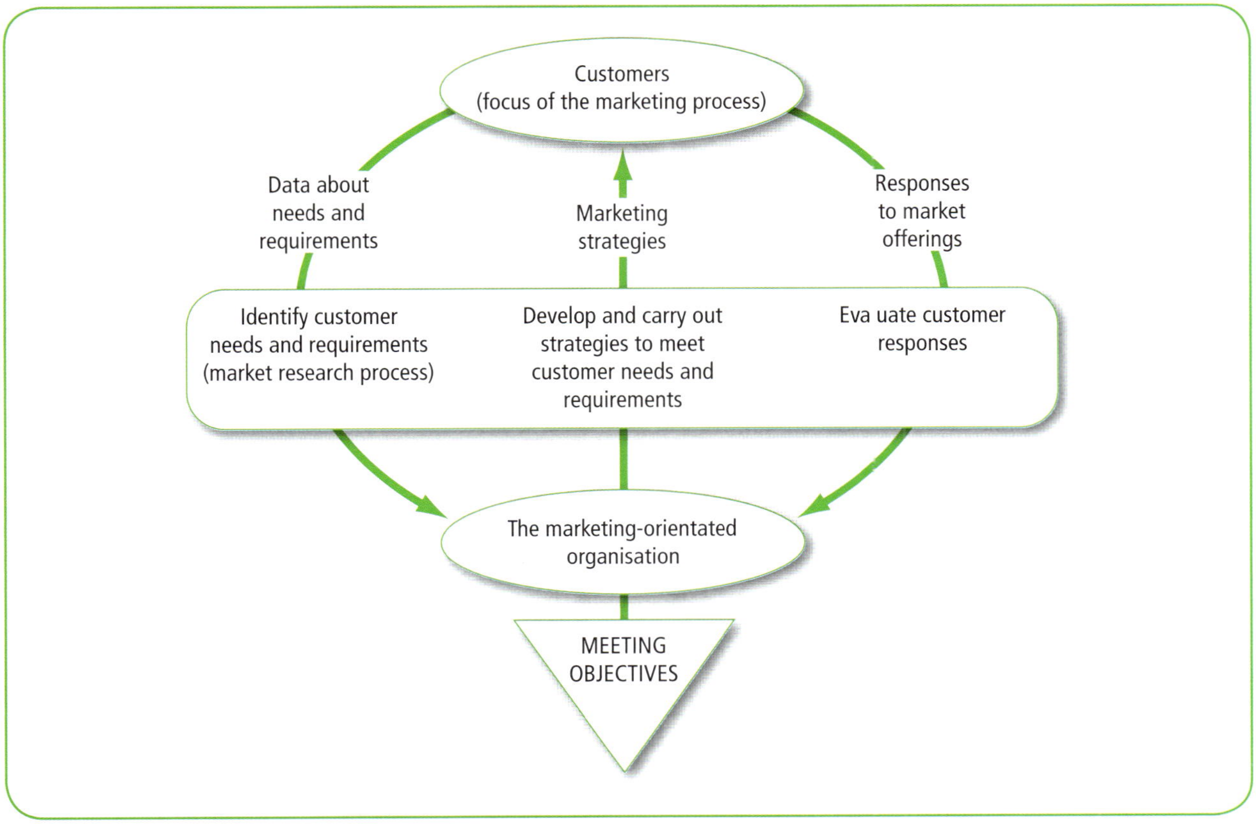
Customers
(focus of the marketing process)
Data about needs and requirements
Marketing strategies
Responses to market offerings
Identify customer needs and requirements (market research process)
Develop and carry out strategies to meet customer needs and requirements
Eva uate customer responses
The marketing-orientated organisation
MEETING OBJECTIVES

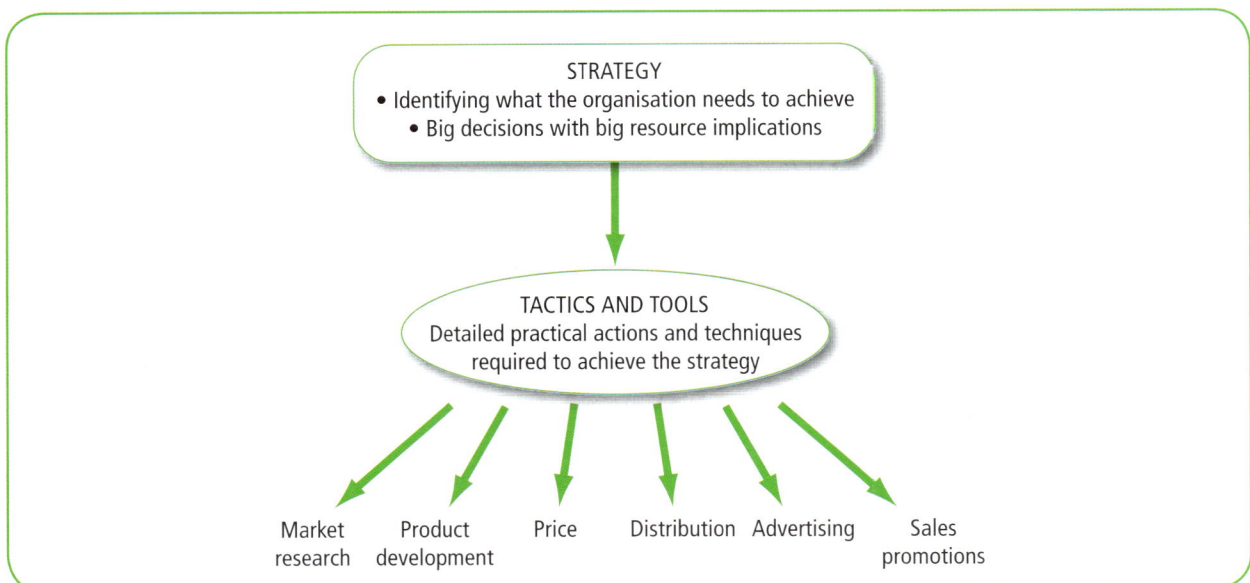

FIGURE 3.5 *The strategic process*

STRATEGY
• Identifying what the organisation needs to achieve
• Big decisions with big resource implications
TACTICS AND TOOLS
Detailed practical actions and techniques required to achieve the strategy
Market research
Product development
Price
Distribution
Advertising
Sales promotions

FIGURE 3.6 *Marketing strategy and tactics*

The terms 'strategy' and 'tactics' are of military origin. Military *strategy* is a general overview that involves the creation of clear aims and objectives and then deciding the key means to achieve these. Military *tactics* are the means used to win a particular campaign or battle.

Having established the marketing strategy, it is possible to decide on the tactics and tools to be used to make the strategy work. For example, this may involve carrying out some detailed market research, developing a product, working out the best price to charge, developing a distribution strategy, running an appropriate advertising campaign or engaging in sales promotional activity.

Planning is at the heart of marketing. It enables decision-makers within an organisation to plan for the present and for the future, and to learn from the past. The three main reasons for planning are to:

1 assess how well the organisation is doing in the various markets in which it operates

2 identify the strengths and weaknesses of the organisation in each of these markets

3 establish goals and objectives, so that resources can be used appropriately.

Assael defines a *marketing plan* as a document invented by marketing managers that:

✳ *'identifies marketing opportunities*

✳ *defines the target market that represents that opportunity*

✳ *develops a mix of strategies directed at this target*

✳ *guides the evaluation of the marketing effort.'*

Marketing objectives are an essential part of the marketing plan as they provide direction for activities to follow. Without clear objectives it is difficult to evaluate what a marketing plan is trying to achieve or whether a plan has been successful. It is usual to translate marketing objectives into quantifiable 'result areas', such as market share, market penetration or growth rate of sales. Some of these may be further broken down into specific sales volumes, value goals or geographical targets.

Marketing objectives may have a time frame and direction. They also provide a basis for evaluation. Marketing must ensure that organisational activities are co-ordinated in a way that marketing objectives are met.

Marketing objectives should therefore be:

1 *Achievable* They should be based on a practical analysis of an organisation's capabilities.

2 *Understandable* They need to be clear so that everyone knows what they are trying to achieve.

3 *Challenging* They should be something everyone has to strive for.

4 *Measurable* Quantification makes it possible to record progress and to make adjustments if marketing objectives are not being met.

We can also relate marketing objectives to the SMART approach used in Unit 1. This stands for:

Specific – objectives should specify what they want to achieve

Measurable – an organisation should measure whether they are meeting objectives or not.

Achievable – the objectives set must be achievable and attainable

Realistic – the objectives must be realistic give the resources used

Time-related – time should be allocated to achieve the objectives.

For example, if market research indicates that people who visit multiplex cinemas are unwilling to stand in the rain queuing for an hour for the last seat to be sold just in front of them, then it is essential for the organisation to find solutions. In Manchester, the UCI multiplex has a bank of 90 telephone operators at the end of a freephone number who take nationwide bookings. Customers can also say where they want to sit. The transaction takes on average 64 seconds. Marketing thus has a responsibility to ensure all aspects of the way in which an organisation operates are geared to meeting consumer requirements.

FIGURE 3.7 *Process of exchange between buyers and sellers*

Developing new products

Being human, all customers are different! But only a few businesses (a tailor, for example, or a firm of architects) can provide products *specifically designed* for each individual customer. Most marketing activities are therefore designed to meet the needs of groups of customers within a market.

A market is made up of actual or potential buyers of a product and the sellers who offer goods to meet buyers' needs. The market for computers is composed of existing owners and prospective buyers of computers, as well as companies such as Apple Macintosh who manufacture them, Microsoft who develop software and Time who distribute them within the marketplace. A market requires a process of exchange between buyers and sellers (see Figure 3.7).

Interaction between buyers and sellers is based upon the notion of the marketing mix. The marketing mix provides a useful way of looking at the marketplace for products. Organisations need to create a successful mix of:

* the right product or service
* sold in the right place
* at the right price
* using the most suitable form of promotion.

The first challenge for any organisation is to find a set of customers and to identify their needs so that appropriate goods and services can be developed. The first element in the marketing mix is the *product*. Once organisations have a product, then all the other elements in this marketing mix can be engaged to meet customer needs. These may

FIGURE 3.8 *The marketing mix*

Find out...

You can see the Next Directory and Knorr websites using www.heinemann.co.uk/hotlinks (express code 1130P, then go to Unit 3).

include developing the *pricing* for the product or service provided, working out how to *distribute* (*place*) goods to the customers, as well as how to *promote* them.

When Next identified a large group of potential customers who could be reached using

CASE STUDY

Falling behind the needs of the customer

For many years, Marks & Spencer (view the website through www.heinemann.co.uk/hotlinks – express code 1130P, then go to Unit 3) had been a British institution, supported by the blind faith of their customers. Their products were the fruits of endless compromises between buyers, managers and suppliers.

The products were a benchmark of British quality – dependable and decent – and stood as a British emblem. But people increasingly came to think that much of this merchandise was dull, and was out of touch with changing fashions. However, at the heart of these products' success was a strong bond between M&S and the British public.

During the 1980s, M&S were probably propped up by good fortune. Men's and women's fashions in the 1980s were based on the older styles of the 1940s and, as more women entered the workforce the ready-made meal became accepted as a comfort food. At the time the alternatives to M&S were probably not attractive enough, but then George at Asda and designers at Debenhams, Zara, IKEA and Gap changed the fashion world, with new merchandise every three weeks instead of M&S's twice-yearly collections. Fashion was also blown apart the moment Next arrived on the scene. Niche-ing, sub-branding and product clustering became the new buzz words. The most fashion conscious of women suddenly became those women in their thirties and forties. They had money, knew about fashion and wanted to make an effort.

During the 1990s M&S emphasised 'value' rather then price, and this provided them with an enviable position in the high street.

However, it was during this time they also got so hung up on quality they forgot about style and fashion. With inappropriate styles, sales fell and even their food halls lost customers. The unthinkable had happened . . . perhaps M&S was not so great after all. The disaffected customers went elsewhere.

In recent years M&S have got into branding, recently buying women's fashion brand Per Una from its creator George Davies for £125m.

Per Una was formed as a joint venture between M&S and Mr Davies. George Davies had a supplier relationship with M&S, but following the purchase the retailer will receive all revenues generated by the brand. The purchase of Per Una was just one of a number of measures unveiled by the new chief David Rose in July 2004 to defeat a potential £9.1bn takeover offer for M&S from retail tycoon Philip Green.

Today, M&S is ripe for acquisition. Valued at more than £9 billion, they have many sites that would be a valuable catch for a predator.

The future of M&S largely depends upon how well their designers are able to push through improvements to core products and win back the confidence of the British public. It is argued today that M&S's biggest problem is public perception and their solution to change such perceptions is through the process of branding.

1 **To what extent were the problems encountered by M&S a failure to understand their customers?**
2 **How have M&S tried to make themselves more market-orientated?**

the Next Directory, they identified a range of different mail order and electronic ways of reaching customers. When Unilever acquired the Knorr brand in 2000, it obtained an evolving family of brands that constantly develop new products based upon the strength of the brand that are sold in more than 87 countries.

In recent years we have seen increasing efforts to meet the individual wants and needs of customers – a process known as *customisation*. This has been particularly noticeable in service industries. Services such as delivering parcels, guarding property or maintaining equipment can be designed to suit a particular customer.

Improving profitability

One distinct objective allied to marketing processes for many organisations in the private sector is that of profitability. In the public sector income and maximising revenue may also be equally important. Shareholders and owners of organisations will inevitably be interested in profits as well as the value of their investment. The **dividend** they receive is a reward for the risk they take in buying shares.

It is probably wrong just to associate most shareholders with trying to make as much profit as possible. Many take a pride in the organisation in which they have invested as well as its reputation. Some of them may be employees or former employees. A number of shareholders

will ask questions of their directors at the **annual general meeting** and in some cases may vote to remove certain directors from the board. Shareholders appoint the board of directors of a company, who in turn appoint the management team.

Many large organisations place considerable emphasis upon 'shareholder value' – that is, making sure that shareholders receive a good return on their investment. The organisation that fails to provide shareholder value will find that its shareholders sell off their shares.

Some customers are worth more to an organisation than others. If a well-established customer decides to shop elsewhere this can have a dire result upon an organisation. For example, when Marks & Spencer decided to source more products from overseas, companies like Courtaulds within the UK were badly affected, and this led to the closing down of factories. A key element therefore within marketing relationships is to appreciate the profitability attached to each customer. If employees understand how much each relationship contributes to an organisation, then they can link their actions to keep customers delighted with products and services in a way that further develops and builds other profitable relationships.

CASE STUDY

Improving market share and profits at Carpetright

Britain's biggest floor coverings retailer, Carpetright, increased its market share and profit margins despite facing sales that were wearing thin. The Essex-based group, which operates stores and concessions across the UK, Ireland, Belgium and Holland, said total sales in the UK and Ireland lifted 8.8 per cent in the 25 weeks to 23 October 2004 against a 9.2 per cent hike in the first 14 weeks of the financial year.

Carpetright, which has 365 stores and 39 concessions in the UK and Ireland, also runs 89 outlets in Holland and Belgium. The group, which employs around 3000 people and has an estimated 26 per cent slice of the UK carpet market, has managed to improve profits despite recent difficult market conditions.

1. **What are Carpetright's marketing objectives likely to be?**
2. **To what extent might market share contribute to its profitability?**

Improving market share

For many organisations their main business objective is to obtain a high market share, and some organisations deliberately set prices that allow them to build such a share. The Boston Consultancy Group argue that organisations with a high market share gain more experience and that such experience is a key asset enabling an organisation to reduce costs per unit and compete more efficiently than their competitors.

A programme of research in the USA produced another theory concerning factors that influence organisational competitiveness. This study was called 'Profit Impact of Marketing Strategies', and is usually referred to as PIMS. This study attempted to analyse the marketing factors that had the biggest impact upon profits. Though a number of conclusions were drawn, the study highlighted the close relationship between market share and profitability.

MARKET SHARE (%)	PROFITABILITY (%)
Under 7	9.6
7–14	12.0
14–22	13.5
22–36	17.9
Over 36	30.2

FIGURE 3.9 *The PIMS study*

The PIMS research showed that organisations with a larger market share were more likely to be profitable (see Figure 3.9). Research took this concept further by showing that high market share and increased performance were the results of moving along a 'learning curve', so that the more an organisation learnt about its position through market research, the better it would perform.

Learning activity

Working in small groups, think of a new product idea. If you were to commercialise this idea, what would your objectives be for the first year? How would you measure whether or not you would be achieving these objectives? Explain why market share is an important marketing objective for many organisations. Why might improving market share be easier in rapidly changing rather than static markets? Provide two examples of organisations that seem to have improved their market share in recent years.

Think of a new product idea that would be useful and relevant to your school or college. Discuss how you could use this idea to make it a commercial reality. What objectives would you have for your idea?

Why are organisations with a large market share likely to be more profitable? One reason is that with high market share and larger levels of output, firms benefit from larger production runs and, when unit costs are reduced, they benefit from increased margins. Though the PIMS study showed that the best competitive strategy for a business was to aim for higher market share, this theory has been criticised for only making weak links between two key variables.

Diversification

This is a strategy for growth which involves developing products or business areas which are outside the organisation's markets. For example, a jeans manufacturer might decide to further develop its labels and brand strengths by going into healthy foods. Some companies deliberately operate a policy of diversification by always trying to identify the most attractive and rapidly developing industries in which to engage. They feel that the best business strategy to guarantee success is to enter attractive and emerging industries, rather than stay in static and slow developing ones.

Whenever an organisation diversifies it is engaging in some activity which is different to its core activities. This can be very useful as a business or marketing objective as it allows the organisation to spread its business risks by entering other markets or delivering other products or services. So, for example, if one product market starts to lose sales, by diversifying this may not damage a business organisation too badly.

Firms might want to diversify if opportunities in new market areas seem attractive or when the organisation wishes to reduce the impact of a trend within an industry.

To diversify an organisation could engage in forward or backward integration whereby the outlets or sources of supplies are joined with the organisation. This is prevalent in the semiconductor businesses where manufacturers of microprocessors join forces with semiconductor producers to ensure a continuous supply.

Alternatively a firm can engage in a conglomerate diversification, which involves the organisation expanding into businesses that have no relationship to its current product, markets or technology. For example, Coca-Cola purchased a movie company as a strategic move to counter a possible decline in the customer segment for its products, such as the youth group.

CASE STUDY

News Corporation – a truly diversified company

It is easy to take the media for granted, but there are some huge media giants out there. One of these is News Corporation. Forever linked with the 'Murdoch' name, and owners of 20th Century Fox, News Corporation has released three of the top five best-performing motion pictures of all time: Star Wars, Star Wars Episode I: The Phantom Menace, and Titanic.

News Corporation is the world's leading publisher of English-language newspapers, with operations in the UK, Australia, Fiji, Papua New Guinea and the USA. Newspapers it publishes in the UK include The Times, The Sun and The News of the World. In the book industry it owns HarperCollins publishers.

News Corporation had total assets as of 30 June 2004 of approximately US$51 billion and total annual revenues of approximately US$21 billion. It is therefore a diversified international media and entertainment company with operations in eight industry segments: filmed entertainment; television; cable network programming; direct broadcast satellite television; magazines and inserts; newspapers; book publishing; and other. It has activities principally in the United States, Continental Europe, the United Kingdom, Australia, Asia and the Pacific Basin.

1 **Describe News Corporation's marketing strategy.**
2 **What benefits do they gain from diversification?**

Relaunching/launching a product

All business organisations have to make critical decisions about products from time to time. For example, if a product has been around for a long time, a decision may have to be made about whether to replace it, or inject life into it, or more crucially whether to let the product fade out of existence.

The life of a product is the period over which it appeals to customers. We can all think of goods that everyone wanted at one time but which have now gone out of fashion. Famous examples from the 60s include hotpants and beehive hairstyles.

The sales performance of any product rises from zero when the product is introduced to the market, reaches a peak and then goes into decline (see Figure 3.10). Most products are faced by a limited life-cycle. Initially the produce may flourish and grow, eventually the market will mature and finally the product will move towards decline and petrification. At each stage in the product life-cycle there is a close relationship between sales and profits so that as organisations or brands go into decline their profitability decreases.

The life-cycle can be broken down into distinct stages. In the *introductory* phase, growth is slow and volume is low because of limited awareness of the product's existence. Sales then rise rapidly during the period of *growth*. It is during this phase that the profit per unit sold usually reaches a maximum. Towards the end of this phase, competitors enter the market to promote their own products, which reduces the rate of growth of sales of the first product.

This period is known as *maturity*. Competitive jockeying – such as product differentiation in the form of new flavours, colours, sizes, etc. – will sift out the weaker brands. During *saturation*, some brands will drop out of the market. The product market may eventually decline and reach a stage when it becomes unprofitable.

The life-cycle may last for a few months or for hundreds of years. To prolong the life-cycle of a brand or a product, an organisation needs to readjust the ingredients of the marketing mix. Periodic injections of new ideas are needed – product improvements, line extensions or improved promotions. Figure 3.11 illustrates the process of injecting new life into a product.

A readjustment of the marketing mix might include:

* Changing or modifying the product, to keep up with or ahead of the competition

* Altering distribution patterns, to provide a more suitable place for the consumer to make purchases

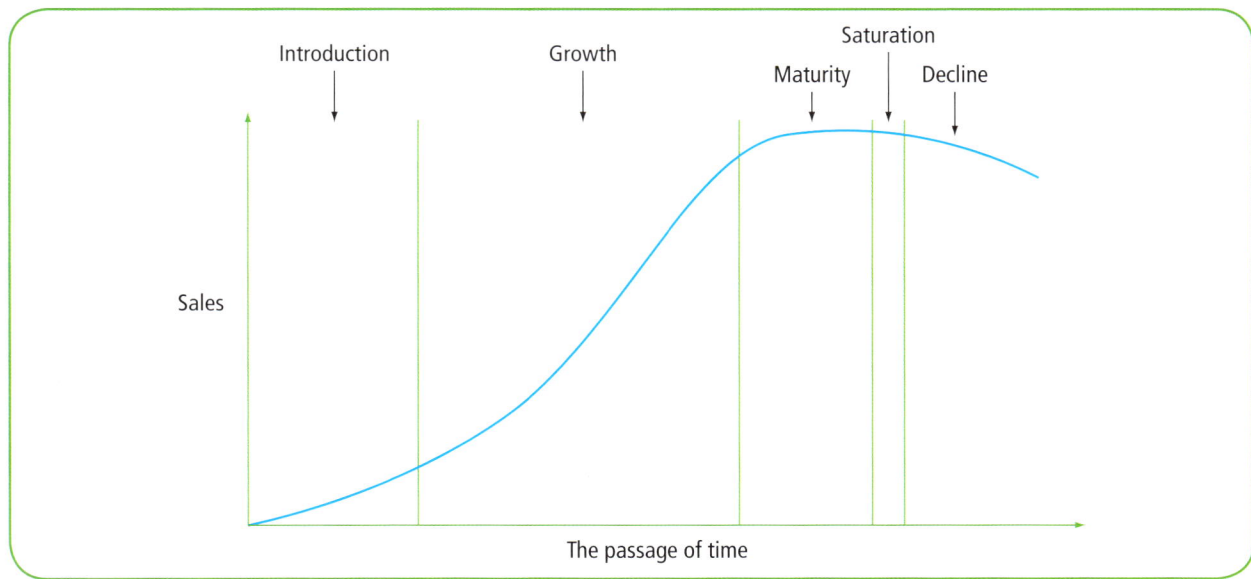

FIGURE 3.10 *Stages in the product life-cycle*

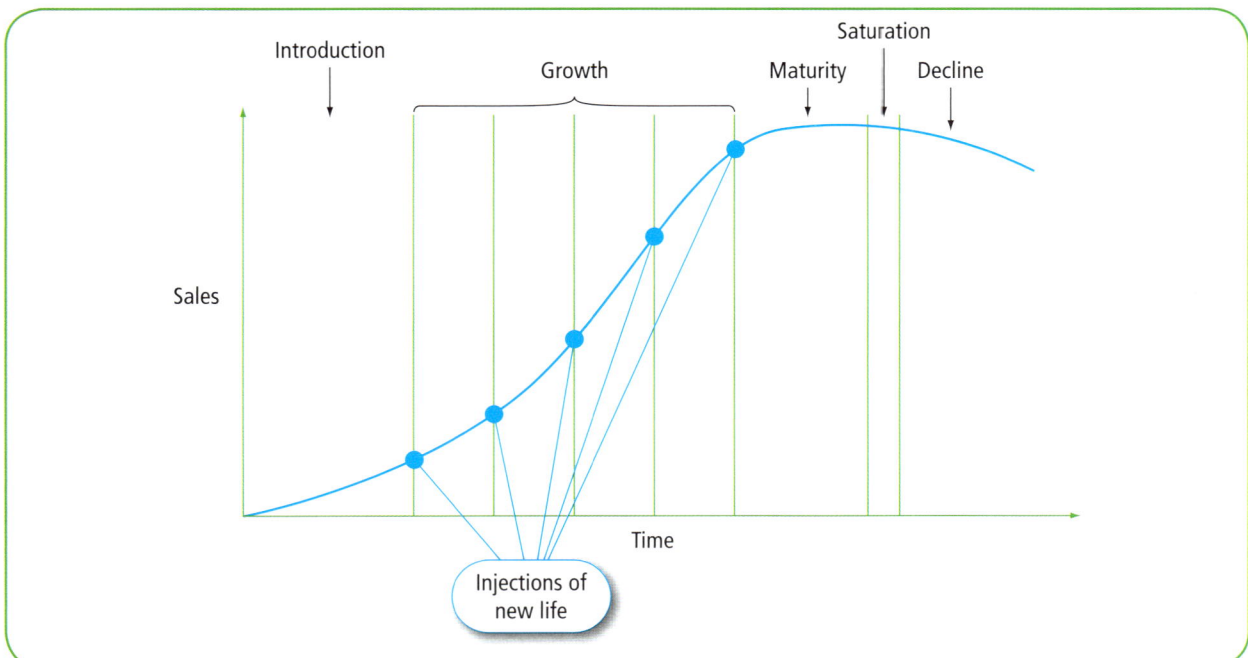

FIGURE 3.11 *Injecting new life into a product*

* Changing prices to reflect competitive activities
* Considering carefully the style of promotion.

Most large organisations produce a range of products, each with its own unique life-cycle. By using life-cycles, marketers can plan when to introduce new lines as old products go into decline. The collection of products that an organisation produces is known as its *product portfolio* (see Figure 3.12).

In Figure 3.12, T_1 represents a point in time. At that point product 1 is in decline, product 2 is in maturity, product 3 is in growth and product 4 has recently been introduced.

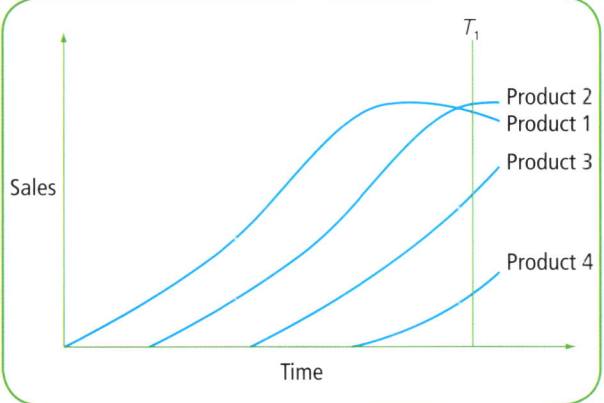

FIGURE 3.12 *A product portfolio*

Examining the life-cycle of a product helps us to appreciate that products go through various phases from infancy to decline. Markets and their structures are changing all of the time. In recent years 'niche marketing' has been popular, particularly with the emergence of branding. Today many organisations have spotted opportunities through the use of the Internet and other technologies to develop their markets.

Earlier we saw that market share is important for business organisations. The Boston Consultancy Group have argued that the faster the growth of a particular market the greater the

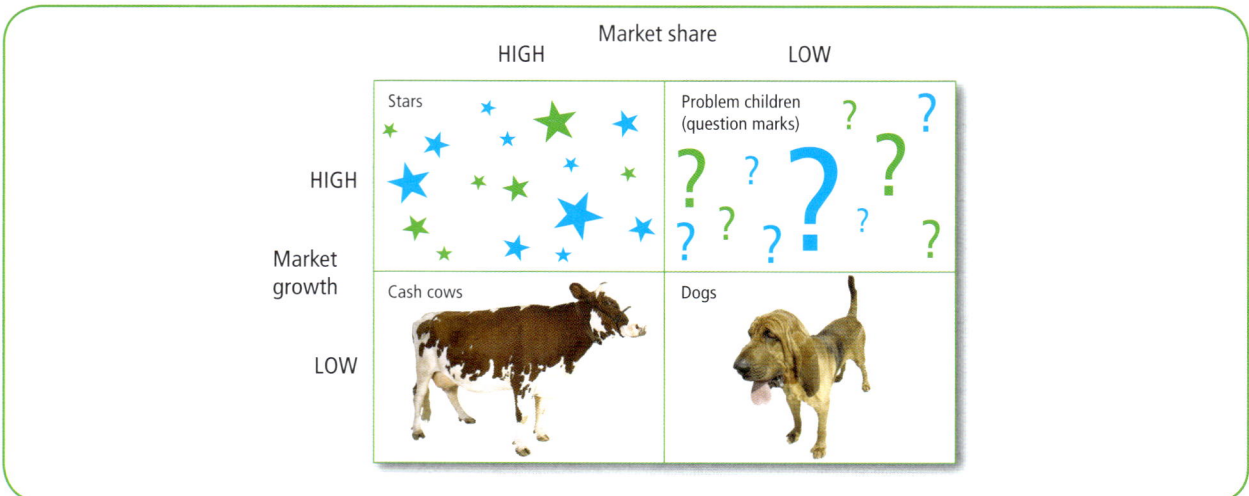

FIGURE 3.13 *The Boston Box or matrix*

cost necessary to maintain position. In a rapidly growing market, considerable expenditure will be required on investment in product lines, and to combat the threat posed by new firms and brands.

The Boston Group developed 'The Boston Box' or matrix, which relates closely to product life-cycles. They identify four types of products in an organisation's portfolio (Figure 3.13).

Problem children

Problem children are products that have just been launched. This is an appropriate name because many products fail to move beyond this phase. Such products are often referred to as *question marks*. Is it possible to develop these products and turn them into the *stars* and *cash cows* of the future? It might be, but first they will require a lot of financial support and this will represent a heavy financial commitment.

Stars

Stars are products that have successfully reached the growth stage in the life-cycle. Although these products too will require a lot of financial support, they will also provide high cash returns. On balance they will provide a neutral cash flow and are good prospects for the future.

Cash-cows

Cash-cows have reached the maturity stage in their product life-cycle and are now 'yielders'.

They have a high market share in markets that are no longer rapidly expanding. Because the market is relatively static, they require few fresh injections of capital, for example, advertising and promotion may be required to inject a little fresh life from time to time. However, the net effect is of a positive cash flow. Cash generated by the cash cows may be used to help the question marks.

Dogs

Dogs are products in decline. These have a low market share in a low-growing or a declining market. As they generate a negative cash flow, they will usually be disposed of.

In order to maintain an effective portfolio development, it is important to have a balance

Learning activity

Using your own experience of a product portfolio from an organisation, identify its:

✳ Question marks

✳ Stars

✳ Cash cows

✳ Dogs.

In each case explain what evidence you have for drawing the conclusions you make. Having done this, look at the portfolio of courses and products offered by your school and college, relating some to the categories above.

of products at any one time. An organisation will require a number of cash cows to provide its 'bread and butter'. At the same time, it is important to develop the cash cows of the future by investing in the question marks. Fortunately the stars should pay their own way. It is also important to identify the dogs and cut them out.

Products in the top half of the Boston Matrix are in the earlier stage of their product life-cycle and so are in high-growth markets. Those in the lower half of the box are in the later stages and so are in markets where growth will have slowed down or stopped.

Ansoff has developed this theory further by outlining a product-market mix. This looks not just at the management of a product portfolio but also more widely at market developments and opportunities. Ansoff's matrix matches existing and new product strategies with existing and new markets (Figure 3.14).

In this way, this matrix suggests five alternative marketing strategies which hinge upon whether the product is new or existing and whether the market is new or existing. These are:

* *Consolidation* implies a positive and active defence of existing products in existing markets.

* *Market penetration* suggests a further penetration of existing markets with existing products. This will involve a strategy of increasing market share within existing segments and markets.

* *Product development* involves developing new products for existing markets.

* *Market development* entails using existing products and finding new markets for them. Better targeting, market research and further segmentation will identify these new markets.

* *Diversification* will lead to a move away from core activities. This might involve some form of integration of production into related activities.

A new product may be one which:

* Replaces an old product

* Opens up a new market

* Broadens an existing market.

It may involve an innovation, a technological breakthrough or simply be a line extension based upon a modification. It is often said that only about 10% of new products are really new. In fact, it is often possible to turn old products into new products simply by finding a new market for them.

There are six distinct stages in the development process for new products. These are:

Step 1 Ideas

Step 2 Screening of ideas

Step 3 Marketing analysis

Step 4 Product development

Step 5 Testing

Step 6 Launch and commercialisation.

As new products go through each of these stages there is a mortality rate (see Figure 3.15).

Product Market	Existing products		New products
Existing markets	Consolidation	Market penetration	Product development
New markets	Market development		Diversification

FIGURE 3.14 *Ansoff's product matrix*

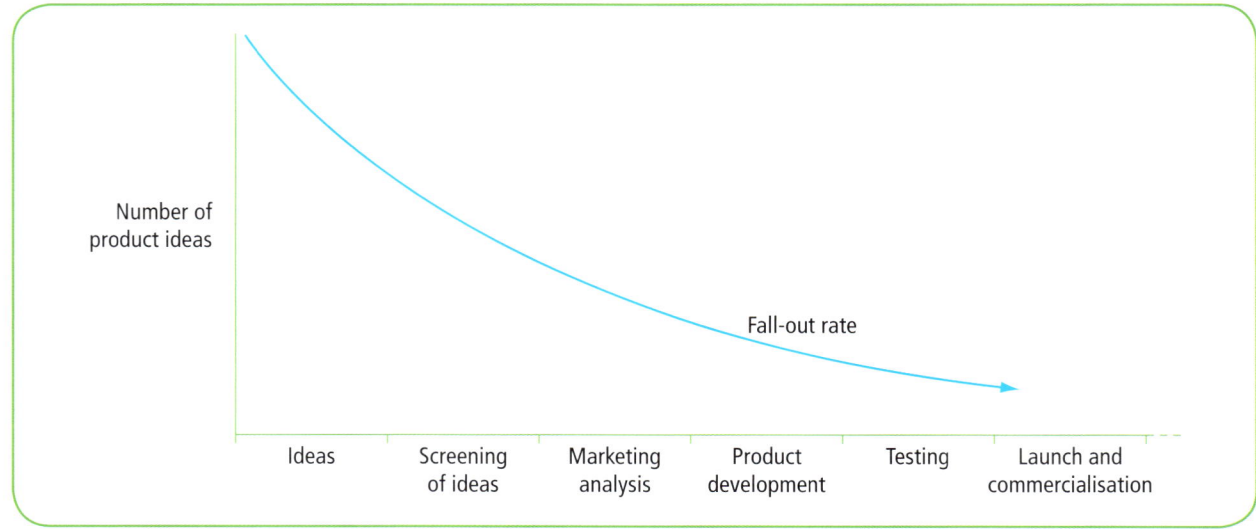

FIGURE 3.15 *Mortality (fall out) during the new product development process*

Step 1 *Ideas*

All new products start from ideas. These ideas may be completely new or simply be an update of an existing product. Ideas may come from:

Research and development – product development and market research working together. Technological breakthroughs and innovations from research are very important.

Mindstorming – involving a few people developing ideas from words and concepts.

Suggestions box – cash incentives may encourage employees to contribute their own ideas.

Sales force – working close to customers, the sales force understands their needs and requirements.

Forced relationships – sometimes one or more products can be joined together to form new product concepts. For example, shampoo and conditioner.

Competitors – monitoring the actions of competitors may provide a rich source of new ideas.

Step 2 *Screening of ideas*

Once ideas have been generated it is important to screen for the ideas likely to be successful and reject the rest. Considerations may include how well the product fits in with others in the product range, the unique elements of any idea that make it competitive, the likely demand for the product and whether or not it could be manufactured economically.

Step 3 *Marketing analysis*

Once the ideas have been screened, further marketing analysis begins. This involves a thorough analysis of the product's market potential. This type of research helps to identify the market volume (units that could be sold) as well as the value of sales expected. It may also help to identify market potential.

Step 4 *Product development*

Having come through the test of marketing analysis it is now time to translate the idea or product concept into a product. Design, innovation and the uses of technology are very important in product development. An assessment of packaging and branding may also be involved.

Step 5 *Testing*

Testing is a vital stage in the product development process. It may involve identifying valuable information through further market research which helps to fine-tune the venture. Test marketing may comprise testing on part of a consumer market or trialling the product to ensure that it meets the required standards.

Segway Scooter

You probably need to be in your thirties or at least your late twenties to remember the antics of Sir Clive Sinclair, inventor of the fabled C5 electric tricycle. When it was unleashed on an unsuspecting public in 1985, the Sinclair C5 was the last word in futuristic transport and caught the attention of all of the British press. Ten months, and £6m of investment, later it was consigned to the commercial scrapheap.

Any of you who have been to the United States recently may have seen the revolutionary Segway scooter, another pioneering new personal transporter. The Segway is the brainchild of American inventor Dean Kamen and has been compared to the C5 for presenting a solution to getting around congested cities. Well it is a case of 'watch this space' as Sinclair, having tested the new Segway, has announced news of a follow-up to the C5, called, not surprisingly, the C6.

Sir Clive is remaining tight-lipped about his new project, describing it only as a 'new product designed at getting people around town'. It is being developed in tandem with a British-based engineering company which specialises in compact electric motors and drive systems. He is convinced there is a gap in the market for his new invention, declaring the Segway unsuitable for British streets.

1 **What are the risks involved with launching innovative new products?**
2 **How might Sir Clive test the market before launching the C6?**

Step 6 *Launch and commercialisation*

The launch is the most important day in the life of a product – it is finally revealed to customers. It may involve rolling from one TV region to another TV region. Today a common technique is to provide sneak glimpses of new products before they are launched.

Increasing brand awareness

A key marketing objective may be to develop brand awareness. A *brand* is a particular product or characteristic that identifies a particular producer.

Many mass-produced products are almost identical. For example, most washing powders are similar, as are different types of margarine. These goods tend to be produced by two or three large companies who encourage sales by creating a brand that differentiates the products in the minds of consumers.

A brand can be a name, a symbol or a design used to identify a specific product and differentiate it from its competitors. Brand names, designs, trademarks, symbols, slogans and even music can be used to distinguish one product from another and allow an organisation to distinguish its products from competing ones.

The business of creating a brand is a particularly important function of marketing. Often people will buy the brand name as much as the product itself. You will see people in supermarkets pick up an item (which they have not seen before) and say, 'this must be a good one because it is made by ....'.

Large organisations swear by the power of the brand. They will fight tooth and nail to raise the status of their brands, and be determined that nothing should affect the power of their brands.

✳ DID YOU KNOW?

Virgin Atlantic became locked in a furious row with airport bosses in Australia over Sir Richard Branson's celebratory stunt following its first flight to Sydney. On arrival, Sir Richard, climbed onto the wing of Virgin's Airbus jet holding a surfboard. He was joined by a group of swimwear models waving a Union flag and an Australian national flag.

There are three different types of brands. These are:

Manufacturer brands Examples of these include Kellogg's Cornflakes, Nescafé Coffee and Heinz Baked Beans. These manufacturer brands associate the producer with the specific product, and the producer will be heavily involved with the promotion of the product.

Own-label brands Examples of these include Tesco, St Michael (Marks & Spencer), Farm Foods (Asda), Sainsbury's own label, etc. These brands are owned and controlled by retailers, and therefore the producers or manufacturers are not associated with the products or involved in their promotion.

Generic brands Such products are extremely rare in the modern competitive market, and those that exist are usually at the lower end of the market with respect to price and quality. These products have no identifiable name or logo. Examples may include plain T-shirts or bin-liners if they have no branded packaging or labels attached that identify the originator.

Organisations seek to create a portfolio of individual products which support the image of a brand. Well-known brand names will therefore emphasise quality throughout the organisation.

A brand which is held in high esteem is worth a lot of money to an organisation. There is a well-

Learning activity

Identify two or three brands of products in a particular market. To what extent could these brands be further developed in a way that exemplifies the attributes of each brand?

known saying in business that, 'an organisation can afford to get rid of its other assets, but not its brand image!'

Market segmentation

Remember that the simplest and most important principle of marketing is that marketing and its related activities should be designed to serve the customers. Serving customers needs with goods and services that do so more precisely than those of competitors in a market-orientated society has today become more important than ever. Whereas in the past, in many markets, all customers were treated to a similar diet of goods and services, organisations now recognise that groups of consumers have different needs, wants and tastes.

Not every person likes the same make of motor car or has the same taste in clothes. Equally, if cost and production time were of no importance, manufacturers would make products to the exact specifications of each buyer. On the other hand, neither can a manufacturer serve all customers successfully if it groups all of their needs and wants together.

CASE STUDY

Special K

Special K is a brand with a unique heritage. Over many years it has evolved as a stand-alone product and Kellogg's have not attempted to create any variants or develop the product further. However, over a period of time products reach their maturity phase of the product life-cycle, and in order to keep the brand fresh it was necessary to revitalise it and extend the growth phase by looking for opportunities to do so.

The solution for Kellogg's was to invest in a series of variants that would support the values of the brand and extend sales of the product. To do this Kellogg's launched cereal bars and also use berries and other variants to provide different taste opportunities for the core product. For Kellogg's this represented low risk and offered a good rate of return.

1 To whom does Special K appeal?
2 Why have Kellogg's invested in a series of variants?

Instead of trying to serve all customers equally, an organisation may focus its efforts on different parts of the total marketplace. Within the total marketplace it is possible to group customers with similar characteristics and divide the market into parts. This is known as market segmentation. Market segments are groups of customers with similar needs and characteristics. The task is to produce and supply different products to suit these segments.

Market segmentation is therefore a process of separating a total market into parts so that different strategies can be used for different sets of customers.

If you attempt to market a single product to the whole population, this is sometimes said to be like using a blunderbuss, firing shots to pepper the whole marketplace.

This is sometimes called *undifferentiated or mass marketing.* A single marketing mix is offered to the whole marketplace. In other words all potential customers are treated as if they have similar characteristics. This may be a relatively cheap way of tackling marketing, but its weakness is that it ignores individual differences.

Market segmentation, using differentiated marketing strategies, tailors separate product and market strategies to different sectors of the market. For example, the market for cars has many segments such as economy, off-road, MPV, luxury, high performance, etc. This approach

Learning activity

Does any market today exist where segmentation does not take place?

When it is not possible to satisfy all of its customers' needs with a uniform product, an organisation will use market segmentation to divide consumers into smaller segments consisting of buyers with similar needs or characteristics so that marketing becomes like firing a rifle instead of a blunderbuss. A rifle with an accurate sight will hit the target more efficiently without wasting ammunition.

recognises that in order to be successful and hit consumer needs, it is necessary to recognise the needs of different groups of consumers and meet them in different ways.

In fact some organisations simply exist to serve highly specialised market segments. They deliberately choose to compete in one segment and develop the most effective mix for that market. This is known as concentrated marketing. For example, Morgan serves the specific and highly esoteric needs of customers who like a car from the past. Jaguar cars are associated with luxury market segments. Similarly, quality fashion retailers today increasingly use brand names

FIGURE 3.18 *Marketing by rifle – hitting the target segment*

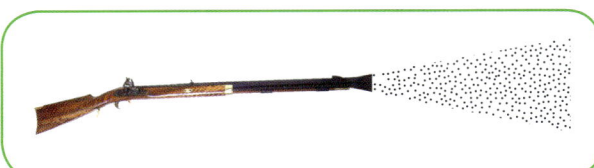

FIGURE 3.16 *Marketing by blunderbuss*

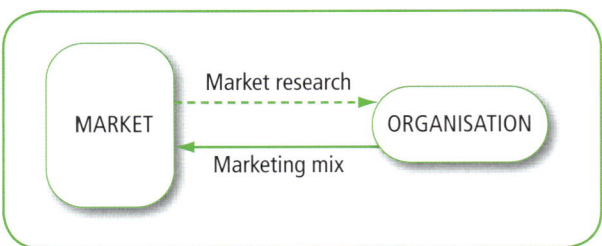

FIGURE 3.17 *Undifferentiated marketing*

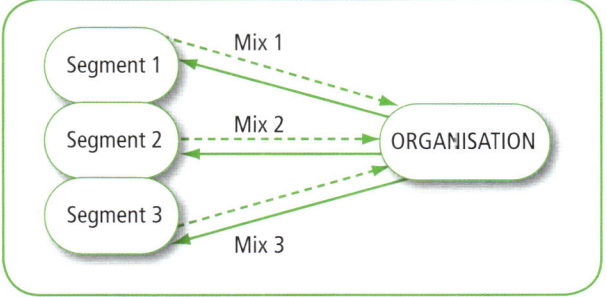

FIGURE 3.19 *Differentiated marketing*

The following diagram illustrates some of the main segments of the tea market, showing examples of teas sold in each segment.

Choose two of the segments and explain how you might use a slightly different marketing mix to appeal to consumers in these segments.

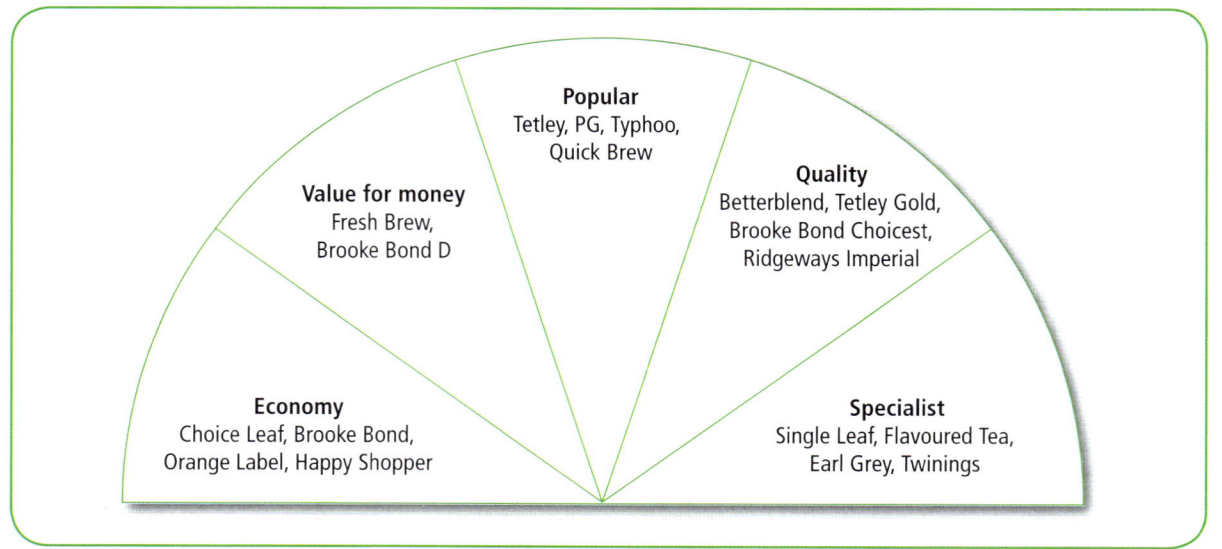

Popular
Tetley, PG, Typhoo, Quick Brew

Value for money
Fresh Brew, Brooke Bond D

Quality
Betterblend, Tetley Gold, Brooke Bond Choicest, Ridgeways Imperial

Economy
Choice Leaf, Brooke Bond, Orange Label, Happy Shopper

Specialist
Single Leaf, Flavoured Tea, Earl Grey, Twinings

FIGURE 3.20 *Segments of the tea market*

to position themselves in particular parts of a market. This is sometimes called niche marketing. A disadvantage is that if sales of a product decline in that segment, the lack of diversification means that this may affect the performance of the organisation.

There are three elements to segmentation – market segments, targeting and positioning.

Market segments

Market segments are groups of customers with similar needs and characteristics. The task is to produce and supply different products to suit these segments.

Targeting

Once segments have been identified, organisations have to identify one or more segments which has a need which can best be met by the organisation. This is known as targeting and may involve mass, undifferentiated marketing or concentrated marketing.

Positioning

Even though parts of the market are divided into segments, and organisations have worked out which ones to target, buyers within each segment will not have identical needs. Positioning involves developing a market strategy through the marketing mix that takes into account the thoughts and perceptions of customers about a product relative to other products and brands. The position is how the product is perceived in the minds of customers. Repositioning involves moving the product away from its current position in the market to another part of the market, where it might compete more effectively. Perhaps the most famous repositioning strategy in recent years is Skoda, who have moved away from a low cost, low reliability position in the market to become a well respected high value brand.

Look at two similar products. Comment upon the similarities and differences of their marketing mixes. To what extent are these due to positioning strategy?

Bases for segmenting markets

Geographic segmentation

This form of segmentation assumes that consumers in different regions may be affected by similar climate, natural factors, population density and levels of income. By dividing markets into regions it is possible to recognise and cater for the needs of customers in the regions. For example, people living in certain countries are assumed to have common characteristics that influence buying attitudes.

Demographic segmentation

Demographic factors, which can be measured with relative precision, have helped many organisations to define a basis on which to segment their market. Because demographic variables can be closely related to customer needs and purchasing behaviour, this helps producers to target their products more effectively. Demographic segmentation may involve dividing the population into discrete segments – for example, by age for clothes retailing, by sex for cosmetics, by family size for different sized packages of breakfast cereals, or in many other ways.

Segmentation by age

Segmentation by age is widely applied. A good example is the way in which banks and building societies develop services for students, young children, elderly customers and so on. Many products are also segmented by gender – clothing, alcohol, cosmetics and cars are segmented in such a way.

Other segmentation

Marketers may also segment according to ethnic background particularly for clothes, food and music. Levels of education can be a segmentation variable – some products clearly appeal to people of higher intellectual ability such as those who read *New Scientist* or *The Economist*.

Geodemographic segmentation

The newest methods of segmentation combine geographic and demographic segmentation principles. These are based on the belief that similar households in a particular locality exhibit similar purchasing behaviour.

The best-known geodemographic method is provided by CACI ACORN in their profile of Great Britain (see Figure 3.21). ACORN stands for A Classification Of Residential Neighbourhoods.

Learning activity

Look at the data below illustrating demographic trends for males within the UK between 1981 and 2002. Comment upon the different sort of products that might follow some of these trends.

	UNDER 4	5–14	15–24	25–34	35–44	45–59	60–64	65–74	75+	ALL
GREAT BRITAIN										
MALES (000s)										
1981	1,706	4,039	4,455	3,933	3,322	4,603	1,345	2,214	1,038	26,655
1982	1,737	3,887	4,514	3,826	3,462	4,554	1,401	2,179	1,073	26,633
1983	1,769	3,759	4,560	3,793	3,559	4,532	1,463	2,117	1,108	26,660
1984	1,773	3,667	4,590	3,818	3,640	4,514	1,515	2,067	1,145	26,729
1985	1,781	3,608	4,594	3,866	3,705	4,501	1,462	2,117	1,176	26,810
1986	1,797	3,542	4,580	3,935	3,778	4,467	1,426	2,152	1,201	26,878
1987	1,818	3,494	4,532	4,025	3,820	4,459	1,395	2,175	1,245	26,963
1988	1,849	3,468	4,443	4,113	3,838	4,490	1,379	2,180	1,277	27,037
1989	1,882	3,477	4,347	4,257	3,854	4,530	1,372	2,193	1,301	27,213
1990	1,901	3,508	4,227	4,379	3,868	4,571	1,365	2,199	1,321	27,339
1991	1,928	3,555	4,095	4,473	3,887	4,614	1,358	2,219	1,337	27,466
1992	1,939	3,609	3,954	4,548	3,816	4,769	1,352	2,243	1,340	27,570
1993	1,926	3,673	3,836	4,599	3,801	4,893	1,341	2,279	1,330	27,678
1994	1,920	3,704	3,749	4,642	3,825	4,992	1,331	2,309	1,319	27,791
1995	1,900	3,726	3,694	4,668	3,879	5,073	1,325	2,276	1,381	27,922
1996	1,866	3,761	3,630	4,677	3,965	5,139	1,322	2,257	1,427	28,044
1997	1,841	3,796	3,582	4,650	4,070	5,193	1,327	2,244	1,466	28,169
1998	1,820	3,817	3,561	4,589	4,181	5,252	1,346	2,236	1,500	28,302
1999	1,796	3,844	3,571	4,512	4,309	5,316	1,366	2,230	1,526	28,470
2000	1,771	3,838	3,598	4,435	4,444	5,379	1,376	2,233	1,552	28,627
2001	1,727	3,771	3,516	3,976	4,214	5,362	1,374	2,245	1,574	27,760
2002	1,686	3,756	3,606	4,004	4,314	5,448	1,376	2,267	1,614	28,072

Source: Office for National Statistics

	ACORN CATEGORY A: THRIVING	POP PROJ 2004 19.9%
1.1	Wealthy suburbs, large detached houses	2.9
1.2	Villages with wealthy commuters	2.7
1.3	Mature affluent home-owning areas	2.8
1.4	Affluent suburbs, older families	3.8
1.5	Mature well-off suburbs	2.7
2.6	Agricultural villages, home-based workers	1.6
2.7	Holiday retreats, older people, home-based workers	0.7
3.8	Home-owning areas, well-off older residents	1.4
3.9	Private flats, elderly people	1.2

Source: 2001 Census Area Statistics © Crown Copyright 2001, © CACI Ltd, 2005

FIGURE 3.21 *Example of ACORN Thriving category*

Psychographic and behavioural segmentation

This form of segmentation divides different groups up on the basis of social class, lifestyle or personality. For example:

1 *Social class* is a socio-economic way of dividing a market according to people's purchasing power and habits. The socio-economic grouping is sometimes called social stratification and each class roughly indicates a pattern of behaviour or consumption habits. One of the best known classifications is the NRS Social Grade Definitions, shown in Figure 3.22.

2 *Lifestyle* influences many of the goods or services that we purchase. Increasingly many make purchases that reflect their various lifestyles. For example, the lifestyle of this author includes healthfood, a love for a particular type of motor car and the occasional glass of Chardonnay.

3 *Personality* is something that we all have. All marketers have to do is to develop goods and services that match the personalities of their consumers. For example, what does it say about someone if they drive an Astra convertible, wear colourful clothes and wear lots of make-up?

4 *Behavioural segmentation* looks at behaviour patterns such as frequent/infrequent purchase and loyalty to a product. For example, one segment of the market may always purchase a product while another may be made up of people who frequently switch between brands. An experienced drinker may stick with Guinness, while an inexperienced one may try out a range of stouts and beers.

3.2 Using appropriate methods of market research

Business activities, by their very nature, are competitive. Within a dynamic business environment producers may be constantly entering and leaving the market. At the same time, changing consumer preferences may provide signals for them to develop new strategies with different products and services. Whereas some organisations will succeed and achieve or surpass their marketing objectives, others will inevitably not perform as well.

Market research is that vital link in the chain between buyers and suppliers. It does this by enabling those who provide goods and services to keep in touch with the needs and wants of those who buy the goods and services.

The American Market Research Association defines market research as:

'The systematic gathering, recording and analysis of data about problems related to the marketing of goods and services.'

We can break this definition down into its various ingredients:

systematic – in other words using an organised and clear method or system

SOCIAL GRADE	SOCIAL STATUS	OCCUPATION
A	Upper middle class	Higher managerial, administrative or professional
B	Middle class	Intermediate managerial, administrative or professional
C1	Lower middle class	Supervisory or clerical, and junior managerial or professional
C2	Skilled working class	Skilled manual workers
D	Working class	Semi-skilled and unskilled workers
E	Those at the lowest level of subsistence	State pensioners or widows (no other earner), casual or low-grade worker

Source: National Readership Survey

FIGURE 3.22 *One form of socio-economic grouping*

gathering – knowing what you are looking for, and collecting appropriate information

recording – keeping clear and organised records of what you find out

analysing – ordering and making sense of your information in order to draw out relevant trends and conclusions

problems related to marketing – finding out the answers to questions which will help you to understand better your customers and other details about the market-place.

All organisational activities take place in an environment where there is some element of risk. For example, last year a firm might have sold 40,000 fridges to a market in Italy. Who is to say that they will sell the 50,000 they plan to sell this year? They may suddenly find new competitors in this market with a much better product than they currently produce, which is being sold at a lower price. Italy may go through a cold spell – there may be problems in the economy that reduce the likelihood that people will change their fridge.

To reduce risk, market research provides an invaluable source of information to help organisations to make decisions and develop strategies for products. For example, it could help them to:

* identify their competitors
* improve their knowledge of consumers and competitors so that changing trends can be identified
* use trends to forecast activities
* monitor their market position and develop plans and strategies
* improve their competitive advantage.

Purpose of market research

All organisations require answers to key questions. Answers help decision-makers to understand the nature of the decisions they have to make about the products they provide and the markets in which they operate.

Questions may include:

How do we define the market? What are its features such as size and character, and what is the nature of competition?

What do customers require? At the heart of marketing should be the ongoing activities of satisfying the needs and aspirations of customers.

CASE STUDY

Connecting the washer to the web

Ariston have developed a washing machine that can communicate with the Internet using its own mobile phone. The margherita2000.com washing machine will be able to send breakdown reports for repair and download new washing cycles from its own website. The householder will also be able to control their washing machine remotely either by using a mobile phone or by logging onto the machine's own website.

The key achievement of this machine is that it is the first of a range of web-connected devices in the home that will be able to talk to each other using a new open communications system called WRAP – WebReady Appliances Protocol. In the first years of the new century, Ariston hope to follow up the launch of the washing machine with a dishwasher, fridge and then an oven.

1 To what sort of audience might the margherita2000 appeal?
2 What sort of market research questions might product planners ask before launching this type of product?

Who are the target groups and how do we reach them? The market may be made up of different groups and segments. Different distribution channels may be used to reach different groups of customers.

What strategies are used by our competitors? It is important to know and understand how the actions of competitors might influence the market.

How do we measure our performance? Market performance may be measured according to a number of key criteria, such as the value or volume of sales as well as brand or market share.

Where is our competitive position? An important feature of marketing analysis is an ongoing review of where the organisation is within the market, its competitive advantage and how changes in its actions might influence market shape and market share.

> *In short, the purpose of market research is to make the process of business scientific, by cutting out unsubstantiated guesswork and hunches!*

Some organisations are creative in their outlook to planning and research. These businesses may anticipate developments in markets and introduce new ideas and new methods to exploit opportunities or minimise problems. In doing this they may take risks to develop new ideas. In contrast other businesses will wait to see what their competitors do before reacting.

Some businesses therefore use market research to move ahead of the competition while others simply see it as a way of keeping up with their competitors. The first type of firm we would describe as being **proactive**, while the second we would describe as **reactive.**

The proactive business will be the first to come up with new ideas, and consequently well placed to exploit their ideas in meeting adventurous marketing objectives such as brand leadership in a new market. Sony are famous for breaking new ground and taking risks through proactive planning and research.

The reactive business does not put itself at the mercy of such risk and can never be in a position to make the same sort of impact as a proactive firm. Equally, it does not fall foul of the mistakes made by proactive firms.

Working in small groups, make a list of:

* five proactive organisations, together with some of their products;

* five reactive organisations and their products.

One of the most important things to remember is that what comes out of market research is only as good as what goes in. Identifying the information required, successfully choosing the most suitable research method and then the type and nature of questioning should all be carefully considered before any project proceeds.

Primary research

Any information that is original and is obtained outside an organisation is referred to as primary data. It is obtained by research conducted by or on behalf of the organisation, is specific to its needs and will involve a range of methods such as discussions, questionnaires and surveys and testing through pilots and field trials.

Questionnaires

Many market research methods depend upon the use of a questionnaire. A questionnaire is a systematic list of questions designed to obtain information from people about:

* specific events

* their attitudes

* their values

* their beliefs.

The quality of the questionnaire is inextricably linked with the survey. A good questionnaire will result in a smooth interview, giving the interviewer a precise format to follow and

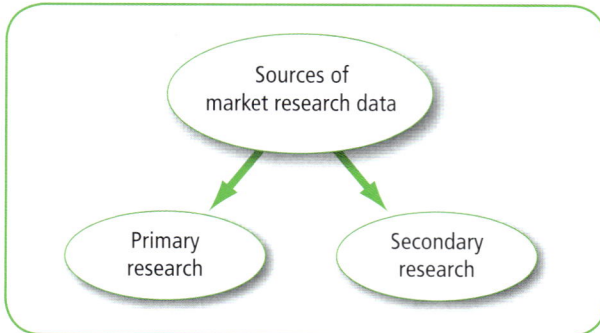

FIGURE 3.23 *Sources of research data*

not ask too many questions

not ask leading or intimate questions

fit questions into a logical sequence

use the language of the target group

not use questions that are confusing or ambiguous

avoid questions relating to sexuality, politics and religion unless they are very relevant.

Sequencing the questions logically is very important. It may be useful to start with a few factual questions that are easy to respond to. Some form of multiple-choice questions may follow these up before introducing questions that require the respondent to think about some of the issues being researched. The questionnaire may be closed with 'filter questions' about the background of the respondent, which help to locate them in the sampling frame.

There is no point including questions that do not relate to the main purposes of the research. The questionnaire should be kept as short as practically possible. More than 40 questions could put off respondents or cause them to provide hasty replies to questions.

The questions in a questionnaire may be 'open' or 'closed'. *Open questions* allow the person answering to give an opinion and may encourage him or her to talk at length. You have to be careful though. Asking questions such as 'What type of music do you listen to?' could lead to such a variety of answers that analysing them would be very difficult. *Closed questions* usually require an answer picked from a range of options (which may be simply yes/no). Most questionnaires use closed questions, so that they can be answered quickly and efficiently, and the answers are easier to analyse (see Figure 3.24).

Sometimes it is necessary to judge the degree of the respondent's feelings on a subject. The best way to do this is to use a rating or response scale. There are various types:

Likert scales show how strongly the respondent agrees or disagrees with a statement (see Figure 3.25).

Rank order scale questions ask the respondent to put a number beside various items in order to

ensuring that he or she obtains exactly the information required in a format that is easy for the researcher to analyse later.

Questionnaire design is critical. Although it is easy to make up questions, it is very difficult to produce a good questionnaire – and a badly designed questionnaire may lead to biased results.

Another problem may arise if very few completed forms are returned, or if those returned are only partially completed. In addition, if the questionnaire is being administered by a number of interviewers, there is always the danger that some may misinterpret questions and introduce their own personal bias in a way that prompts certain answers from respondents.

If you were asked to write a questionnaire, where would you start? The starting point would be to think about the focus of your questions. For example, what information do you require and why do you need it? You would also need to think about the target audience that you wish to examine. It would be important to question all of the people who are likely to have relevant opinions or information.

When people give up their own time to answer the questions on a questionnaire, it is useful to tell them who you are and why you are undertaking this research. This is not only polite but will also put the respondent at ease and may facilitate co-operation. The language used and the number of prompts and examples to support the points made within the questionnaire need to be considered.

A good questionnaire will:

ask questions which relate directly to information needs

Please indicate with a tick which types of music you listen to regularly (tick all that apply):

- ☐ Classical
- ☐ Easy listening
- ☐ Jazz
- ☐ Blues
- ☐ Golden oldies
- ☐ Popular
- ☐ Heavy metal
- ☐ Punk
- ☐ Indie
- ☐ Rap
- ☐ Dance
- ☐ Swing
- ☐ Hip Hop
- ☐ Other (please specify) _ _ _ _ _ _ _ _ _ _ _

FIGURE 3.24 *A closed question*

put them in some sort of order of preference, as shown in Figure 3.26.

An **intention-to-buy** asks respondents to indicate by ticking a box how likely it is that they will buy some items in the future (see Figure 3.27).

Semantic differential scales use two words describing the opposite ends of a scale, with a series of points highlighted between. The

These are all considerations when choosing where to buy a new computer. Put them in rank order with 1 by the most important, 2 by the second most important and so on down to 5 against the least important.

Wide choice	2
Helpful sales staff	3
Value for money	1
After-sales service	4
Quick delivery	5

FIGURE 3.26 *A rank order scale question*

If a textbook was available covering this unit/module, I would:

Definitely buy	Probably buy	Not sure	Probably not buy	Definitely not buy
1 ☐	2 ☐	3 ☐	4 ☐	5 ☐

FIGURE 3.27 *An intention-to-buy question*

respondents are asked to indicate where on the scale their opinion lies (see Figure 3.28).

Put a cross in the box that shows how strongly you agree or disagree with each of the following statements:

	Strongly agree	Agree	Neither agree nor disagree	Disagree	Strongly disagree
This AS course has prepared me well for work		X			
The lecturers at college are well prepared			X		
The lectures at college are interesting	X				
I was well prepared for my assignments				X	

FIGURE 3.25 *A Likert scale*

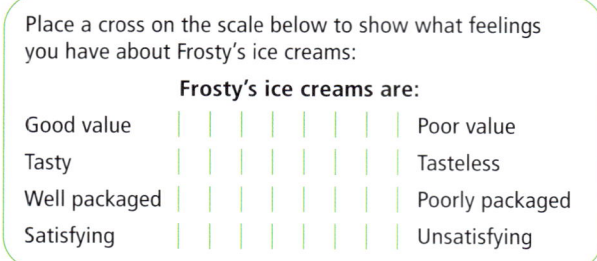

Place a cross on the scale below to show what feelings you have about Frosty's ice creams:

Frosty's ice creams are:

Good value | | | | | | | Poor value
Tasty | | | | | | | Tasteless
Well packaged | | | | | | | Poorly packaged
Satisfying | | | | | | | Unsatisfying

FIGURE 3.28 *A semantic differential scale*

Frosty's ice creams are:

	1 2 3 4 5 6 7 8 9 10	
Good value	✗	Poor value
Tasty	✗	Tasteless
Well packaged	✗	Poorly packaged
Satisfying	✗	Unsatisfying

FIGURE 3.29 *Comparing respondent replies*

Frosty and Polar ice creams are:

Good value ✗ ✗ Poor value
Tasty ✗ ✗ Tasteless
Well packaged ✗ ✗ Poorly packaged
Satisfying ✗ ✗ Unsatisfying
Polar   Frosty

FIGURE 3.30 *Comparing product strengths and weaknesses*

Once the respondent has completed such a question, the points can be joined up to produce a profile of that product. Comparing replies from a number of respondents provides a useful profile of how the product is viewed by customers (see Figure 3.29).

It is then possible to compare products or brands by superimposing two or more profiles on one scale, to identify the strengths and weaknesses of each. An example of this is shown in Figure 3.30.

The purpose of a closed question is to get people to commit themselves to a concrete answer. The problem with open questions is that

Learning activity

Think back to any questionnaire or form which you have recently filled in. (If necessary, use your course enrolment form as an example) What was the purpose of the form or questionnaire? Was it simple or easy to understand? Do you feel that it was well designed? If not, why not?

they are difficult to analyse. Closed questions tie respondents down so that they have to make a decision within a range of choices.

To help interviewers operate a questionnaire, a **prompt card** is sometimes used. This means that, if several or all of the questions in the questionnaire have the same range or set of answers, these can be numbered and then the respondents answers can be recorded as numbers (see Figure 3.31).

Some questionnaires are designed so that respondents can concentrate on the questions that are relevant, and the skip over the questions which do not relate to them (see Figure 3.32).

Dolland & Aitchison	01
Specsavers Optical Superstores	02
Boots Opticians	03
Vision Express	04
Rayner & Keeler	05
Optical Express	06
G. C. Bateman	07
Co-op	08
Scrivens	09
Others	10

FIGURE 3.31 *A prompt card*

Question 6 **Do you have a bank account?**
☐ YES
☐ NO
If your answer is **NO**, proceed to question 20

FIGURE 3.32 *A question that permits a respondent to skip to the next relevant part of a questionnaire*

Use the questionnaire below to discuss your feelings about one product which you regularly purchase (Product A):

Total performance of Product A (including product, sales, support, price, etc.):

Dissatisfied ☐ ☐ ☐ ☐ ☐ ☐ ☐ ☐ ☐ ☐ **Very satisfied**
        1   2   3   4   5   6   7   8   9   10

Compared to one year earlier, is Product A's total performance:

☐ Better   ☐ Worse   ☐ Same

Why?

[blank box]

What one thing can_____ do to improve the performance of Product A in meeting your total needs?

[blank box]

Explain how the answers you have provided for this brief questionnaire might be used.

What information has it provided?

Comment upon the structure of the questions.

How easy would it be to analyse and interpret the information it provided?

Observation

This involves looking at how consumers behave in the shopping environment. Information like this can help marketers to make decisions about packaging, or influence the choice of point-of-sale materials designed to attract the attention of shoppers. It may also help to make decisions about where to place particular products in a shop – the process of putting products in a store in the right place at the right time is known as **merchandising**. This is particularly important in the retail trade.

Today a number of electronic devices can be used to monitor customers' individual responses. For example:

✱ a psycho-galvanometer measures perspiration and this may be used for a variety of forms of testing

✱ an eye camera may record reactions such as visual stimulation

✱ a tachistoscope exposes material for a short period and then measures responses.

Product testing and test marketing

It is possible to use tests within the marketplace as a form of primary research. For example, an organisation may test a new product in a television region that is regarded as being representative of the wider market. One major problem with test marketing is that it alerts competitors to new ideas. However, at least it does help an organisation to anticipate the ways in which consumers will respond to a new product idea or concept.

In test marketing the organisation will need to decide upon the size and make-up of the sample it is using. They will also need to give consideration to the length of time that is appropriate for the test in order to provide valid and reliable results. Research indicates that the longer the period for which products are test marketed, the more accurate the forecasts that can be made about their likely success.

An alternative to test marketing is to use a consumer panel to find out consumer attitudes to a product or the strength of preferences.

Focus groups

Focus groups are an inexpensive method of obtaining useful qualitative information from consumers. For example, under the guidance of a chairperson, a group of users of the same product may be invited to provide opinions on its use. Members of a focus group might be members of the public who have opinions on certain products and services. They may be drawn from a certain market segment or from an industry. Focus groups are very good at testing customer reactions to product developments or proposals.

A good leader is essential for a focus group. He or she will introduce key topics for discussion, keep order and ensure that every group member has the opportunity to make a contribution. The main benefit of such groups is that new ideas and opinions can be 'bounced off' each group member to refine them and prompt further creative thought. A group requires a note taker. It may also be audio or video-taped.

CASE STUDY

Like other manufacturers, Vauxhall has to cope with a rapidly changing world and to keep pace it begins planning the next model even as the wraps are coming off a new launch.

This begins with a series of 'clinics' where the reaction to a new shape is tested out on a number of preselected motorists. These motorists are recruited by an outside agency from owners of cars in the target group together with a small number positioned above the group (who may be persuaded to trade down) and below the group (who may be persuaded to trade up). They will be people who have no connection with the motor or advertising industries.

Confidentiality is very important at this stage, so the cars are not badged and the respondents are not told which manufacturer is conducting the clinic. This also avoids any personal prejudices against a particular marque coming into play.

1 Why do Vauxhall use focus groups or clinics?
2 What sort of issues are they likely to raise at such groups?
3 Who might be targeted to attend such groups?
4 How would Vauxhall probably use this information?

See more on the Vauxhall website through www.heinemann.co.uk/hotlinks (express code 1130P, then go to Unit 3).

Consumer panels

Another market research method is to set up panels of consumers, which consist of groups of consumers who agree to provide information about their attitudes or buying habits.

A consumer on a *home audit panel* will discuss consumer issues during a series of personal visits by a researcher. The great advantage is that this type of panel will supply information over a long period of time from a willing participant who may agree to sample, test or use a range of products or who is simply asked to respond to questions on consumer issues.

Another type of panel are those that involve the collection of electronically-generated information. For example, one such panel is provided by the Broadcasters' Audience Research Board which estimates the number of people watching TV programmes. Members of this panel are selected in a way that makes sure that they are representative of all television households. Once a prospective panel member agrees to join the panel, their television sets and video recorders are then monitored by a meter which collects information about their viewing habits. Members register their presence in a room by pressing a button on their peoplemeter handset when they enter a room and then the meter captures information related to their viewing.

According to BARB:

'The Broadcasters' Audience Research Board (BARB) is responsible for providing estimates of the number of people watching television. This includes which channels and programmes are being watched, at what time, and the type of people who are watching at any one time. BARB provides television audience data on a minute-by-minute basis for channels received within the UK. The data is available for reporting nationally and at ITV and BBC regional level and covers all analogue and digital platforms.

Viewing estimates are obtained from panels of television owning households representing the viewing behaviour of the 24+ million households within the UK. The panels are selected to be representative of each ITV and BBC region. The service covers viewing within private households only.

Panel homes are selected via a "multi-stage, stratified and unclustered" sample design. What this means is that the panel is fully representative of all television households across the whole of the UK.'

Set up your own consumer discussion panel. Provide respondents with a suitable form and then ask five people to monitor their purchases over a fortnight. Think of some appropriate questions and then interview each person to discuss their purchases. Record your results.

For more information on BARB, visit their website using www.heinemann.co.uk/hotlinks (express code 1130P, then go to Unit 3).

Organisations that buy Homescan information from Nielsen can understand exactly who their customers are. They find out about what products customers are buying day by day, so that they can tailor this knowledge to develop promotions and their advertising for the days when the right customers come in store. They can assess a new product launch. By using Homescan they can evaluate the retail distribution of a new product and understand the factors behind its build in volume and market share. It also provides an opportunity to track products to find out factors that might be undermining their performance. This all helps to measure the tactical and strategic objectives of a marketing campaign and to refine and develop precise elements of marketing strategies. For example, it might help to answer questions such as:

CASE STUDY

Waving the wand

A C Nielsen's electronic consumer panel is known as Homescan. It brings a new dimension to consumer analysis providing a powerful insight into the behaviour of customers. In a sophisticated and competitive marketing environment, this type of panel provides instant and precise data using barcode technology. Launched in June 1989, Homescan became the first panel in Europe to use in-home scanning.

See more about Homescan on A C Nielsen's website through www.heinemann.co.uk/hotlinks (express code 1130P, then go to Unit 3).

Households are chosen to mirror demographics within regions to provide accurate representations of purchasing across the country. Each household is equipped with a small hand-held scanner, referred to as a wand. After each shopping trip they record the date, the items bought, any promotional offers which applied, the price, the quantity and the store used.

The wand asks a series of questions to prompt the panellist. Scanning each product's barcode enables its 'fingerprint' to be recorded and provides A C Nielsen with a precise record of consumer purchasing. The information is then transferred directly, via telephone modem links, to Nielsen's host computer. Collecting daily purchasing data provides speed and precision to marketing.

Homescan includes all grocery purchases brought into the home from any outlet. The panel includes 10,500 households throughout the UK, including Northern Ireland.

1 What is the purpose of Homescan?
2 How might A C Nielsen use this data?

Has the relaunch succeeded in regaining lapsed buyers?

What is the best way to target mailing activity?

How does advertising expenditure help which brands?

Where do consumers buy?

How loyal are consumers?

In October 2004 A C Nielsen announced that it had completed the first phase of the expansion of its U.S. Homescan consumer panel, bringing the panel size up to 91,500 households creating a rich source of consumer insights.

As part of its *Homescan MegaPanel* initiative, A C Nielsen expanded the size of its Homescan panel from 61,500 households, with a second phase set to increase the size of the panel to 125,000 households by the end of 2005.

According to A C Nielsen, 'The expanded panel will allow for the development of specialty panels consisting of households with babies, households with teens, and others, all of which will help clients better serve specific niches and identify new ones. The *MegaPanel* will also allow for improved sales measurement within fast-growing retail channels such as mass merchandisers, dollar stores, warehouse clubs stores, and pet specialty stores.'

Trade audits

Sometimes the best and easiest form of market research is simply to discuss issues with customers to make sure that their experiences match their expectations. This is known as a trade audit. Trade audits involve an analysis of consumer experiences. For example, at the end of your course you may be asked to fill in a questionnaire so that you can provide feedback about each of your modules and discuss your experiences.

Marketing/trade auditing is used as a means of assessing past performance so that an assessment can be taken about future courses of action. As an internal audit it enables an organisation to understand how it stands in relation to its customers and where its strengths and weaknesses lie. David Mercer sets out the following list of key points of information that need to be collected for the marketing audit:

Who are the customers? What are their key characteristics and what differentiates them from other members of the population?

What are their needs and wants? What do they expect the product to do and what are their special requirements and perceptions?

What are their attitudes and what are their buying intentions?

Trade or marketing audits will therefore be concerned with:

* reviewing all of current marketing activity, focusing upon how well the marketing mix meets the needs of existing customers

* a review of marketing systems from the customers' standpoint to assess how well their needs are being catered for.

Secondary research

Secondary marketing information is effectively anything that has previously been published. It can be built from both *internal* and *external* sources.

Internal sources of secondary data

Internal information is information already held within the organisation, more often than not held in databases. A database is a large amount of information stored in a way that it can easily be found, processed and updated. Users may access the database across an organisation

Information on existing customers will form the core of the database, with sales invoices probably being the most valued source of data. The invoice is created for financial purposes but it contains a considerable amount of customer data that can be made immediately available for others. For example, it might contain information such as:

Customer title	gender, job description, other forms of identification
Customer surname	ethnic coding
Customer address	geographic coding
Date of sale	tracking purchase rates and repurchasing patterns
Items ordered	product category interests
Quantities ordered	heavy / medium / light users
Price	value of customer
Terms and conditions	customer service needs.

One way in which organisations in the retail industry keep and analyse data from customers is by the use of loyalty cards. It would be possible to match the postcode of the customer with the nature and type of purchases they might make, and then to use this information as a base for making product and merchandising decisions within a store.

External sources of secondary data

External data exists in the form of published materials collected by somebody else. It can provide a broader dimension to data previously collected.

For example, external information can be used to enhance existing knowledge. Postcodes may help to group customers geographically. By identifying and labelling certain characteristics of a customer, a company may be able to make assumptions about their needs. Two examples of useful external sources are:

Domestic socio-economic data Customers are classified according to their house type, the assumption being that a certain lifestyle is associated with that type of house.

Industrial classification Organisational customers can be classified according to the nature of their activities. Certain types of organisations can then be expected to have predictable demands for services.

External information can complement an organisation's own information by providing direct comparison with competitors, by putting performance within the context of the economy as a whole, and by identifying markets offering potential.

Government statistics

The principal suppliers of government statistics in the UK are:

ONS (Office for National Statistics)
DTI (Department of Trade and Industry)
DfES (Department for Education and Skills)
GSS (Government Statistical Service)
OECD (Organisation for Economic Co-operation and Development)
Visit the websites of these organisations through www.heinemann.co.uk/hotlinks (express code 1130P, then go to Unit 3).

Some of the key publications include:

Monthly Digest of Statistics – summary information on many economic trends.
Regional Trends – regional profiles, households, labour, living standards, etc.
Labour Market Trends – topical articles, hours worked, sickness, training, vacancies, disputes, earnings and unemployment.
Social Trends – trends in labour markets, incomes, and spending by item and by region.
Family Spending – details on who earns and spends what.

New Earnings Survey – earnings listed by industry, area, occupation and others.
National Food Survey – expenditure on and consumption of food by income group and region.
Population Trends – family statistics including births, marriages and deaths, etc. in regions.
Annual Abstract of Statistics – population, social conditions, production, prices, employment.
Bank of England Quarterly Bulletin – articles on financial trends.
General Household Survey – social and socio-economic issues.
Retail Prices Index – changes in UK prices.
Census of Production – data about production by firms in all industries.
Eurostat Publications – a variety, covering economic, industrial and demographic changes across Europe.
Indicators of Industrial Activity - production, employment and prices across a variety of industries and compared worldwide.
Business Monitors – statistics concerning output in different business sectors. *The Retailing Monitor* is of particular interest, covering what is being bought by region.

Media and other sources

Another useful source of information is the *media*. Whilst unlikely to yield detailed data, the media may present a series of stories about key market sectors or larger organisations. Sources include:

CASE STUDY

Applying to be a market researcher

Market researchers organise the collection of public and business opinion about products, services or organisations. They may also conduct market research interviews and test new questionnaires.

Tasks and duties

If you apply to be a market researcher you may be asked to:

Discuss information with clients

Design surveys and questionnaires

Organise and manage surveys

Liaise with field workers and their supervisors

Supervise survey staff

Conduct interviews

Undertake comprehensive secondary research and generally develop an understanding of how such knowledge could be used to support decision-making processes.

Skills

Market researchers need good research skills and the ability to think logically so that they can design good surveys and questionnaires. They need mathematical and statistical ability and computer skills, to analyse and interpret their data.

Organisational and time-management skills are important in this work. Market researchers should also have good written and oral communication skills and they should be good listeners. It is also important to have creative thinking ability to be able to find solutions to problems.

Knowledge

Market researchers should know about questionnaire design, survey methods and marketing techniques. They should also know how to interpret statistics. They should understand how humans behave and think, and they need to be aware of different sampling and interview methods.

It is important for market researchers to have some knowledge and understanding of the businesses or industries they research. Market researchers need an understanding of marketing, business or research methods.

Personal qualities

Market researchers need to be able to work well under pressure, and juggle many tasks within a project. Accuracy is important, and they should be culturally sensitive when designing questionnaires and managing survey projects. They should be team players and honest. The ability to manage tasks and take responsibility are important for this job. Market researchers must also be able to keep information private.

Appearance

As market researchers spend a lot of time dealing with people such as clients, respondents and other professionals outside the organisation, their appearance is important.

Write a list detailing your experiences of market research.

Newspapers – broadsheets such as *The Times* and *The Financial Times* are both authoritative sources. However, they do not take into account the value of local papers and local circumstances.

Magazines and trade journals – the obvious ones are *The Economist* and *The Grocer*.

TV and radio – these include specialist news and current affairs programmes.

Teletext – this provides a variety of current information across many topics.

Trade associations publish information for their members concerning their particular fields, and there are associations for almost all trades.

The Internet has rapidly become an invaluable research tool providing a rich resource for information from a multitude of sources. As a resource it is predicted to continue to grow rapidly and become much more central to the workings of organisations not just in terms

Using the case study, draft a person specification for a market research post.

Look at the requirements for market researchers. Think about how you might or might not fit the bill for such a post. Draft a letter of application for the post of a market researcher at an organisation you have some knowledge of or interest in.

of 'Internet marketing' but also as a business resource. Try visiting MORI through www.heinemann.co.uk/hotlinks (express code 1130P, then go to Unit 3). Many organisations such as Boots or Nestlé have their own *intranet*. Unlike the Internet which is available to all, an intranet is a data sharing facility within an organisation.

There are a number of *commercial market research companies* offering a range of services and selling data that they acquire from a variety of sources. For example, Mintel is a commercial research organisation which, in return for a fee, provides a monthly journal containing reports on consumer markets – for example, bread, alcoholic drinks and financial services. Information includes areas such as market size, main competitors, projected growth, market share of main competitors, advertising spend of main competitors and other trends. Mintel also produces in-depth reports on certain markets and the website is available through www.heinemann.co.uk/hotlinks (express code 1130P, then go to Unit 3).

The types of reports produced by agencies include:

Retail Business Market Surveys These are published monthly and each carries details of certain industries. It is important for those involved in market research to be able to access those relevant to their particular field. Each copy will carry an index of industries investigated. There will be details on market size, market sectors, price trends, sales abroad, advertising and promotion, consumption, distribution, branding and prospects for the industry.

Key Note Reports carry even more information with specific information upon each industry.

Retail Audits Some organisations such as Retail Audits collect data of retail sales through supermarkets and larger chains and then sell the information to organisations wishing to buy it. These figures enable producers to work out the market shares of their markets, the sales of different products and the effects of any recent strategy such as a price change or a promotional campaign.

Quantitative and qualitative data

The information gathered through market research may be described as being either **qualitative** or **quantitative** in nature. Qualitative information informs the organisation about the opinions and preferences of individuals and cannot always be interpreted statistically. For example, in response to a qualitative interview about cakes one person might feel that the cake is too moist and rich, while another might think that

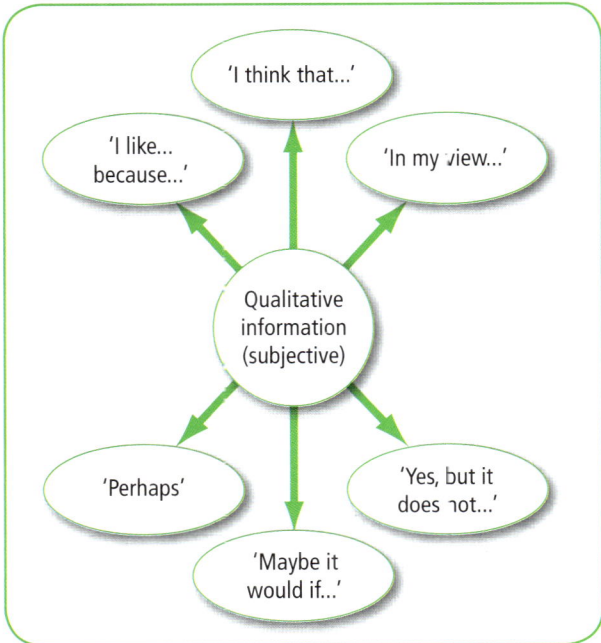

FIGURE 3.33 *Qualitative information*

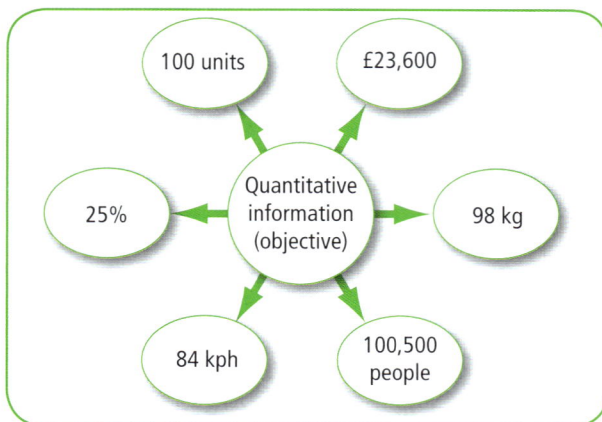

FIGURE 3.34 *Quantitative information*

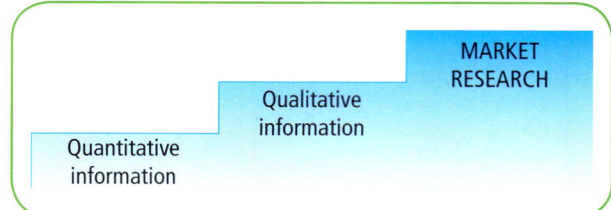

FIGURE 3.35 *Supporting quantitative data by qualitative information*

it has a rich taste. Qualitative research is therefore about descriptions. This type of information is difficult to categorise and measure because it is based upon personal views deemed to be subjective.

On the other hand quantitative information is research that produces figures that can be examined statistically. For example, 15 out of 20 people might prefer one brand to another. As this is considered to be based upon hard facts, it is considered to be objective.

Many research methods supply both qualitative and quantitative information, and the two are closely interlinked. Qualitative information provides the context within which quantitative facts operate. The 'What do you think about…?' approach gives people the opportunity to offer a variety of opinions, reasons, motivations and influencing factors. A *group discussion*, for example, allows different opinions to be offered, which will frequently lead to a consensus, giving an idea of the popular view. People enjoy offering their opinions on subjects as diverse as the current political climate and the taste of a particular margarine, and what this gives the researcher is an overall view of that particular audience's reaction to a proposition.

Quantitative data helps to produce an idea of the size and overall shape of markets and the effects of strategies on the demand for goods and services. Qualitative data helps to take this process further to show how goods and services have met the needs of current and potential customers (Figure 3.35).

There are two broad areas in which market research can take place. If information does not already exist in an identifiable form it will have to be collected first-hand. This is known as **primary research**. Any information that is already published outside an organisation is known as **secondary research data.**

Validity, use and limitations

Planning the data collection process helps to ensure that data is reliable. In *primary research* it is important to think about what you are trying to achieve from the survey. If you are unclear about what you are trying to achieve, the results will be equally unclear. It is also important with this type of research to beware of vague objectives. Choosing the correct sampling method and research technique is particularly important.

Although there may be a ready availability of *secondary research* data, it has to be remembered that the information has been collected by someone else and will not be specific to the needs of a particular organisation. It may also be dated.

Whatever technique is used for collecting data, it is important to ensure that the research is both reliable and valid. A research technique is considered reliable if it produces almost identical results in successive or repeated trials. To have validity a research technique must measure what it is supposed to measure and not something else! A valid market research method provides data that can be used to test what is being sought.

As market research takes place, it provides a wealth of data that has to be collected, processed and analysed. Research may be carried out by the organisation's own market research staff or by staff from an agency. Alternatively secondary data may be bought in the form of reports. Clearly, primary collection of data is likely to be of greater cost than simply buying data. Data collection is not only expensive, but also subject to error. The process, therefore, has to be carefully monitored and managed.

The final stage in the market research process is to interpret the findings and draw conclusions. These are then reported back to managers and other decision-makers. Many different statistical techniques may be used to support this process. Clearly, if managers are to make decisions based upon the data they will want to know that the research process was carried out properly and that they can rely upon the data before deciding what action to take.

Interpretation and generalisation from data

The real benefit of market research information is determined by how much it improves the marketer's ability to make decisions. Good quality information will enable decisions to be made which satisfy the needs of the target market and also help the organisation to achieve its goals.

The use of market research represents a change from problem-solving by intuition to decision-making based on scientific gathering and analysis of information. The great advantage is that market research systematically provides information upon which managers may base product decisions.

Market analysis may, therefore, be used to identify:

* Changes in the markets for different products and businesses

* Profit opportunities

* The need to make changes to the product mix.

Changes in the markets for different products and businesses

The size and potential of any market must be constantly monitored for change. Analysis of sales trends as well as the size and potential of any market must be considered important. If the total size of the market is known, an organisation can thus work out what percentage of the market it has (market share) and then develop a strategy

Find out...

Check current developments in television from the Independent Television Commission through www.heinemann.co.uk/hotlinks (express code 1130P, then go to Unit 3).

FIGURE 3.36 *Market growth*

which helps it to increase its proportion of the market.

Market analysis may also be used to predict changes in the potential of the market both in the short- and long-term. Few markets are static and, as changes take place, it is important to understand about potential buyers as well as existing buyers.

There are three digital platforms of digital television. These are Terrestrial (DTT) with OnDigital, Digital Satellite Television currently served by BskyB and Digital Cable Television. Digital television currently has 9% penetration in UK homes. For example, for the marketers of digital television, it is important to know about the numbers of households who do not have digital set-top boxes as well as those who have them. They need to think about how long it will take to reach buyers who do not have digital services.

In high-growth markets it is usually easier to meet growth objectives, and these markets are often considered to be more profitable. Low-growth markets, by their very nature, are more static and may even be declining. As the market size approaches the market potential, growth slows and competition usually intensifies.

Profit opportunities

As products go through their product life-cycle, the profitability of different products changes.

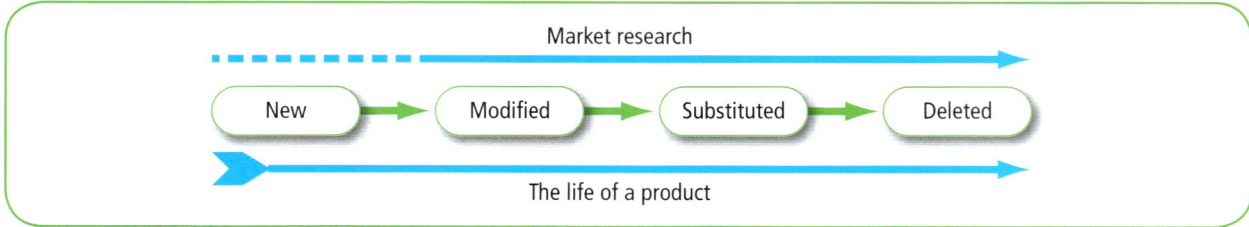

FIGURE 3.37 *Using research during the life of a product to make key product decisions*

Marketing analysis helps to direct an organisation towards those activities where profitability and other business objectives can best be satisfied.

The need to make changes to the product mix

The product mix comprises all of the products an organisation provides for its customers. Research will help managers to understand the sort of decisions they have to make about the product mix. For example, it might:

* identify opportunities for growth and development for new and existing products

* show how new products could replace existing products. This is known as *product substitution*

* show how some products are in decline – by modifying a product it may be possible to slow down its decline and sustain its profitability

* indicate that because a product is no longer satisfying a number of customers it ought to be deleted.

Changes in consumer behaviour

The process of buying a good or service is not as simple as it might appear. A customer does not usually make a purchase without thinking carefully about his or her requirements. Wherever there is choice, decisions are made and these are influenced by complex motives.

Market research will help an organisation to understand why customers make particular decisions, particularly through the analysis of buying patterns, who buys, what they buy, how they develop preferences and how they buy. Analysing these changes will help an organisation to cater more closely for customers' needs.

Changes in the activities of competitors

An organisation must at all times be aware of its competitors and the nature of what they are doing. Competition exists when two or more organisations act independently to sell their products to the same group of consumers. In some markets there may be a lot of competition, signified by an abundance of products and services so that consumers have a massive choice. These markets are characterised by promotional activities and price competition.

In other markets competition is limited and consumers are only able to choose from a limited range of products and services. In these circumstances consumers may feel that prices are too high – they are not getting value for money.

Direct competition exists where organisations produce similar products that appeal to the same group of consumers. *The Daily Star* competes directly with *The Sun*; and if you want to have a wall built, all the builders in your area looking for this type of work are in direct competition.

Even an organisation with no direct competition may face indirect competition as potential customers may consider different ways of meeting the same need. Instead of buying a motor car, they might buy a moped; instead of buying a box of chocolates on Mother's Day, they could buy a bunch of flowers – or send their mother a lottery ticket! See the National Lottery website through www.heinemann.co.uk/hotlinks (express code 1130P, then go to Unit 3).

Changes in the effectiveness of other marketing mix ingredients

Market research will also provide valuable information about the use of other marketing mix ingredients. For example, what are customers

Learning activity

Look at the market for one particular type of product. For example, it could be cars, electricity, confectionery or even beer. Comment upon how organisations within this market behave. What sorts of decisions have some of them recently made? What type of information would they have had available before they made these decisions?

perceptions of price, how effective is advertising, do distribution systems cater for customer requirements, what would be the effect on demand of changes in pricing policies?

3.3 Choosing an appropriate marketing mix

The marketing mix provides us with a useful way of looking at the marketing of products. Organisations need to create a successful mix of:

✱ the right *product* (or service)

✱ sold in the right *place*

✱ at the right *price*

✱ using the most suitable form of *promotion*.

As we have seen this simple mix is often referred to as the four Ps of product, price, place and promotion. This rather straightforward way of looking at what has become an increasingly complex business environment has at times been felt to be a little simplistic and limiting in terms of the real mix and what should be the fullness of our understanding. In recent times, therefore,

it has been expanded to include three more Ps to become a 7P mix with the additional elements of:

✱ *people*

✱ *provision* of customer service

✱ *process management*

People

People are widely recognised to be the greatest asset of the modern organisation. The governing principle, whether recognised or not, is that everybody who works for an organisation is a customer, either inside (the internal customer) or outside (the 'traditional customer') the company. Both kinds of customer expect to be supplied with the product or service they need, on time and as specified. This principle holds good for everyone in the company, whatever their level of skill and experience, whether their 'product' is answering a telephone or masterminding a major new project. It works to everyone's benefit. In doing so it provides the individual with genuine responsibility and scope for initiative, and it virtually guarantees that the organisation's performance will be improved.

Provision of customer service

Customer service has become increasingly important in a rapidly changing market-place. It has become more closely linked with the core product. Customer service is associated with developing bonds with customers in order to create long-term relationships that lead to advantages for all groups. It does not just happen. It is a process which involves pre-transaction, transaction and post-transaction considerations. Emphasis upon customer service will change from one product to another. For example, when manufacturing goods such as bread or shampoo customer service may involve developing strong customer relationships with many of the large retailers. In a pure service industry such as hairdressing or insurance, there are no tangible goods, and so customers will view nearly all of the benefits they get on the basis of the service they receive.

Learning activity

Make a study of consumer choice for a particular type of product which is sold in a supermarket. How many different types and brands of the product are on sale? How do the types and brands compete against each other? To what extent do consumers benefit from having this choice? Identify the different segments for this type of product. Does variety lead to increased quality? What are the other benefits of variety? What are the drawbacks of having so much choice?

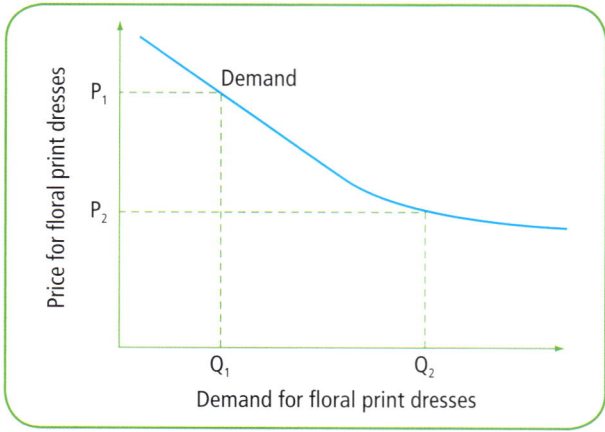

FIGURE 3.38 *Demand curve*

Process management

This involves all of the procedures, tasks, mechanisms and activities through which a product or service is delivered to a customer. It is clear that in a modern organisation processes are a key part of the marketing mix, involving developing priorities and ways of meeting customer needs. Processes might involve key decisions about customer involvement and employee discretion. In today's rapidly changing business environment, in order to meet consumer needs more closely, it is marketing that should determine the processes that link manufacturing with the customer.

The marketing mix is therefore a series of controllable variables that an organisation can use in order to best meet customer needs and ensure that an organisation is successful in the markets in which it serves.

Pricing and the techniques of pricing

The Oxford English Dictionary defines prices as the *'sum or consideration or sacrifice for which a thing may be bought or attained'*. Price is the only element of the marketing mix that directly generates incomes – other elements of the marketing mix are costs. The importance of price in the marketing mix varies. In low-cost, non-fashion markets price can be critical (for example, in the sale of white emulsion and gloss paint). In fashion markets, such as clothing, it can be one of the least relevant factors. Certain products are designed to suit a

particular segment (e.g. economy family cars), while others perform a specific function regardless of price (e.g. sports cars). For consumers with limited budgets, price is a key-purchasing criterion, while for those to whom 'money is no object' price is less important.

The first pricing task is to create an overall pricing goal for an organisation which is in line with the marketing strategy, and then determine objectives for each of the product lines.

The price charged for a product is associated with a given level of sales. We can illustrate this relationship by means of a demand curve (see Figure 3.38).

The curve in Figure 3.38 shows the levels of demand for a floral print dress sold at different market prices. As with most products, customers for floral dresses would be prepared to make more purchases at a lower than a higher price. The normal way to express customer sensitivity to price changes is through a measure known as **price elasticity of demand**. This is the measure of how much quantities purchased will alter in response to given price changes. Demand is said to be **elastic** if the change in quantity demanded is of a greater proportion than the change in price that initiated it.

For example, if the price of a particular brand of washing powder fell by 10 per cent and there was an increase in sales of 20 per cent, the demand for the product would be said to be elastic; the change in price led to more than proportionate response in quantity demanded.

Pricing objectives	Percentage of firms
Target profit or return on capital employed	67
Prices fair to firm and customers	13
Prices similar to those of competitors	8
Target sales volume	7
Stable sales volume	5
Target market share	2
Stable prices	2
Other	1

FIGURE 3.39 *Firms' pricing objectives*

$$\text{Price elasticity of demand} = \frac{\% \text{ change in quantity demanded}}{\% \text{ change in price}}$$

When a relative change in the quantity sold is less than the relative change in price, demand is said to be **inelastic**. For example, if a price increase of 10 per cent results in a 5 per cent fall in sales, price elasticity will be –0.5.

Price elasticities vary with the level of competition. The more competition in the market, the more likely it is that demand for a particular product line will be elastic. Price elasticity also varies during the product life-cycle. In the early days, when there is little competition, price inelasticity will be the rule within a sensible price range. However, as products mature, elasticity will increase in the competitive price range.

D. Shipley noted preferences among the principal set of pricing objectives of firms as shown in Figure 3.39.

Once pricing objectives have been established, organisations need to establish an appropriate pricing strategy.

Penetration pricing

Penetration pricing is appropriate when the seller knows that demand is likely to be elastic. A low price is therefore required to attract consumers to the product. Penetration pricing is normally associated with the launch of a new product for which the market needs to be penetrated (see Figure 3.40).

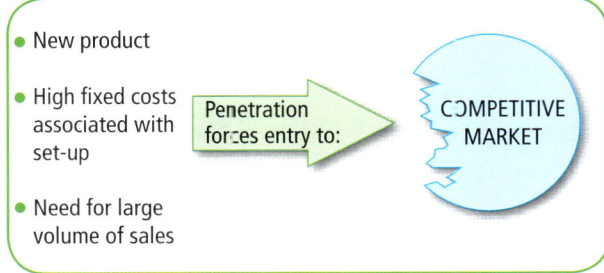

FIGURE 3.40 *An environment appropriate for penetration pricing*

Because a price starts low, even though a product will be developing market share, the product may initially make a loss until consumer awareness is increased.

A typical example would be that of a new breakfast cereal or a product being launched in a new overseas market. Initially it would be launched with a relatively low price, coupled with discounts and special offers. As the product penetrates the market, sales and profitability increase. Prices then creep upwards.

Penetration pricing is particularly appropriate for products where economies of scale can be employed to produce large volumes at low unit costs. Products which are produced on a large scale are initially burdened by high fixed costs for research, development and purchases of plant and equipment. It is important to spread these fixed costs quickly over a large volume of output. Penetration pricing is also common when there is a strong possibility of competition from rival pricing.

Skimming

At the launch of a new product, there will frequently be little competition in the market, so that demand for the product may be relatively inelastic. Consumers will probably have little knowledge of the product. Skimming involves setting a reasonably high initial price in order to yield high initial returns from those consumers willing to buy the new product. Once the first group of customers has been satisfied, the seller can then lower prices in order to make sales to new groups of customers.

This process can be continued until a larger section of the total market has been catered for. By

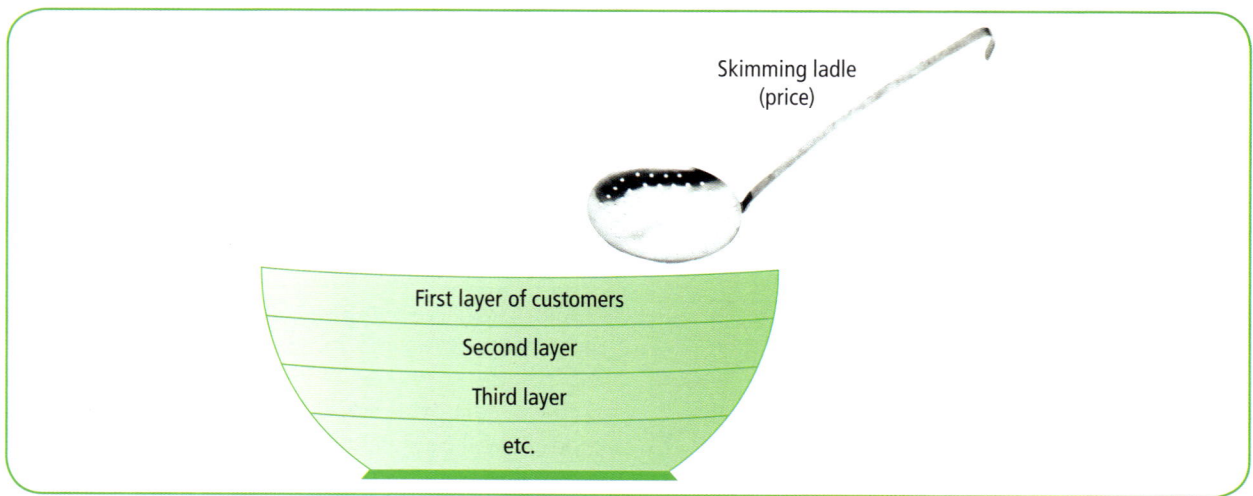

FIGURE 3.41 *Skimming*

operating in this way, the business removes the risk of underpricing the product.

The name 'skimming' comes from the process of skimming the cream from the top of a milk product (Figure 3.41).

Cost-plus pricing

Any study of organisations in the real world shows that many businesses use no other basis than a **mark-up** on the cost of providing the product or service concerned. Information about costs is usually easier to piece together than information about other variables such as likely revenue. Firms will often therefore simply add a margin to the **unit cost.**

The unit cost is the average cost of each item produced. For example, if an organisation produces 800 units at a total cost of £24,000, the unit cost will be £30. Talk to many owners of small businesses and they will tell you that they 'cost out' each hour worked and then add a margin for profits; or they will simply mark-up each item sold by a certain percentage. For example, fashion items are frequently marked up by between 100 and 200 per cent.

The process of cost-plus pricing can best be illustrated in relation to large organisations where **economies of scale** can be spread over a considerable range of output.

For a large organisation, unit costs will fall rapidly at first as the overheads are spread over a larger output. It is therefore a relatively simple

calculation to add a fixed margin (e.g. 20 per cent) to the unit cost. The organisation is able to select an output to produce and to set a price that will be 20 per cent higher than the unit cost of production (see Figure 3.42).

Whilst cost-plus pricing is very popular, there are many dangers associated with it. If the price is set too high, sales may fall short of expectations; and if the price is set too low, then potential revenue is sacrificed. However, the greatest danger of cost-based pricing is that it indicates a *production-orientated approach to the market*. Emphasis on costs leads to tunnel vision that looks inwards at the company's product rather than outwards at the customers' perception of the product.

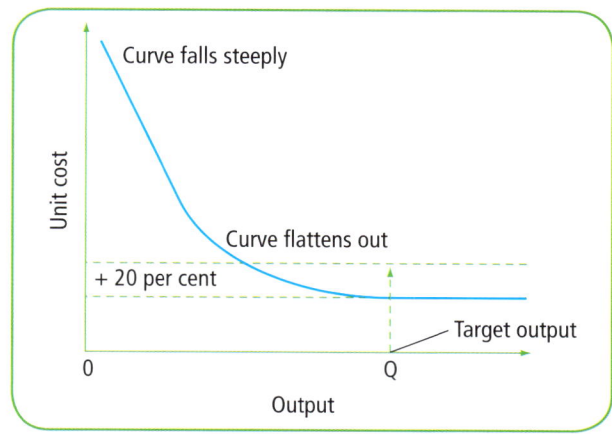

FIGURE 3.42 *Select a target output OQ and then add 20 per cent to the unit cost to get price*

Why is the margin for luxury goods such as designer goods and fashion accessories likely to be higher than for cigarettes or newspapers?

There is a strong link between value and price. **Delivery of value** is an important ingredient of an exchange. Marketing has been described as 'selling goods that don't come back to people who do'. If the seller does not provide customers with a significant value proposition, whatever the price, goods may be returned or customers will not come back.

In the longer term, the success of business organisations (and individuals) will depend on their ability to provide customers with **value for money** through the exchange process.

Most customers compare prices with the perceived quality or value provided by the goods and services they purchase – they are concerned with the value proposition provided by the organisation and its relationship to the price they have paid. For example, some customers are value orientated and want to pay low prices for acceptable quality; some buyers want high quality and are willing to pay more for it. Many of today's retailers are using emphasis upon 'value' as a form of competition. Instead of focusing simply upon price, they provide customers with a better value package – more for the same price – than other competitors in that segment of the market.

It is therefore important to price according to the nature of customers in the marketplace. On the one hand you may lose customers by charging too high a price – with a low value proposition if customers feel that they are not getting value for money. On the other hand you may lose custom from charging too low a price – potential customers may feel that the low price indicates lower quality than they are seeking.

Compare two products or services for which roughly similar prices are charged. Explain which product or service represents a better value proposition.

Competition-based pricing

In extremely competitive situations, costs have to be treated as a secondary consideration in short-term price determination. This is particularly true when competing products are almost identical, customers are well informed and where there are few suppliers.

The nature and extent of competition is frequently an important influence upon price. If a product is faced with direct competition, then it will compete against other very similar products in the marketplace. This will constrain pricing decisions so that price setting will need to be kept closely in line with rivals' actions. In contrast, when a product is faced by indirect competition (i.e. competition with products in different sectors of the market) then there will be more scope to vary price. This opens up the possibility for a number of strategies. For example, a firm might choose a high-price strategy to give a product a 'quality' feel. In contrast, it might charge a low price so that consumers see the product as a 'bargain'.

An individual organisation might try to insulate itself against price sensitivity by differentiating its products from those of rivals. Markets are sometimes classified according to the level of competition that applies. For example, an extreme level of competition is termed **perfect competition** (it exists in theory rather than in practice). The other extreme is **monopoly** where a single firm dominates a market. In the real world, most markets lie between these extremes and involve some level of imperfection.

If a perfect market could exist there would be no limitations to new firms entering the market, and buyers would know exactly what was on offer and would incur no costs in buying from one seller rather than another. Products would be almost identical. In a monopoly situation, only one firm exists and barriers prevent new firms from entering the market. The seller has considerable powers to control the market.

FIGURE 3.43 *Competition*

In imperfect markets, there may be few or many sellers. Products are usually **differentiated** and consumers do not have perfect information about the differences between products.

Where organisations seek to reduce competition and make their products better than their rivals, the development of monopolistic powers enables them to push up prices and make larger profits. The level of competition is thus a key determinant of price. Where there are many close competitors, there is little scope to charge a price which is above the market price. Organisations in such markets are *price takers.*

In a situation where there is no competition, the seller can often charge a relatively high price. In other words they are a *price maker*. However,

Learning activity

Categorise the following examples into:

Penetration pricing
Skimming
Cost plus pricing
Value-based competition
Competition-based pricing

In each instance explain why you have categorised the example in the way in which you have:

1 A new book comes onto the market in hardback form at £25, two months later it comes out in paperback at £15, the following year it comes out in a 2nd edition at £10.

2 In order to improve its competitive position in the high street, a major retailer creates a series of sub-brands designed to improve the ways in which its customers view its products.

3 A breakfast cereal manufacturer introduces a new type of cereal at a low price in order to attract customers to buy the product.

4 A garden centre sets a margin of 30 per cent on all of its stock.

5 A company launches a revolutionary piece of software.

6 In a fiercely competitive market, a business simply looks at the price charged by others before setting its own price.

Learning activity

Identify a number of products known to you and discuss the pricing strategies used by the product or service provider.

the seller cannot charge more than the consumer is prepared to pay. At the end of the day consumers can spend their income on alternative products. Between these two extremes, we find hundreds of different markets. In some the consumer has more power, in others it is the seller.

Product

The product is the most important element in an organisation's marketing mix. According to Sally Dibb et al (1994), 'A product is everything, both favourable and unfavourable, that is received in an exchange.' We shall see later that this is supported through the total product concept. That is, the product is the organisation itself, the brand and everything it does to satisfy customer needs including the very tangible item (physical product), if there is one, as well as all of the accompanying intangible benefits that are sometimes less obvious and more difficult to identify.

As we saw on page 143, *brand* is part of a particular product and includes characteristics that identify it with a particular producer. Brands are very important.

Product features, advantages and benefits

Customers as a rule do not buy features, they buy what those features can do for them – the problems they solve, the money or the time they save, etc. A product is really a bundle of benefits. A key aspect of marketing is to make sure that products create the benefits that a consumer desires in a particular product and that the product offering is better than those of competitors. Associated with this is the need to make sure that the market fully understands the range of benefits on offer, through strong communications.

When we understand the benefits that customers are looking for in a product, we are best placed to know why they will buy it – and hence focus our marketing accordingly. For example, in buying toothpaste the benefits that customers may be looking for include:

* Flavour and product appearance

* Brightness of teeth

* Decay prevention

* Price / value for money

* Appealing brand name and confidence in brand.

Knowing that these are the benefits the consumer requires enables the organisation to focus its efforts on creating products that will produce one or more of them, and then promotion can be used to highlight the organisation's ability to create these benefits.

There are often clear and *tangible features* (things you can touch and see) associated with a product. Tangible features might include shape, design, colour, packaging and size.

Intangible features are not so obvious. These include the reputation of an organisation, the brand image, after sales service, availability of spare parts, service centres and so on.

It is also argued that products provide advantages for customers through three different dimensions. These are:

Generic dimensions – these are the key benefits of a particular item. For example, shoe polish should, we hope, clean shoes. Freezers should store frozen

FIGURE 3.44 *Product features may be tangible or intangible*

food. Hairdressers should be able to cut and style hair, including that of this author!

Sensual dimensions – these have an impact upon the senses. They might include design, colour, taste, smell and texture. The sensual benefits are frequently highlighted by advertisers. This is clearly the case when advertising food and drinks – 'smooth and creamy', 'the amber nectar' and so on.

Extended dimensions – a wide range of additional benefits are included here. Examples are servicing agreements, credit facilities, guarantees, maintenance contracts and so on.

With any group of products there is a distinct mix of items. They may include:

A *product item* is a specific model, brand or size of a product that an organisation sells, for example, a 2kg box of Uncle Ben's Long Grain Rice.

A *product line* is a group of closely related product items, with similar characteristics and/or applications, for example a line of Uncle Ben's Rice items, including short grain, long grain and pudding rice.

A *product mix* is all of an organisation's product lines, e.g. including rice, flour, sugar, pickles and other lines. Any product mix can be described according to its width, length, depth and consistency.

Width is the number of different product lines on offer. For example, Coca-Cola has 'stuck to the knitting' and produces quite a narrow range of soft drinks including Sprite, Fanta and Coca-Cola. In contrast, a company like Unilever has a wide range of products from Walls ice-cream and Birds Eye frozen foods to many different types of soap powders and cleaning agents. Having a narrow range of products enables you to benefit from economies of large-scale production whereas breadth enables an organisation to benefit from diversification. Broadening a line to create breadth means extending it beyond its current range.

Length is the total number of items on offer. The decision on the number of lines to offer is very important. Too many lines and you may overstretch yourself, and even start to compete

Learning activity

When the car manufacturer Volkswagen bought a 31% share in Skoda in 1991, the leading Skoda model was the downmarket Favorit. Not only were substantial changes made to the Favorit, but in 1995 a new, more upmarket Felicia was added to Skoda's lines with great success.

against your own lines. Line stretching involves increasing the product line, either by moving into higher-quality items or moving downmarket.

The process of line filling involves filling in gaps in product lines. For example, confectionery manufacturers regularly develop new chocolate bars to fill perceived gaps in their range of products. Line rationalisation involves cutting out lines that are not central to the organisation's major focus of interest, or those that have lost popularity.

Depth is the number of variants of each brand, for example, the number of different sizes, models or flavours within a product line. Detergent companies like Procter & Gamble or Unilever offer many different sizes of soap powder boxes as well as lots of different kinds of soap powder, all targeted at slightly different groups of customers. It makes sense for a large company to offer a product for all occasions in order to aim for a position of leadership. However, it is important not to cannibalise the sales of your own products. Deepening a product would mean adding more lines within your existing range. Line pruning means cutting the depth of a product line by reducing the number of alternative sizes, models or flavours in the line.

Consistency is the closeness of the relationship between each product line.

Creating the optimum product mix means having the right balance in terms of width, depth, length and consistency. An effective product mix should yield a balanced profit contribution from

Learning activity

Examine the annual report of a well known public company, e.g. Cadbury Schweppes. Comment on the width, depth and consistency of their product mix.

a number of lines – although there will always be some products that are the highest yielders.

Organisations need to decide whether they have the right mix at any one point in time while having an eye on future changes. Key concerns are: Should we stick to the narrow range of lines in which we are successful? What are our current strengths and weaknesses? What are the opportunities and threats of diversifying? How can we avoid competing with ourselves?

Place

In simple terms, the place element within the marketing mix is probably the most underestimated element. It provides the basic structure for the customer needs to be satisfied.

For example, physical distribution involves getting a product from A to B. Physical distribution management is an important part of the place process. It helps an organisation to meet customer needs profitably and efficiently. In doing so it enables manufacturers and distributors to provide goods for customers at the right time, in the right place and in the condition required. It may also reduce the **lead-time** – from when a

customer first makes an order until the time when that order is delivered.

Logistics is the process of integrating materials management and physical distribution management, and involves a whole series of activities from moving raw materials through to manufacturing processes and moving finished goods to the final consumer.

Physical distribution must balance the need for customer service against the need to minimise costs. On the one hand to maximise customer service an organisation may need a lot of stock and warehouse space, efficient staff and rapid transport mechanisms, while on the other to minimise costs they need low stock levels, limited storage space, few staff and slower transport. Designing a physical distribution system therefore

CASE STUDY

Research Machines

Founded in 1973 by Mike Fischer and Mike O'Regan, RM plc is the UK's leading provider of commercial education services and a pioneer in the application of technology to education. The Group's first educational microcomputer was launched in 1977, and schools, colleges and universities have become the main market for RM since then. In recent years RM has expanded its range of products and services to include interactive whole-class teaching services, teacher training, ICT-based needs assessment and school management information systems.

According to RM, 'In the 1990s it became clear that the educational community was looking for more from their suppliers than simple technological expertise. RM rose to the challenge. Looking beyond the technology, the Group formed long-term partnerships with both educationalists and other learning technology companies. These partnerships allow us to deliver genuine learning productivity. It is a strategy that has worked as our market leadership shows. RM's passion is education and its aim is to explore and exploit the potential of IT to improve educational standards. Today, RM is expanding its relationships with customers further by providing a diverse range of education services.'

1 What makes RM different to many other IT organisations?
2 In marketing terms describe how RM has developed the products it offers.

involves trading off costs against service, or inputs against outputs.

Inputs involve all of the distribution costs such as freight costs, inventory costs, warehousing costs and other service costs. It is important to know exactly what each of these costs are and control them in order to minimise waste. This may involve a detailed analysis of labour time, transport time, and other factors spent on each product.

Outputs can be primarily measured in terms of the value of services provided for customers. Distribution can provide a clear competitive benefit in meeting customer needs, for example by offering a quick and efficient service. Every business must decide how it is going to use distribution and relate this to their competitive advantage. Weaknesses in distribution would clearly need to be compensated for by strengths in other areas of the marketing mix.

The physical distribution system that an organisation selects will largely depend upon the scale of operations and the size of an organisation's market. A business handling a lot of international mail, for example, might locate near a large airport. Key decisions about physical distribution may include the following:

Inventory – a business that wants to maximise customer service will have the highest inventory costs, because it needs to hold stock to meet all requests. The key inventory decisions are when and how much to order. The danger of keeping too little in stock is that an organisation could lose custom because of dissatisfaction with the quality of service.

Warehousing – a key decision is where to locate warehouses, and how many to have.

Load size – should units be transported in bulk or broken down into smaller units for delivery? Again, an organisation will have to trade-off customer convenience and the cost of distribution.

Communications – it is important to develop an efficient information processing and invoicing system.

Channels are the networks of intermediaries linking the producer to the market. Whereas direct selling methods are *zero-level channels* which do not use an intermediary, indirect selling methods use one or more channels of distribution through which goods are transferred from the producer to the end user. These channels consist of one or more individuals or organisations who help to make the products available for the end user (see Figure 3.45).

Intermediaries such as *wholesalers* stock a range of goods from competing manufacturers to sell on to other organisations such as retailers. Most wholesalers take on the title to the goods and so assume many of the risks associated which include:

Breaking bulk Manufacturers produce goods in bulk for sale but they might not want to store

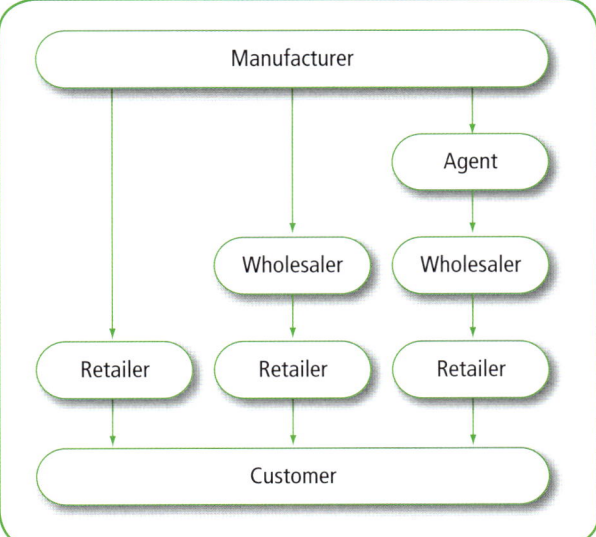

FIGURE 3.45 *Indirect sales channels*

the goods themselves. They want to be paid as quickly as possible. A number of wholesalers buy the stock for them and generally payment is prompt. The wholesaler then stocks these goods, along with others bought from other manufacturers, on the premises, ready for purchase by retailers.

Simplifying the distribution process The chain of distribution without the wholesaler would look something like Figure 3.46. Manufacturer 1 has to carry out four journeys to supply retailers 1, 2, 3 and 4, and has to send out four sets of business documents, and handle four sets of accounts. The same situation applies to each of the manufacturers, so that in total 16 journeys are made and 16 sets of paperwork are required.

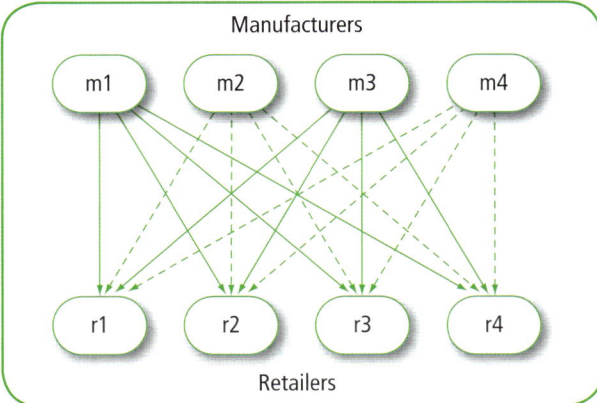

FIGURE 3.46 *The distribution chain without the wholesaler*

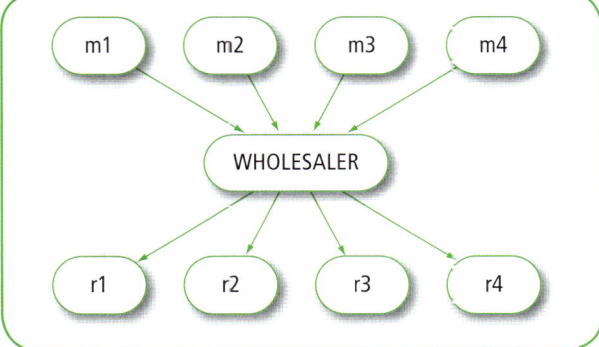

FIGURE 3.47 *The distribution chain with the wholesaler*

This is a simplification because in the real world thousands of different transactions might be involved!

An intermediary can simplify costs and processes of distribution by cutting down on journeys, fuel and other costs as well as cutting down on paperwork such as invoicing and administration.

The chain of distribution with an intermediary such as a wholesaler would look something like Figure 3.47. Clearly everything is simplified.

Storage Most retailers have only a limited amount of storage space. The wholesaler can be looked upon as a cupboard for the retailer. Manufacturers are able to unload finished goods on the wholesaler, which then act as a conduit to the retailers.

Packing and labelling The wholesaler will in some instances finish off the packaging and labelling of goods, perhaps by putting price tags or brand labels on the goods.

Offering advice Being in the middle of a chain of distribution, wholesalers have a lot more information at their fingertips than either the retailer or manufacturer. In particular, wholesalers know which goods are selling well. With this in mind they can advise retailers on what to buy and manufacturers on what to produce.

By contracting out the process of distribution, a company can concentrate on its core functions.

The French word *retailer* means 'to cut again'. We have already seen that the wholesaler breaks down bulk supplies from the manufacturer. The retailer then cuts the bulk again to sell individual items to customers. In the modern retailing environment, *the physical environment* for selling to end-users has become increasingly complex and in tune with customer focus and needs.

Daewoo, for instance, distributed cars in the UK without using a traditional local car dealership network. The use of telephone, modem and the Internet as well as fax are also providing the consumer with new ways to view and purchase products. **Telemarketing** is now being used to sell products such as insurance and pensions, which were previously sold by a one-to-one personal interview. The availability of satellite TV channels, has promoted the introduction of **home shopping**, with the American company QVC launching an English-speaking shopping channel within Europe. Simultaneously, the Internet is increasingly being used for **electronic commerce**, selling goods to consumers. This new channel of distribution is being investigated by many other organisations who are already involved in the distribution chain such as supermarkets. See, for example, the Tesco website through www.heinemann.co.uk/hotlinks (express code 1130P, then go to Unit 3). These imaginative approaches to distribution are being viewed as a major new opportunity to meet customer needs within a rapidly changing physical environment.

This physical environment for retailing largely depends upon:

Ownership Who owns the retail unit? Does a sole trader independently own it? Is it owned by a large multiple with shareholders? Is it a co-operative or a franchised outlet?

Range of merchandise Does the retail outlet specialise in a range of goods or does it have a spread of interests? Examples of specialised outlets include ice-cream parlours, furniture stores and fast-food outlets. Woolworths is an

Learning activity

Use either your own experience or the experiences of people known to you to discuss the advantages and disadvantages of using the Internet for shopping.

Learning activity

Draw a plan of your local shopping area. Make a list of the different types of retailers in the area.

example of a more general outlet. Harrods at one time claimed to sell everything from 'a pin to an elephant'.

Pricing policy Some retail outlets concentrate on the bottom of the price range. They offer discounts and low prices, buying in bulk and selling in large quantities. The early policy of Jack Cohen, founder of Tesco, was 'pile them high, sell them cheap'. In contrast, other retail outlets aim for an upmarket price image. This is true of fashion shops, clothing and jewellery stores.

Location This has become increasingly important in recent years. Low-price stores frequently choose locations where business rates and other site costs are minimised. In contrast, large multiples and department stores need a town-centre location, or a site near a major road. Small 'corner' shops need a healthy volume of custom for their livelihood – their strength is in offering local convenience. The growth of out-of-town centres has provided further opportunities to create a range of retailing opportunities for customers, including multiplex cinemas and restaurants.

Size Many variety stores are now over 50,000 sq. ft. in area, but superstores and hypermarkets have areas from 25,000 to 100,000 sq. ft.

There are many different ways of meeting customer needs through different forms of distribution. These include:

Independent traders According to the Census of Distribution, an independent trader is a retail organisation with fewer than 10 branches. A typical number is one or two branches. The market share for these has been declining, particularly in food.

Multiple chains These are usually owned by large companies, with a high degree of control from a head office. Some multiples are classified as specialist stores concentrating upon a narrow range of items, while others are variety chains such as Marks & Spencer and Littlewoods. Key features of multiples are:

* centralised buying
* concentration on fast-moving lines
* merchandise is widely known
* located in busy shopping areas
* volume sales enable prices to be low
* shops project a strong corporate image
* many key functions are centralised.

Supermarkets A supermarket is defined as a store with at least 2,000 square feet (or about 200 square metres) of selling area, using mainly self-service methods and having at least three check-out points. The layout of the store is designed to speed customer flow, and reduce time spent shopping.

Hypermarkets These are very large supermarkets, usually either out-of-town or on the fringes of towns or cities. They have a massive selling area and offer a wide range of household goods at discount prices. As well as food and clothing, they stock lines as diverse as DIY equipment, motoring accessories, children's toys and hardware.

Department stores The definition of a department store, as used by the Census of Distribution, is a store with a large number of departments and employing more than 25 people. They are to be found upon 'prime sites' in the centre of most towns and cities. The key feature of a department store is that it is divided into separate departments, providing a range of shopping opportunities, within pristine sales areas, so that all shopping can take place under one roof. They have a reputation for selling high-quality branded goods.

Discount stores Today, specialist companies such as Comet and Currys concentrate upon selling large quantities of consumer durables at discount prices. The aim of these stores is to produce a high level of total profit through fast turnover of stock. Many of these stores offer a range of credit services and other facilities to complement their customer offer.

Learning activity

Look at the business information pages in a broadsheet newspaper over a two-week period and collect articles that refer to organisations involved in retailing activity. Discuss how each article or statement describes recent changes in retailing activities.

Co-operative retail societies There are fewer than thirty cooperative retail societies in various parts of the UK. These aim to provide more than business services, to support the community in a variety of ways.

Catalogue shopping Organisations such as Argos and Index publish a catalogue listing all of the goods they sell. Customers visit their high street stores in order to collect their goods. Goods are not generally on display, with the majority of the store's space allocated for stock. Though the physical environment for these types of outlets is not particularly attractive for consumers, the low running costs means that they benefit from low prices.

Home shopping There are three main sectors. Agency mail order catalogues such as Freemans and Great Universal stores bypass intermediaries. Individuals become agents and either buy for themselves receiving a commission or sell goods on to friends and family. Direct mail catalogues such as Next Directory have become increasingly popular methods of ordering goods, usually paying by credit card. Interactive television, the Internet and television shopping channels have massive potential to change our shopping habits in recent years. As consumers become more confident in using them, they have the potential to serve a range of different needs and requirements.

Learning activity

Compare and contrast the physical environment of two retailing organisations. Look, for example, at their size, location, number of branches, pricing structure, market position, range of goods, associated services and support for their customers. Carry out a short shopping survey to find out what type of organisation customers prefer to use for a range of different selected products.

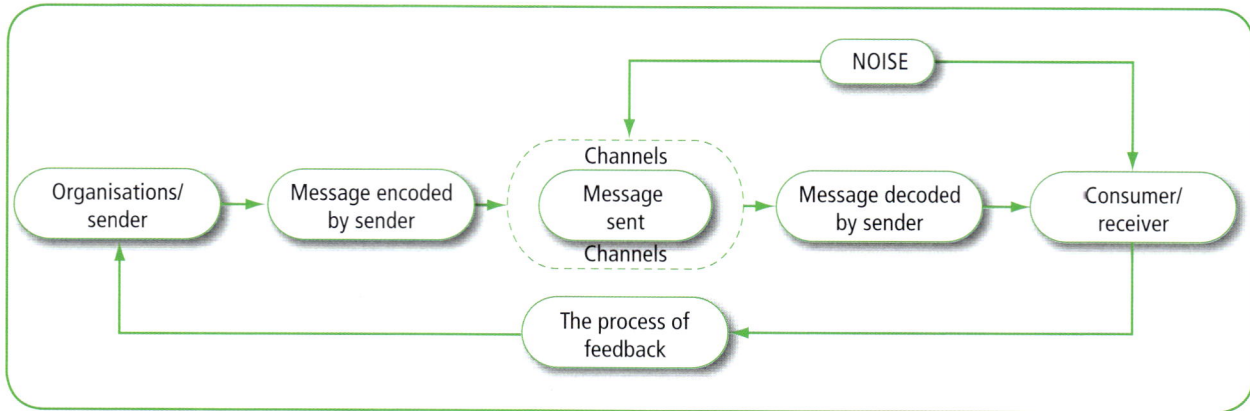

FIGURE 3.48 *The communication process*

Promotion

Promotion includes all of the techniques that an organisation uses to communicate with other individuals and organisations. Organisations are the *senders* in the communication process and *consumers* are the *receivers*. A sender will put information in the form that a receiver can understand. This might involve oral, visual, verbal or written messages to transmit the ideas. This process is called *encoding*. The sender will also choose a particular medium to use to send the message to the receiver (e.g. television, radio, newspapers). If the consumer interprets the message as required, it should have the impact that the seller wished for.

Though the message flows through to the receiver there is no guarantee that the receiver will either receive the full message or understand it. This is because the process may be subject to some form of interference, which affects the flow of information. This is known as *noise* and may lead to the downfall of the message. It will take the form of any barrier which acts as an impediment to the smooth flow of information and may include linguistic and cultural differences between the sender and the receiver. For example, one leaflet put through your door may be lost amongst a sea of direct mail from other organisations.

To increase the chances of a message getting across, an organisation needs to think carefully about the target audience. For example, it is important to channel the message through the most appropriate media. It might also be necessary to repeat the message several times rather than rely on one transmission.

Once the audience has been identified the communicator also needs to think about the sort of response required. If, for example, the final response required through the communication process is purchase, there may be six phases to the buyer-readiness process (see Figure 3.49).

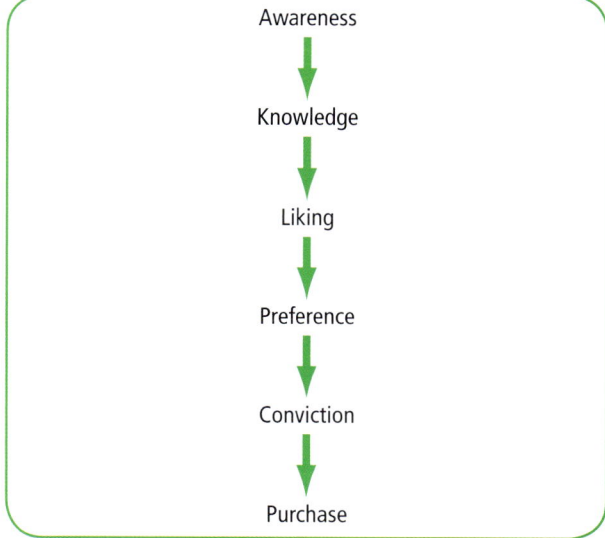

FIGURE 3.49 *Buyer-readiness phases*

It is important, therefore, that the promotion mix takes into account each of these stages with different types of promotional activities.

Advertising

Advertising is a method of communicating with groups in the marketplace in order to achieve certain objectives. Advertisements are messages sent through the media which are intended to inform or influence the people who receive them (see Figure 3.50).

It can be defined as a **paid-for** type of marketing communication that is **non-personal**, but aimed at a specific **target audience** through a **mass media channel.**

According to the American Marketing Association advertising is 'any paid form of non-personal presentation and promotion of ideas, goods or services by an identifiable sponsor'.

Advertising must be a directed communication at a targeted market, and should draw attention to the characteristics of a product, which will appeal to the buying motives of potential customers. The ultimate purpose of advertising for organisations is to enhance buyers' responses to its products by channelling their desires and preferences to their products ahead of their competitors.

Within this purpose there may be a range of advertising objectives. For example:

* promoting goods and services
* to assist with selling
* to increase sales
* to develop awareness of new products, or developments to existing products
* to provide information that may assist with selling decisions

* to encourage a desire to own a product
* to generate enquiries
* developing the image of the organisation
* to provide information to a target audience
* to soften attitudes
* to assist with public relations activities
* to change views
* to provide a better external environment
* to develop support from a community.

Advertising is often classified under one of three headings:

Informative advertising conveys information and raises consumer awareness of the features and benefits of a product. It is often used in the introductory phase of the product life-cycle, or after modification.

Persuasive advertising is concerned with creating a desire for the product and stimulating purchase. It is used with established and more mature products.

Reinforcement advertising is concerned with reminding consumers about the product, and is used to reinforce the knowledge held by potential consumers about the benefits to be gained from purchase.

The starting point for an advertising campaign is to produce an advertising plan. This will involve allocating a budget to a range of activities designed to meet advertising objectives. There are seven steps in an advertising campaign. These are:

Step 1   Identify the target market
Step 2   Define advertising objectives
Step 3   Decide on and create the advertising
         message

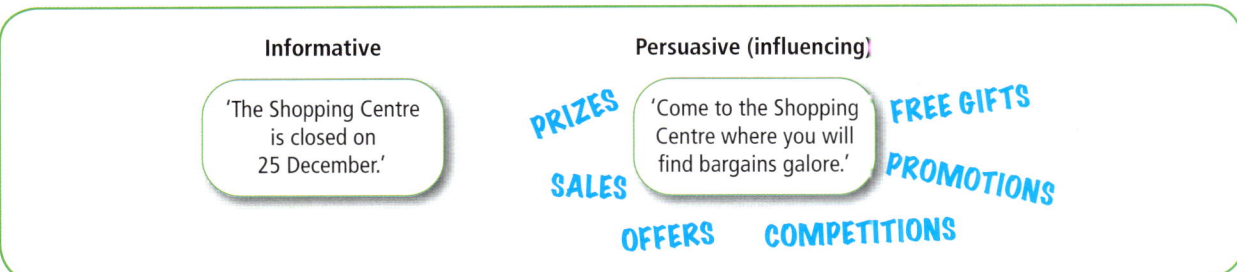

FIGURE 3.50 *The difference between informative and persuasive (influencing) advertising*

Compare and contrast two advertising campaigns, where one is clearly trying to promote goods and services and the other is trying to improve an image by developing public support for its activities. Comment upon how their approaches to advertising are similar, and then where they are different.

Step 4   Allocate the budget
Step 5   Develop the media plan
Step 6   Execute the campaign
Step 7   Evaluate the effectiveness of the campaign

Advertising messages may be sent through a variety of media forms, such as TV, radio, cinema, posters, billboards, flyers, transport advertising and the press. For more information about advertising look at the World Advertising Research Center website through www.heinemann.co.uk/hotlinks (express code 1130P, then go to Unit 3).

At all stages in the advertising process it is important to assess how effectively advertisements have contributed to the communication process. In order to measure objectives DAGMAR have become a fundamental part of good advertising practice. This stands for:

Defining **A**dvertising **G**oals for **M**easured **A**dvertising **R**esults

In other words, before any advertising campaign is started, an organisation must define its communication objectives so that achievements can be measured both during and after the campaign.

Printed media make up by far the largest group of media in the UK. The group includes all newspapers and magazines, both local and national, as well as trade press, periodicals and professional journals. There are about 9,000 regular publications in the UK which can be used by the advertiser. They allow the advertiser to send a message to several million people through the press or to target magazines of special interest such as *Business Education Today*, which allows the advertiser to communicate with people in the teaching profession. As a result the media allows for accurate targeting and positioning. Think of all of the hobbies, lifestyles and backgrounds of readers of such magazines. Types of customers are identified by analysing readership profiles.

CASE STUDY

The top six advertisers 2003

ADVERTISING EXPENDITURE

RANK	COMPANY	TOTAL £'000S	TV %	RADIO %	PRESS %	OTHER %
1	Procter & Gamble	192,405	76.2	6.1	12.5	5.3
2	COI Communications	143,137	59.4	16.9	23.8	7.9
3	BT	96,882	53.8	6.2	31.3	8.7
4	L'Oreal Golden	92,447	72.4	0.2	21.4	6.1
5	Ford Motor Company	79,015	48.5	6.5	28.6	16.4
6	Lever Fabergé Personal Care	70,626	66.5	2.2	12.7	18.6

Source: Nielsen Media Research

1 What do the allocations of expenditure tell you about the nature and types of advertising undertaken by each of these advertisers?
2 What forms of advertising might fall into the 'other' bracket?
3 Why do you think the six companies have such a large advertising spend?
4 If you were working for one of these companies, how would you evaluate the effectiveness of such a spend?

The benefit of printed media is that long or complex messages can be sent and, as the message is durable, may be read repeatedly. If an advertisement appears in a prestige magazine it may take on the prestige of that particular publication.

Broadcast media includes commercial television and commercial radio. Television is the most powerful medium – reaching 98% of households and viewing figures for some programmes can exceed 20 million. Television advertisements are, however, high cost and advertising messages are short-lived.

Direct mail

Direct mail is personally addressed advertising that is delivered through the post. By using direct mail an organisation can establish a direct relationship with its customers or prospective customers. Direct mail has been the third largest medium for over 13 years and now represents 14.3 per cent of all advertising expenditure in the UK. 5,418 million direct mail items were mailed in 2004 and £2,468.63 million was spent by advertisers on this medium in the same year. It

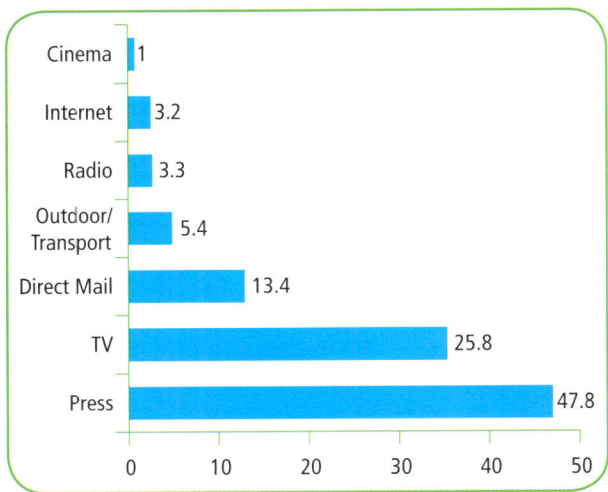

Source: World Advertising Research Center/DMIS

FIGURE 3.51 *Share of Total Advertising Expenditure in 2004*

is estimated that consumer direct mail generates nearly £27 billion worth of business every year.

Public relations

The forces in an organisation's external environment are capable of affecting it in a variety of ways. The forces may be social, economic, political, local or environmental and might be represented by a variety of groups such as customers, shareholders, employees and special interest groups. Reacting positively to such forces and influences is very important.

Public relations is the planned and sustained effort an organisation makes to establish, develop and build relationships with its many publics (see Figure 3.52).

The purpose of public relations (PR) is therefore to provide an external environment for an organisation in which it is popular and can prosper. Building goodwill in such a way requires behaviour by the organisation which takes into account the attitudes of the many people who come across it and its products.

Whereas many of the other promotional methods are *short-term*, public relations is long-term, as it may take a long time for an organisation to improve the way people think more positively about its products and activities. For example, just think about the sort of public relations problems that chemical and oil companies have in a world where consumers have become increasingly environmentally conscious.

The launch of the Millennium Dome in Greenwich in the Year 2000, instantly saw many of the newspapers launch an offensive against some of the activities as they sought to investigate whether the cost of the Dome was money well spent. This was a typical public relations problem for those operating the Dome, who then had to emphasise its positive attributes. In the political arena, talking positively about activities is sometimes known as 'spin'.

According to Frank Jefkins, PR involves a transfer process which helps to convert the negative feelings of an organisation's many publics into positive ones (see Figure 3.53).

There are may different types of public relations activities:

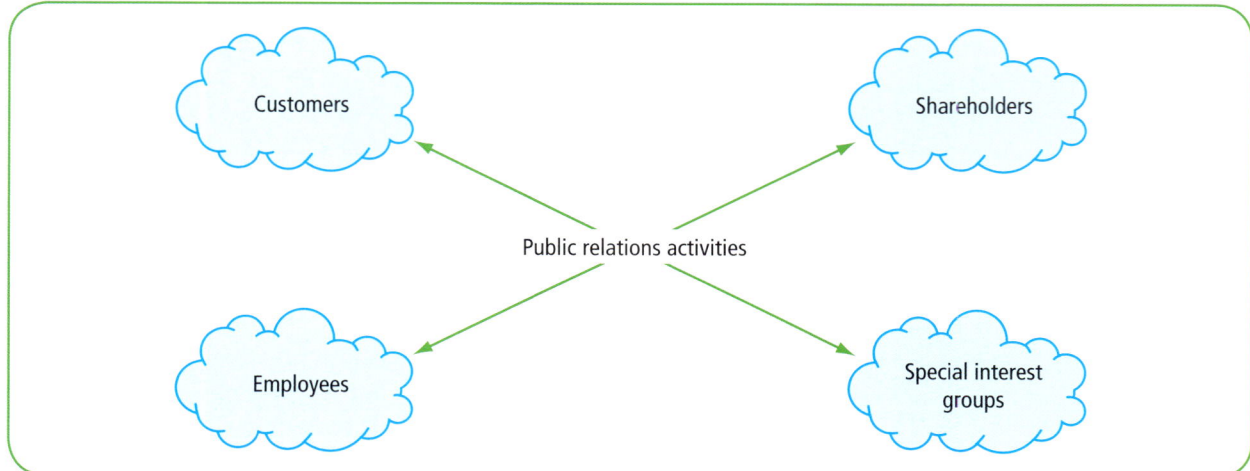

FIGURE 3.52 *Public relations activities*

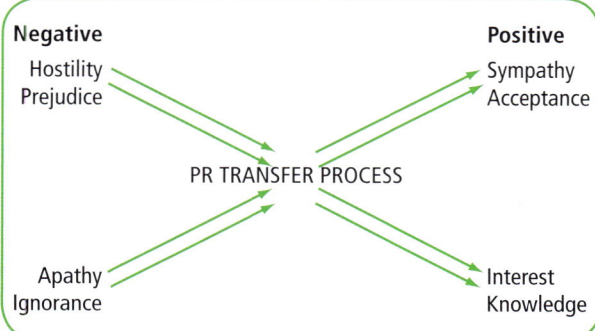

FIGURE 3.53 *The PR transfer process*

Charitable donations and community relations are good for an organisation's image, often provide lots of good publicity and also help to promote and provide for a good cause.

Hospitality at top sporting events is a popular method used by organisations to develop their customer relations. For example, there are opportunities to entertain customers at events such as the FA Cup Final, Wimbledon and the Grand National.

Press releases covering events affecting the organisation – such as news stories, export achievements, policy changes, technical developments and anything which enhances the organisation's image.

Visits and open days are a popular method of inviting people to various events to improve their understanding of what the organisation stands for.

Sponsorship of sporting and cultural events is viewed as a useful opportunity to associate an image with a particular type of function. For example, the NatWest Trophy and the Embassy World Snooker Championship.

Lobbying of ministers, officials and important people from outside interest groups, so that an accurate portrayal can be made of a problem or a case, may help to influence their views of the organisation.

Corporate videotapes have become an increasingly popular way of providing interested parties with a 'view' of an organisation's activities.

Minor product changes, such as no testing on animals or environmentally-friendly products may provide considerable PR benefits.

Sales promotions

Sales promotions describes a category of techniques which are used to encourage customers to make a purchase. These activities are effectively short-term and may be used:

* to increase sales
* to help with personal selling

* to respond to the actions of competitors

* as an effective alternative to advertising.

The Institute of Sales Promotion defines sales promotion as follows:

Sales promotion is the function of marketing which seeks to achieve given objectives by the adding of intrinsic, tangible value to a product or service.

The essential feature of a sales promotion is that it is a short-term inducement to encourage customers to react quickly, whereas advertising is usually a process that develops the whole product or brand.

As you walk down a town High Street or through a shopping mall, you will see many different examples of sales promotions. Such promotions may serve many different purposes. For example, competitions, vouchers or coupons and trading stamps may be designed to build customer loyalty and perhaps increase the volume purchased by existing customers. Product sampling is a strategy that is often used to introduce new products into the marketplace. Clearance sales of overstocked goods will increase turnover during part of the year in which business might otherwise be slack. Many sales promotions are undertaken in response to the activities of competitors to ensure that an organisation remains competitive. Sales promotions can be divided into two broad areas:

* promotions assisting with the sale of products to the trade

* promotions assisting the trade in selling products to the final consumer.

Selling into the pipeline is an expression used to describe promotions which move products from the manufacturer into the distribution system.

Selling out of the pipeline describes promotions which trigger the end-user to make a purchase (see Figure 3.54).

There are many different types of sales promotion:

Dealer loaders are among the inducements to attract orders from retailers and wholesalers. They may include a 'free case' with so many cases bought. For example, thirteen for the price of twelve is known as a 'baker's dozen'.
Competitions may interest dealers and consumers. For dealers they may be linked to sales with attractive prizes for the most successful dealer. Scratch cards, free draws and bingo cards are popular promotional methods for consumers.
Promotional gifts such as bottles of spirits, clocks, watches or diaries are considered useful bounty for dealers.
Price reductions and *special offers* are usually popular with consumers. They can, however, prove expensive as many consumers would otherwise have been prepared to pay the full price.
Premium offers may offer extra product for the same price. *Coupons* which offer money off or money back may also be attractive incentives for consumers. These may appear in magazines, be distributed door-to-door or appear on the side of a pack.

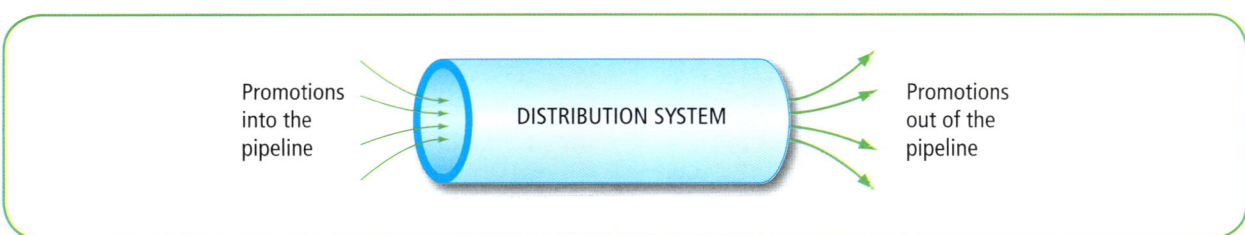

Promotions into the pipeline → DISTRIBUTION SYSTEM → Promotions out of the pipeline

FIGURE 3.54 *Selling into and out of the pipeline*

Charity promotions can be popular with younger consumers, who collect box tops or coupons and send them to a manufacturer, which then makes a donation to charity.

Loyalty incentives are today an increasingly used form of sales promotion. Dealer's loyalty might be rewarded with bigger discounts, competitions and prizes or even have their names published as stockists in advertisements. For consumers, loyalty incentives such as loyalty cards and points may provide 'cash back', free gifts or a variety of other tangible benefits.

Direct selling

Most days of your life you are involved in some form of selling activity. It might be persuading a friend to come with you to the pictures, or asking a relative to buy something for you. What you are doing is using your relationship to sell your ideas to someone else.

Personal or direct selling involves interaction between individuals or groups of individuals.

The objective of personal selling is to make a sale, and it is the culmination of all of the marketing activities that have taken place beforehand. It involves matching a customer's requirements with the goods or services on offer. The better the match, the more lasting the relationship between the seller and the buyer.

The role of personal selling will vary from business to business. It is a two-way process which can be one of the most expensive areas of the promotional mix. This personal communication element can be very important

as the final sale might come only as a result of protracted negotiations.

Personal selling is important in both consumer and organisational markets. However, in consumer goods markets, advertising often helps the process and is often the driving force which *pulls* a product through the distribution network. In organisational markets on the other hand, personal selling may have to work harder to *push* the product through to the market (see Figure 3.55).

The main benefit of personal selling is the ability to communicate with and focus on customers individually and with precision. For example, if you go into a travel agency and ask for details about a holiday, the sales assistant may explain and point out the features of various packages and any discounts or promotions they might offer. All of the other areas of the promotional mix are targeted at groups of people.

Although we have mental stereotypes of the typical salesperson, selling involves special skills. Whereas there is a tendency to downgrade this role in the UK, in many countries (Germany for example), sales staff require a high degree of technical competence and are generally accepted to be part of the corporate elite. Salespeople are key intermediaries who present information to customers and then provide feedback on customer needs.

Sales staff are representing an organisation and so need to reflect a positive image from that organisation. It is important that they do not offend customers by their appearance – the mode of dress should match the nature of the products and the organisation. For example, a sales assistant in a fashion store should wear something up-to-date, whereas an insurance salesperson should wear more formal clothes. It is often said that the way we look determines the ways others look at us!

Similarly, effective speaking will help to create the appropriate image and situation for the sale

Learning activity

Make a list of situations in which you have recently been involved in some form of personal selling. Explain how the selling process took place in each instance. Did you have any responsibilities to the other person(s) involved in the exchange process?

FIGURE 3.55 *The push-pull effect*

Product knowledge

After-sales service

Communications skills

Sales administration

Point-of-sale service

Customer care

FIGURE 3.56 *Stages in the selling process*

to take place. Good grammar, vocabulary, diction and voice tone may help to reflect the degree of professionalism required for the sale to take place.

Many organisations spend more on personal selling than on any other area of the promotional mix, and within organisations large numbers of individuals may find that personal selling forms part of their role. Personal selling may involve individuals developing special skills and using them in many different operational situations. To do so, sales staff need to know their products and be well trained in selling techniques (Figure 3.56).

Selling in a highly competitive world means that preparation has never been so important. Though it has been said that salespeople are born and not made, nevertheless skills, knowledge and training can improve performance. Training is designed to build on people's selling skills and to use their personal abilities and understanding to follow the psychological stages of the sales process. Product knowledge is vital, as it allows for feedback from the prospective customer's questions about the product's technical specifications, benefits and functions.

Knowing their customers may help to determine how sales staff communicate with them. For example, some customers may prefer

to be addressed with the more formal Mr or Mrs while others like to be called by their first name.

Probing is important in the early stage of a sales presentation, in order to find out the prospect's needs and where his or her priorities might lie. The salesperson can then try to match the product or service with the prospect's requirements. This may involve elaborating on the product's advantages, concentrating on aspects such as savings in costs, design ingredients, performance specifications, after-sales service, etc.

During the presentation, the salesperson must constantly evaluate whether the product is appropriate to the needs of the prospect. It is unethical to sell something that is not needed – although this may often happen! The large and more complex the order, the more complex the negotiations over supply. In many different situations it is important to provide a number of services to help with the process. For example, these might include:

* product demonstrations
* performance specifications
* sales literature
* samples
* a meeting to discuss details
* credit facilities
* sales promotions.

The prospective customer may have a variety of objections to the purchase. These objections may be genuine, or as a result of a misunderstanding. There might be reluctance to make a commitment at this stage. Logical, well-presented arguments and incentives may overcome such objections.

Timing is crucial to the sale. A salesperson must look for *buying signals* which indicate that the prospect is close to a decision, and almost ready to put a signature on an order form and discuss the contractual arrangements.

It is always important to *follow up the sale with post-sale support*. Promises that might have been made during the negotiations will have to be fulfilled. If the salesperson guarantees delivery by a certain date, that date must be held. Servicing arrangements must be efficiently carried out, and

Using an example known to you, show how strong after-sales service may help to promote repeat purchasing patterns.

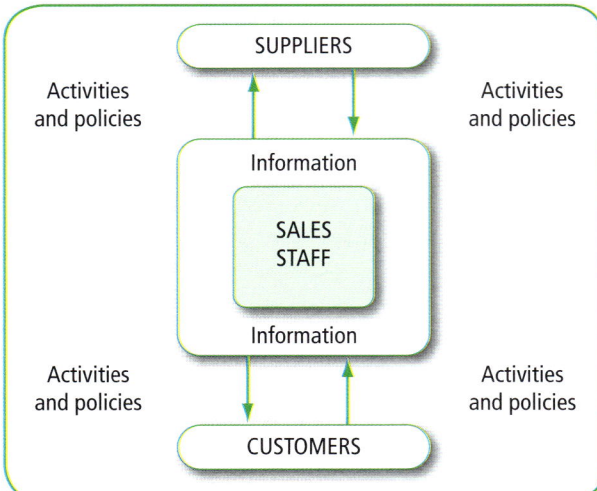

FIGURE 3.57 *The information link between customers and their suppliers*

any problems dealt with. Contacting customers to see if they are happy with the product will encourage repeat buying and improve the supplier's concern for its customers.

Sales staff may also have a number of other related functions. Communication, for example, is an important role. Sales staff act as an information link between suppliers and their customers. As a result, personal selling involves a boundary role – being at the boundary of a supplying organisation and also in direct and close contact with customers. The role is often not only one of selling but also one of interpreting the activities and policies of each organisation to the other (see Figure 3.57). A considerable amount of administration may also therefore accompany the selling role. For example, reports, schedules and computerised information such as inventory details are a part of daily life for a salesperson.

Comprehensive records on customers should be kept and updated after each visit. Keeping sales records enables the salesperson to respond exactly to each customer's individual needs. Knowledge of competitors and their products enables the seller to respond to queries about the relative merits and demerits of products.

3.4 Other factors influencing the marketing mix

Every organisation involved in marketing activity is faced with a number of constraints that may limit their activity. They then need to work within these constraints.

Costs

Internal constraints relate to the resource capabilities of an organisation such as costs. For example, an organisation might identify potential customers but how capable is it in meeting their needs? It might not have the resources to do so.

For example, in recent years Coca-Cola has developed a global presence. It has been able to do this by ploughing more money into long-term investment. Coca-Cola invests 70 per cent of its profits and achieves a staggering rate of growth.

When a company wants to develop new products or services it needs the resources to finance expansion. The bigger the scale of the development projects, the more resources are required. Sometimes companies finance expansion by selling off existing assets – for example, ICI has moved into higher value-added chemical products, such as components for lip-glosses and eye shadow. To finance this move it sold off a number of its existing heavy chemical plants which had low long-term profit potential.

In addition to financial resources, business organisations need the skills and know-how for a range of marketing activities. Increasingly, companies rely on buying in expertise from outside the organisation.

External constraints involve a series of factors within the business environment in which an organisation operates that limit in one way and another their activities. These will include:

Consumers If an organisation is not market-focused or if consumers are not interested in a product, then it will be difficult to market.
Competitors It may be difficult to market a product for which a competitor already has an advantage.

Becoming millionaires!

Dan and his younger brother Ron are experienced market traders, flitting from one market to another across south-east London. They are self-motivated entrepreneurs whose main aim in life is to become millionaires. As small businessmen, they do not always find life easy!

Dan was recently offered the opportunity to buy some of the latest DVDs, which were claimed to be 'kosher'. These are a big opportunity to expand the business, with an up-to-date consumer product that will bring the punters in. The great benefit is that if customers are interested in the DVDs, Dan knows that he can do a deal with some quick-boiling kettles he bought a few months ago that he has had trouble getting rid of. The kettles look smart but take 15 minutes to boil.

Dan's real problem is that he has not got the 'readies' to buy the DVDs. Ron is always 'skint' and cannot help. He is wondering about whether to sell off the van to provide him with the capital. The problem then would be that they would have to buy an alternative form of transport such as 'company mopeds', but this may have the alternative benefit of allowing them to start some courier work.

Another idea Dan has to expand the business is to use Ron's expertise in information technology to set up training courses. Though Ron was very good with computers, he has not used one for 5 years, and feels that if Dan is going to do this, they need to buy in help from another person.

1 **What internal, and external constraints make life more difficult for Dan and Ron?**
2 **What might be a better business strategy for them?**

Economy In a period of economic recession when consumer have falling incomes, it may be difficult to market a luxury product.

The Law There may be a number of laws constraining the activities of a business and making it difficult for them to do well.

The market-focused company will fully research all of these constraints and try to find solutions that enable it to turn weaknesses into strengths and threats into opportunities.

Political, economic, legal and environmental factors

One of the key influences upon the effectiveness of the marketing mix is the business environment. It is quite possible for an excellent business idea to do badly mainly because of factors outside the control of the entrepreneur. The process of 'knowing the other' is often referred to as 'scanning the environment'.

Examining the business environment helps an organisation to develop appropriate marketing strategies including the marketing mix. Important external forces that influence the marketing strategy might include:

the customer – buying behaviour of customers including why they buy, their buying habits and the size of the market.

the industry – the behaviour of organisations within the industry. e.g. retailers and wholesalers, their motivations and the structure and performance of organisations within the industry.

competitors – their position and behaviour.

the government and regulatory bodies – their influence over marketing and competitive policies.

Selection of an appropriate marketing mix involves creating the best possible match between the external environment and the internal capabilities of the organisation. Though the elements of the marketing mix are largely controllable by marketing managers within an organisation, many of the changes and forces within the business environment are not. The success of the marketing programme therefore depends upon how well an organisation can match its marketing strategies and marketing mix to the external business environment in which that business is operating.

Developing an appropriate marketing strategy involves creating the best possible match between the external environment and the internal capabilities of the organisation.

PEST model

One useful way of analysing an organisation's external environment is by grouping external forces neatly into four areas by using a PEST analysis. PEST stands for **P**olitical, **E**conomic, **S**ocial and **T**echnological influences, all of which are external (see Figure 3.58).

Carrying out a PEST analysis involves identifying the key factors external to an organisation which are in a state of flux and are likely to have an influence on the organisation in the coming months and years.

Whereas identifying these factors is relatively easy, assessing their ongoing impact and effect is more difficult. An effective PEST analysis will be based on detailed research using all of the latest

journals and publications. For example, if certain taxes are likely to be lowered, how much are they likely to be lowered by? What will be the impact on the sales of each product? Figures need to be as accurate as possible – if interest rates are expected to go up, how much will they go up? How long will they be raised for? What will be their impact upon sales and costs?

Political, legal and fiscal factors Business decisions are influenced by political, fiscal (taxation) and legal decisions. For example, although in recent years many people have been encouraged to become self-employed, there has been a feeling by many of these people that they are over-regulated. These influences might include:

* changes in the tax structure
* privatisation
* the influence of unions
* changes in the availability of raw materials
* duties and levies
* regulatory constraints such as labelling, quality, safety.

Economic factors Though the economic environment is influenced by domestic economic policies, it is also dependent upon world economic trends. Rates of economic growth, inflation, consumption patterns, income distribution and many other economic trends determine the nature of products and services required by consumers, as well as how difficult it becomes to supply them! Influences might include:

* inflation
* unemployment
* energy prices
* price volatility.

Social/cultural factors To understand the social and cultural environment involves close analysis of society. Demographic changes such as population growth, movements and age distribution will be important, as will changes in cultural values and social trends such as family size and social behaviour. Factors might include:

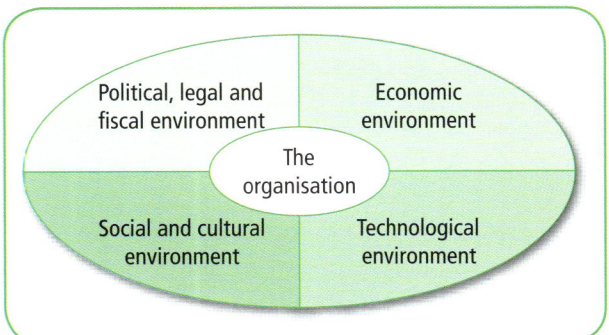

FIGURE 3.58 *The wider business environment*

* consumer lifestyles
* environmental issues
* demographic issues
* education
* immigration/emigration
* religion.

Technological factors In marketing goods and services, organisations must become aware of new materials as well as developments in manufacturing and business processes. At the same time organisations have to look at the nature of their products and, in particular, their cost-effectiveness as well as their performance in relation to competition. Factors might include:

* new technological processes
* energy saving techniques
* new materials and substitutes for existing materials
* better equipment
* new product developments.

Learning activity

This activity is best undertaken when working in a small group. The starting point is to identify an organisation which you are going to use as the centrepiece for a PEST analysis. It would be useful if you knew somebody working for the organisation who will be able to provide you with some of the information you require. Meet the person to discuss each of the PEST forces influencing their business. This is the starting point for your analysis. Use the Internet and a reference library to find out more to support the points made through the interview. Present your findings back to the class, and then discuss the impact that all of these external forces have had upon the strategic decisions made by the organisation over recent years.

Forces external to the organisation are rarely stable, and many of these forces can alter quickly and dramatically. It is important to recognise that while some of these forces will be harmful to marketing efforts, others will create new opportunities.

ASSESSMENT EVIDENCE

Having left school/college you have been given a unique opportunity to start a small business with a close relative who, having been left a substantial amount of money by his aunt, wants to put it to good use. This is a really unique opportunity for you. Your relative has a range of practical experience, but has recently left his job because he wants to do something different and work for himself rather than for other people. He has offered you both a salary and a profit share if the business becomes successful, and just wants to do something that is exciting but successful at the same time.

Although you share the enthusiasm of your relative, you are more guarded about the process of setting up the business. The relative has suggested buying an existing business but you would prefer to set something up from scratch, as you feel that you would both then not only feel like owners of the business but also be owners of the ideas.

You want to use your understanding of business organisations to help you start this business, and you're interested in using your experience of marketing not only gained through this module but also through the part-time employment you have had.

Mindstorm your idea for the business. Your idea could be based upon either an existing or new product and business proposition. In doing so identify the aims of the business and discuss your business idea within the context of the industrial context that you will serve.

Describe the customers you intend to serve. In doing this describe the market you intend to work within and the processes of segmentation that you will use.

Undertake market research for your product/service idea. Your market research should include both primary and secondary sources. Discuss how you will use the market research and the conclusions it is enabling you to draw.

Construct a marketing mix for your product/service/business idea. Try to link your marketing mix not just to the segments that you will serve and the needs of your customers but also link the marketing mix to the findings from the research you have undertaken.

Evaluate your actions and proposals so far. This involves you justifying what you have done and making judgments about the potential for your ideas.

In order to score the higher level marks for your coursework you need to provide considerable evidence of the widespread research that you have undertaken. Remember to integrate and use knowledge from your research AND from other areas that you are undertaking on this course. For example, you should show that you have thought about the particular form of business ownership that your business has as well as all of the stakeholders that it serves.

As you work on this:

* make sure that you show a good understanding to provide a detailed explanation of the product or service you intend to develop

* show that you understand the purpose of marketing aims and objectives and can develop a marketing mix that can successfully enable you to achieve these aims and objectives

* carefully construct a picture of your target market and think about how the market you service has been segmented

* collect an extensive amount of data from your market research, both primary and secondary

* consider how you intend to analyse your market research data in order to draw some meaningful conclusions

* try to show how your marketing mix matches the findings from your market research

* use the marketing Ps as a framework for your analysis and attempt to show your depth of knowledge when identifying and choosing an appropriate strategy

* make sure that you have evaluated your marketing mix successfully. Try to justify and support all of the decisions you have made with relevant data

* make comparative decisions of other products or services either direct or indirect to help to justify the decisions you have made.

Glossary

Accounting Identifying, measuring, recording and reporting information relating to the activities of an organisation.

Advertising Standards Authority (ASA) Independent body that exercises control over all advertising in the UK.

Aim A business aim is the general end purpose that it is working towards, e.g. our aim is to become the UK's Number 1 ……..

Ansoff H. I. Ansoff was born in Vladivostock in December 1918 with an American father and a Russian mother. He went on to become a leading US industrialist, developed his career as a university professor and became famous for his work upon business strategies.

Appraisal Interview between a manager and a subordinate / colleague to establish priorities and targets for the future as well as to review previous and current performance.

Assets Things that an organisation owns, as well as other items that may be owed to the business.

Auditing Making lists and keeping records. E.g. an environmental audit records all processes, activities etc that have an impact on the environment.

Auditors Professional accountants who provide independent scrutiny and report on an organisation's financial position.

Authorised capital The value of shares that a company is allowed by law to sell in total.

Balance sheet A snapshot of what an organisation owns and owes on a particular date.

Board of Directors Group chosen by shareholders to represent their interests. The Chair of a company is the main representative of the shareholders.

Break-even point The point at which sales levels are high enough not to make a loss, but not high enough to make a profit.

Budgets Financial plan that helps businesses to set targets and control expenditure.

Capital This is provided by the owner of the business and is therefore deemed to be owed to the owner by the business.

Cash The liquid asset that enables an organisation to buy the goods and services it requires in order to add value to them.

Charity An organisation set up for a particular charitable purpose e.g. for educational or religious purposes. The organisation is overseen by a group of trustees. It does not make a profit although it can make a surplus.

Coach	Someone who provides help and guidance to a less experienced colleague by monitoring and assessing their performance in a constructive way.
Code of Practice	A written set of requirements setting out how activities will be carried out.
Corporation Tax	The first charge on profits paid to the Inland Revenue.
Company	An organisation that is a corporate body in law and which is owned by shareholders.
Consumers	People who use/consume a product.
Consumer protection	Laws, bodies and actions whose purpose is to look after the interests of consumers.
Contribution	Selling price per unit less variable costs per unit.
Control	Control refers either to the act of managing and making decisions in a business, or in keeping an organisation on plan or working to previously decided programmes.
Corporate Social Responsibility	CSR is the process of making sure that an organisation (a corporate body) looks after the community and wider society e.g. through charitable work.
Culture	The typical pattern of behaviors that characterise working relationships in an organisation e.g. friendly or cold, bureaucratic or laid back etc.
Cross-functional team	A team within an organisation made up of people from a range of specialisms.
Curriculum vitae	A specially prepared list of a job applicant's qualifications, previous job history, experience, etc.
Current assets	Sometimes called 'circulating assets', these are short-term assets because their form is constantly changing.
Current liabilities	Debts a business needs to repay within a short period of time (normally a year).
Customers	People who buy a product.
Database	Large amount of information stored on a computer so that it can easily be found, processed and updated.
Deed of Partnership	A legal document setting out the relationship between partners in a partnership e.g. how to share profits.
Desktop mapping	Viewing and analysing data geographically, with information superimposed in layers on digital maps.
Development	Identifying and seeking to meet the needs of individuals in the workplace e.g. by providing them with opportunities to expand their job role.
Diversification	Spreading interests over a variety of products/activities.
Dividend	A share of the company's profit paid to shareholders.
Empowerment	Giving more decision making responsibility to those lower down in an organisation.
Ethics	Moral principles or rules of conduct getting things 'right'.

Financial accounting	Concerned with the recording of financial transactions and the preparation of financial reports to communicate past financial performance.
Fixed assets	These tend to have a life-span of more than one year. They comprise items that are purchased and generally kept for a long period of time.
Flat organisation	An organisational structure that has relatively few layers of command.
Focus groups	Small groups of customers who are able to discuss their needs in some depth.
Fringe benefits	Additional benefits on top of pay e.g. a company car or other perks.
Function	A specialist component of an organisation e.g. the marketing function of a company.
Gap analysis	Analysing what is happening in the business environment
Global warming	The raising of air and sea temperatures as a result of pollution, the emission of greenhouse gases, etc.
Good	The term used to describe something which gives a consumer value e.g. a physical good such as a bread roll or a curry. The term 'good' is sometimes used just to include physical items with the term service being applied to an intangible provision of benefits.
Government department	A body set up by the government to run a particular activity or service. It is staffed by government officials known as civil servants.
Human Resource Management (HRM)	Involves seeking to help individuals to meet their own work needs while at the same time helping the organisation to achieve its objectives.
Induction	The process of introducing an individual to the workplace, routines, colleagues and processes.
Issued capital	The value of shares that a company has issued at any one time. This will typically be less than the authorised capital.
Job analysis	The process where an employer looks at what is required within the current job; this can be done in a number of ways including looking at the job description, observing someone in the job or through a questionnaire.
Job description	The list of working conditions for a job, e.g. pay, hours and duties.
Legislation	Laws often created by Acts of Parliament.
Liabilities	These include anything that an organisation owes.
Liquidation	This occurs when a business can no longer pay its debts.
Liquidity	Being able to meet financial obligations.
Long-term liability	Sometimes called a deferred liability, this is not due for payment until some time in the future.

Management accounting	Involves looking to the future using a knowledge of past performance, where relevant, to aid the management of the business.
Market	The range of means by which consumers can buy a particular product or alternative to it.
Market penetration	This involves making more sales to customers, without changing products in any way
Market research	'The systematic gathering, recording and analysis of data about problems related to the marketing of goods and services' (American Market Research Association)
Market segment	The result of dividing up large heterogeneous markets with similar needs into smaller markets (segments) according to shared characteristics.
Market share	The percentage of sales within a market that is held by one brand or company.
Marketing	'The management process responsible for identifying, anticipating and satisfying customer requirements profitably' (Chartered Institute of Marketing)
Marketing mix	A series of variable factors such as the four Ps (product/price/place/promotion) used by an organisation to meet its customers' needs
Marketing objectives	The targets that the organisation seeks to meet through its marketing activities.
Marketing plan	A plan that uses the marketing mix to identify and then meet consumers' requirements.
Marketing strategies	Long-term plans designed to enable an organisation to identify and meet the wants and needs of its customers.
Matrix	Type of organisational structure in which a particular unit or individual is accountable to more than one line manager or function.
Mentor	An individual that provides advice, guidance and support to a colleague in the workplace.
Method study	Examining the way in which work is carried out to try and ascertain superior methods to do the work.
Modern Apprenticeship	Government funded scheme combining education, training and the development of practical skills for work related occupations.
Motivation	The personal drive to achieve targets and get things done.
Municipal enterprise	A government body that runs a particular activity on a local level and is usually financed by some form of taxation or government grant.
Objective	A component part of an overall business aim. Sometimes objectives are quantified (numbers are attached to the objective e.g. to increase production by 10% this year).
Overtrading	Expansion that damages cash flow.
Ownership	The act of being a part owner of a business e.g. shareholders are the owners of a company.

Performance Related Pay (PRP)	Pay that is tied to the achievement of targets, objectives and other measurable outcomes.
Person specification	List of attributes needed by a person to perform a job, such as personality type or experience.
Pilot	To gauge the market reaction before a test is viable.
Positioning	Placing a product within the overall market e.g. at the 'no frills' end or at the 'luxury' end of the market.
Primary information	Information an organisation compiles by its own efforts perhaps commissioning a market research agency.
Private sector	That part of the economy that is owned by private individuals e.g. one person businesses, partnerships and companies.
Process	An activity involved in turning raw inputs into more finished outputs.
Product life-cycle	Key stages in the life of a product e.g. launch, introduction, growth, maturity, decline.
Public company	An organisation owned by shareholders. The shares can be bought and sold on the Stock Exchange.
Public sector	That part of the economy that is owned by the government on behalf of citizens.
Qualitative	Research associated with consumer responses, feelings, attitudes and descriptions usually from a limited number of respondents (people).
Quantitative	Research associated with figures or numbers that help to make the research more objective usually from a large number of consumers.
Questionnaire	Systematic list of questions designed to obtain information from people about specific events, their attitudes, their values and their beliefs.
Recruitment	Taking on employees.
Recycling	Making use of material and 'waste' products so that they can be reused again.
Registrar of Companies	Individual responsible for listing, recording and approving the details of companies. Companies House is located in Cardiff.
Rights issue	A cheap way of issuing new shares by giving existing shareholders the right to buy them.
Sample	Questioning a selection of respondents from the target market.
Secondary information	Published data collected by another organisation and not specific to the project in hand.
Selection	Choose employees to take up a position from a number of possible choices.
Self-regulation	Individuals, organisations, and industries controlling the way they behave rather than responding to external pressure/laws. For example, the advertising industry in this country regulates advertising through the Advertising Standards Authority.

Service	There are two main types of services:
	1. Services to people – i.e. intangible benefits such as hairdressing, watching a film at the cinema, receiving personal insurance cover.
	2. Services to businesses such as the transport of goods, the insurance of business items, etc.
Sex Discrimination Act	Legislation setting out how the two sexes can be treated equally (in a non-discriminatory way).
Shortlist	A list drawn up which shows the best candidates from all the candidates who have applied for a post.
Sole trader	a one-person business. The one person may employ others but he or she is the sole owner.
Spreadsheet	Table of numbers which can be organised and altered on a computer according to preset formulae.
Stakeholder	A person or group with an interest or concern.
Strategic choice	Setting out a menu of strategic options, comparing the options provided by the menu and choosing the best option from the menu.
Strategic implementation	Putting the chosen marketing strategy into action.
Stock Exchange	A market for shares that have already been issued to shareholders. They can then sell off existing shares and buy others. Typically the work of the Stock Exchange today is carried out by computer screen trading.
Tall organisation	An organisation with lots of layers in it.
Tangible	Something that you can touch and see i.e. a physical good.
Targeting	Developing strategies for particular segments.
Trading account	Shows how gross profit is arrived at (Net sales − Cost of sales = Gross profit).
Training	Activities designed to help an individual work more effectively within an organisation depending on their training needs.
Trade union	Body set up to represent the organised rights of labour in the workplace. Being united (a union) gives individual employees greater strength to bargain with employers than if they were working on their own.
Variance analysis	A process of analysing where actual performance differs from budgeted performance.
Voluntary organisation	An organisation managed and staffed by unpaid voluntary workers.
Working capital ratio	This shows how easily the business can pay its short-term debts and is the ratio of current assets to current liabilities.

Index

Page numbers in italics refer to illustrations and diagrams.